HEGEL'S
PHENOMENOLOGY
OF SPIRIT

Studies in Phenomenology and
Existential Philosophy

Martin Heidegger

HEGEL'S PHENOMENOLOGY OF SPIRIT

Translated by

Parvis Emad and

Kenneth Maly

Indiana University Press

BLOOMINGTON & INDIANAPOLIS

Preparation of this book was aided by a grant from the Program for Translations of the
National Endowment for the Humanities, an independent federal agency.

Published in German as *Hegels Phänomenologie des Geistes*
© 1980 by Vittorio Klostermann, Frankfurt am Main

Manufactured in the United States of America

Library of Congress Cataloging in Publication Data
Heidegger, Martin, 1889–1976.
  Hegel's Phenomenology of spirit.

  (Studies in phenomenology and existential philosophy)
  Translation of: Hegels Phänomenologie des Geistes.
  1. Hegel, Georg Wilhelm Friedrich, 1770–1831.
Phänomenologie des Geistes.   2. Spirit.   3. Consciousness.
4. Truth.   I. Title.   II. Series.
B2929.H3513   1988   193   87–45440
ISBN 0–253–32766–0
1   2   3   4   5   92   91   90   89   88

Contents

TRANSLATORS' FOREWORD   viii

Introduction
The Task of the Phenomenology of Spirit as the First Part of the System of Science   1

§ 1. *The system of the phenomenology and of the encyclopedia*   2

§ 2. *Hegel's conception of a system of science*   9

   a) Philosophy as "the science"   9

   b) Absolute and relative knowledge. Philosophy as the system of science   13

§ 3. *The significance of the first part of the system with regard to the designation of both of its titles*   17

   a) "Science of the Experience of Consciousness"   18

   b) "Science of the Phenomenology of Spirit"   23

§ 4. *The inner mission of the phenomenology of spirit as the first part of the system*   26

   a) Absolute knowledge coming to itself   26

   b) Misinterpretations of the intention of the *Phenomenology*   28

   c) Conditions for a critical debate with Hegel   30

Preliminary Consideration   32

§ 5. *The presupposition of the* Phenomenology: *Its absolute beginning with the absolute*   32

   a) The stages of spirit's coming-to-itself   34

   b) Philosophy as the unfolding of its presupposition. The question concerning finitude and the problematic of infinitude in Hegel   36

   c) Brief preliminary remarks on the literature, on the terminology of the words *being* and *beings*, and on the inner comportment in reading   39

FIRST PART

Consciouness

Chapter One   Sense Certainty   45

§ **6. Sense certainty and the immediacy**   46

  a) Immediate knowledge as the first necessary object for us who know
     absolutely   46

  b) The being-in-and-for-itself of the subject-matter and the con-
     templation of absolute knowledge. "Absolvent" absolute knowl-
     edge   49

  c) The immediacy of the object and of the knowing of sense certainty.
     "Pure being" and extantness   53

  d) Distinctions and mediation in the pure being of what is immediate
     in sense certainty. The multiplicity of examples of the this and the
     this as I and as object   58

  e) The experience of the difference between immediacy and media-
     tion. What is essential and not essential in sense certainty itself.
     The this as the essence, its significance as now and here, and the
     universal as the essence of the this   60

  f) Language as the expression of what is universal and the singular
     item which is intended—the ontological difference and dialectic   63

§ **7. Mediatedness as the essence of what is immediate and the dialectical
     movement**   66

  a) Intention as the essence of sense certainty. The singularity and
     universality of intending   66

  b) The immediacy of sense certainty as non-differentiation of I and
     object. The demonstrated singular now in its movement toward
     the universal   69

  c) The infinity of absolute knowledge as the being-sublated of the
     finite and as dialectic. The starting point of a confrontation with
     Hegel's dialectic—the infinitude or finitude of being   72

  d) Points of orientation regarding the problem of the infinity of being:
     The absolvence of spirit from what is relative. The logical and
     subjective justification of infinity   75

Chapter Two   Perception   81

§ **8. Consciousness of perception and its object**   81

  a) Perception as mediation and transition from sense certainty to
     understanding   81

  b) The thing as what is essential in perception. Thingness as the unity
     of the "also" of properties   84

c) The exclusive unity of the thing as condition for having properties. The perceptual object's having of properties and the possibility of deception   87

§ 9. *The mediating and contradictory character of perception*   89

a) The possibility of deception as the ground of the contradiction in perception as taking and reflection   89

b) The reciprocal distribution of the contradictory one and "also" of the thing to perceiving as taking and reflection   91

c) The contradiction of the thing in itself—being for itself and being for an other—and the failure of the reflection of perception   93

Chapter Three   Force and Understanding   97

§10. *The absolute character of cognition*   97

a) Absolute cognition as ontotheology   97

b) The unity of the contradiction of the thing in its essence as force 101

c) Finite and absolute cognition—"Appearance and the Supersensible World"   105

§11. *The transition from consciousness to self-consciousness*   112

a) Force and the play of forces. Being-for-itself in being-for-another 112

b) The appearance of the play of forces and the unity of the law   116

c) The infinity of the I. Spirit as λόγος, I, God, and ὄν   124

SECOND PART

Self-consciouness

§12. *Self-consciousness as the truth of consciousness*   129

a) "The Truth of Self-certainty"   129

b) The significance of the transition from consciousness to self-consciousness   131

§13. *The being of self-consciousness*   136

a) The attainment of the self-being of the self in its independence 136

b) The new concept of being as inhering-in-itself, life. Being and time in Hegel—*Being and Time*   141

CONCLUSION   149

EDITOR'S EPILOGUE   150

GLOSSARY OF GERMAN TERMS   154

TRANSLATORS' FOREWORD

The work presented here is an English translation of Martin Heidegger, *Hegels Phänomenologie des Geistes*—Volume 32 of the *Gesamtausgabe (Complete Edition)*—which constitutes the lecture course given by Heidegger at the University of Freiburg during the winter semester of 1930/31. The German edition, edited by Ingtraud Görland, was published in 1980 by Vittorio Klostermann Verlag.

The text of this lecture course occupies an important place among Heidegger's writings on Hegel. There are several crucial discussions of Hegel—in Section 82 of *Being and Time* and in the essays "Hegel's Concept of Experience"[1] and "Hegel and the Greeks"[2]—as well as brief analyses of Hegel spread throughout Heidegger's writings. However, the present text represents Heidegger's most substantial treatment of Hegel published so far. Bypassing the preface and the introduction to Hegel's work, this lecture course explicates Sections A ("Consciousness") and B ("Self-Consciousness") of the *Phenomenology of Spirit*.[3]

The Character of the Text: A Reading. What distinguishes the following text, setting it apart from a commentary in the usual sense, is the fact that in this lecture course Heidegger offers a simple reading of Sections A and B of the *Phenomenology of Spirit*. If one looks at Heidegger's reading of Hegel from the outside, without taking into account what actually transpires in it, then the reading might be characterized as an interpretation of the chapters "Sense Certainty," "Perception," "Force and Understanding," and "Self-consciousness." But what actually transpires in this interpretive reading is a careful and meticulous unfolding of the movement of thinking that is called "the phenomenology of spirit." This reading reveals the phenomenology of spirit as a thinking which gathers itself up in a gradual, always conscious and always self-assured manner. The emergent unfolding of this gathering of "the phenomenology of spirit" marks the simplicity of Heidegger's reading.

What we read in the text presented here in translation is not the establishment of a position or the expression of an intellectual superiority that is out to score points for or against Hegel. The interpreter of those sections of the *Phenomenology of Spirit* finds here a reading in which the process of the phenomenology of spirit becomes alive again. That Heidegger intended this—rather than a survey of various interpretations of Hegel's thought—is shown by the fact that he assigns a limited space to the discussion of works *about* Hegel. The process of the phenomenology of spirit can come to live again independently of an extensive and thorough treatment of the Hegel literature. As the work of thinking progresses, and as we are drawn into the movement of thinking, it becomes increasingly clear how little *this* movement depends on the vast and growing literature on Hegel.

This does not mean that Hegel scholarship should be forfeited. Rather, in its powerful stroke, Heidegger's reading reveals from within how necessary it is to inaugurate one's reading of the *Phenomenology of Spirit* prior to and independent of the debate created by the secondary literature on that work. What we learn from the example that Heidegger provides is that the movement of thinking that occurs as the *conditio sine qua non* of coming to terms with the *Phenomenology of Spirit* needs to be initiated each time anew. Instead of being on the lookout for what this or that one has said about this work, the reader should initiate his or her own reading. What safeguards this reading from deteriorating into a subjective rendition of the *Phenomenology of Spirit* is not the authority of the secondary literature, but the essential character of this work as a work of thinking.

The simplicity of the reading which is at stake here and the movement which this reading is to bring about can be reached only when the *Phenomenology of Spirit* is taken as a work of thinking. The phrase "work of thinking" should not be mis-taken as a platitude on the basis of which the *Phenomenology of Spirit* might be seen as the product of Hegel's intellectual efforts. The phrase "work of thinking" refers to the work-character of the work *Phenomenology of Spirit*, to its ἔργον, which is never experienced in a *mere* reading of the text.[4] It is important to bear in mind that this ἔργον (in which the attentive reader participates) is not something added to the work as a supplement. A philosophical work such as Hegel's *Phenomenology of Spirit* exists as the ἔργον which it brings to light from within itself.

The priority which Heidegger ascribes to the work as a work of thinking helps us to understand why the familiar characterization of the *Phenomenology of Spirit* as a *product* of Hegel's intellectual efforts is far from adequate. When we take the work to be the product of Hegel's intellectual effort, then we are immediately confronted with the question: Who is Hegel? Is he the focal point of any number of biographical studies? What is fundamentally objectionable in this characterization is that it immediately opens the door for an assessment of the *work* in terms of biography—in terms of a correlation between work and life. By considering the work as a by-product of life, we reduce the work to an outgrowth of subjectivity, thus blocking access to the ἔργον (to what is going on), which is summed up in the word *work*.

We might, then, distinguish the several meanings of the word *work*— and along with that the concomitant root issues involved: (1) the work that we have as a *product* of Hegel's efforts, (2) the work as the *book* that we have (the *Phenomenology of Spirit* as a text-work), and (3) the work of thinking that is going on in the text-work, a work of thinking that our attentive reading can participate in. The first meaning of work—as product—Heidegger dismisses as peripheral, nongermane, and utterly external to the movement of thinking that his reading is intended to stimulate. The second meaning of work—as text-work—comes up whenever Heidegger makes reference to the work as *text*. The third meaning of work as process, as the movement of thinking, is the root issue and is central to Heidegger's concern in this lecture course. Because of a certain style used in German—of not necessarily italicizing titles of books—these last two meanings (the ones that actually bear on Heidegger's reading) are not distinguished in the German edition: The words "die Phänomenologie des Geistes" (not italicized in German) can refer to the book *Phenomenology of Spirit* or to the process or movement of "the phenomenology of spirit." In order to provide an English translation in accord with standard English style, we had to determine in each instance *which* of the two senses was meant. This became a matter of interpretation, a task that the German edition could avoid.

In order to see the originality of the work, we must go beyond the legacy of Romanticism and historicism, which assumes a direct correlation between life and work and reduces the work to an accomplishment of human subjectivity. When Heidegger began a lecture course on Aristotle, instead of giving the customary account of the philosopher's life, he chose merely to say: "Aristotle was born, he worked, and he died."[5] Thus, he intimates that biographical data do not provide a reliable starting point for entry into the work of a philosopher. Any view which assumes that a work is born out of life is an explanation offered *about* the work instead of an attempt to come to grips with its originality. The notion of the "history of the evolution of a work in the course of the development of the life of an author" tends to lead away from what occurs in the work—it is a *mis-leading* notion. The unexamined assumption concerning the nature of the work as a by-product of life is a way of explaining the work away rather than coming to terms with its original character. This explanation tends surreptitiously to annihilate the work's questioning power.

As Heidegger returns to the originality of the work as a work of thinking, as he demands that the reader be guided by the ἔργον (which *is* the work) rather than by the desire to place the work alongside other biographical peculiarities of the author, he leads the reader back to the original togetherness of thinking and questioning. Thus, Heidegger points beyond the correlation of life and work to the work's independent stature as a work of *thinking*.

It is certainly naive to want to explain anything in the *Phenomenology of Spirit* by going back to the events of Hegel's life in Jena before 1807. For understanding what goes on in this work, curiosity about Hegel's life in that period is a bad guide. Rather, it is the *Phenomenology of Spirit* as a work that made that life to be Hegel's life. As a work of thinking, the *Phenomenology of Spirit* inheres in itself: Its independence forbids external and biographical explanations. It is good to pause for a moment and to wonder about the phenomenology of spirit as that which claimed Hegel's "attention" in the midst of the events that made up his life in Jena. What is it that occurs in the work of the phenomenology of spirit that made this life to be Hegel's life? Is it not the overriding concern with the phenomenology of spirit that stamps life with a Hegelian mark? The response to this question should come from a direct exposure to the ἔργον of thinking, which, as the phenomenology of spirit, leads the way in Hegel's life. This is to suggest that, in opposition to romantic and historicistic views, we should see life in the light of the work. If we take up the questions that make up the very fabric of the phenomenology of spirit (or of the *Phenomenology of Spirit*), then we gain access to a plane from which the written history of the life of Hegel (his biography) appears in a new light. It is from such a plane that we understand Heidegger when he asks: "Is it not rather such that the work makes possible an interpretation of the biography?"[6] This question is a warning that the work should be viewed not as a by-product of life, but rather as a central light which colors and tunes the contingencies and inevitabilities that are called life.

The independent and integral character of the work of thinking is central for Heidegger's own work and applies to the works of others as well. In order to preserve this independent and integral character and to stress the need for taking up the work as it claims one's thinking in its immediacy, the volumes of Heidegger's *Gesamtausgabe* are published without an interpretive introduction and a commentary. This is a significant point and has direct bearing on the character of the present text. Thus, it needs to be addressed briefly here.

When we come to a work of thinking, we should entertain no illusion as to what awaits us in reading the work. We do not come to grips with a work if we seek refuge in the convenience which an introduction or brief commentary provides. Either we are prepared for confronting the task with *all* its demands, or we are simply not yet prepared. No interpretive introduction or commentary will change that. We must be sincere with ourselves. More than anything else, a work of thinking calls for sincerity. Such a sincerity already knows that the labyrinthian device of an introduction cannot circumvent the actual encounter with the work of thinking. We must face the work as it is. If we fail to do so, if we get into the work in accordance with the suggestions made in the introduction, then we run the risk of learning later that those suggestions are peripheral, external to the work, and inappropriate. Thus, they will need correction. But since the correction of those views or suggestions is accomplished by getting into the work itself, then why not begin with the work in the first place? That is why volumes of the *Gesamtausgabe* of Heidegger's works are not supplemented with an introduction or brief commentary. Instead, the reader should face the work in the freedom in which the work comes forth as a work of thinking. This freedom is not preserved when the work is considered to be a riddle whose basic solutions are expected to be found in a brief commentary or introduction.

The text of *Hegels Phänomenologie des Geistes* appears without an introduction or brief commentary, because nothing should stand between this work and its readers, who attentively participate in the work of thinking therein. This present text needs *not* to have such a commentary or introduction, because the character of this text—as a reading that participates in the movement of the work of thinking that is opened up for us in the text-work—demonstrates above all else the inappropriateness of such an introduction. There is no question that, when an introduction is added to a work, a specific way of reading the work is suggested. But this specific way of reading the work is *not* the only way to read the work. An exceptional and extreme case—but nevertheless relevant—is Jacques Derrida's French translation of Husserl's *Ursprung der Geometrie*. When Derrida supplements his translation of this work with an introduction and commentary, he suggests a certain way of reading this work, which is certainly not the only way to read it. Whatever the merits of Derrida's commentary—and these merits are certainly there—there is no doubt that his introduction and his comments stand between the reader and Husserl's work. By contrast, we can say: The absence of an introduction in the original edition of *Hegels Phänomenologie des Geistes* safeguards the independence of the work of thinking as it occurs in the space of freedom that is necessary for the flourishing of the work itself.

The Tension of Translation. The work character of the work of thinking, whether it is the *Phenomenology of Spirit* by Hegel or *Hegel's Phenomenology of Spirit* by Heidegger, is primarily manifest in the language of the work. In both Hegel and Heidegger, this language takes on a unique character. In order to say what needs to be said, both Hegel and Heidegger speak a rigorous and precise language that goes beyond the traditional language of philosophy. In this new territory that language traverses, as it is molded in the works of Hegel and Heidegger, thinking itself enters new territories. It is easy to accuse both Hegel and Heidegger of taking inappropriate measures with language, of wanting to be deliberately abstruse, obscure, and unclear. This accusation comes from the reluctance to recognize that in both philosophers language manifests new territories of thinking. If we grasp the urgency of what these philosophers want to think, then we realize that they cannot say what they think without saying it in their own way.

But precisely this demand that the *work of thinking* places on both Hegel and Heidegger, as language was molded in their thinking, sometimes leads to virtually insurmountable difficulties for the translator. The difficulties in translating Hegel and Heidegger arise mainly in pointing, *in another language*, to the territories that these thinkers have opened up. It goes without saying that there is no general rule or universal method for doing this. Beyond bending and twisting the existing resources of a language, in order to let it fit the needs of what is being translated, we as translators are mindful of the realms or territories that this work opens up. (The desire to deal as adequately as possible with these difficulties prompted us to work closely with the French translation of this volume, by Emmanuel Martineau.)[7]

Aware of these difficulties and with an eye or ear toward letting those difficulties resonate for the reader of this English translation, we offer here the following reflections on significant tensions that arose in our work of translation and how we have chosen to resolve them:

1. As already mentioned, the phrase "die Phänomenologie des Geistes" appears in the German edition without italics. Sometimes it refers to Hegel's text and is a *title*; and sometimes it refers to the process or movement of the thinking that is underway: the phenomenology of spirit as the very work of thinking. In each case we have tried to determine which sense of the phrase was operative. In this translation, *Phenomenology of Spirit* (in italics and capitalized) refers, obviously, to the Hegel text, whereas the phrase "the phenomenology of spirit" (without italics, in lower case, and without quotation marks) refers to that movement in thinking that is the *work* of the phenomenology of spirit. (The same problem, distinction, and solution apply to the *Logic*—Hegel's text—and to "logic"—the movement of logic in the work of thinking.) We are aware that there is interpretation involved in this procedure and, moreover, that we are thereby making a distinction that the German edition—and perhaps even Heidegger himself—did not or did not need to make. (Does the work of thinking that we the readers participate in suffer more *with* the distinction or *without* it?)

2. In consultation with the French translation, we have occasionally changed the paragraph divisions in order to make possible a smoother and more readable text.

3. The use of italics in the translation varies from that in the German edition. Italics in Heidegger's original text serve to emphasize certain things within the context of oral delivery and are less appropriate for the written text. Moreover, italics are part of the language and should be used according

to peculiarities of the particular language. Thus, our italics are not always those that appear in Heidegger's text. We found that at times we could not wisely carry the italics over into our English rendition. On the other hand, we found that at times the English requires italics when the German does not. Thus, in some instances our use of italics varies from the original German, based on our understanding that the use of italics is not just a technical aspect that exists independently of the specific language being used, but is part and parcel of the language itself, one of its gestures.

4. We used A. V. Miller's translation of Hegel's *Phenomenology of Spirit*, while making emendations to that translation. At times we found it necessary to deviate from the English Hegel terminology—e.g., that used by Miller—because we had to adjust his rendition to the context of Heidegger's work with Hegel's text, and thus to the context of our translation.

5. Given these various issues in general and within that context, we offer the following reflections on significant tensions within individual words:

absolvent. There is no English equivalent for this word. It is, of course, not really a German word either. The term *absolvent* is crucial for the work that Heidegger does with Hegel's text. Thus, we kept the word in our translation, without ignoring entirely the possibilities offered by such English words as "detachment" or "the act of detaching." The term *absolvent* must be distinguished from "the absolute" (*das Absolute*). *Absolvent knowing*, for example, carries with it at all times several connotations: in the process of being absolved/detached, in the process of the absolute, becoming absolute.

aufzeigen. Throughout this translation, we have translated *aufzeigen* as "showing up"—and not, as is commonly done, as "pointing out." It seems to us that the term "showing up" better accounts for the process of appearing, manifesting, shining—which is of utmost concern for Hegel and for Heidegger's reading of Hegel.

dieses and *diesig*. A common word in German, *dieses* is used in Hegel's text to indicate that he wants to think something which is not yet thought in traditional ways of thinking about a thing. When Hegel says "*dieses*," he wants to think a thing as it is on its way to becoming an object for consciousness. When Heidegger uses the words "*diesig*" or "*das Diesige*," he is reconsidering this same process and finds that to be "*dieses*" a thing must have the character of a *dieses*, must be *diesig*. Only thus can a thing be on its way to becoming an object for consciousness. Thus, we have translated *diesig* as "having the character of a this." (Similar explanations can be offered in regard to other terms, such as *hiesig* and *ichlich*.)

einzeln. English has two possibilities: *particular* or *individual*. The nuance of each of these words in English is perhaps more a matter of style than of anything else. We have translated *einzeln* consistently as "particular," even though we are aware that a case can be made for the appropriateness of the word *individual* in some instances.

gleichgültig. It is our judgment that Hegel uses this word in *two* senses: as "indifferent" and as "with equal weight or force." In each instance we have chosen one or the other, trying to be mindful of this difference.

meinen, das Meinen, and *das Meine.* First, *meinen* and *das Meinen* can sometimes be translated into English as "meaning," but more often as "intending." We have used both English words. Second, the connection that these words have in their German rootedness is impossible to maintain in English translation. The reader simply needs to remember that the words are rooted together in German.

die Mitte. This is a crucial technical term for Hegel. It presented us with a special difficulty, in that the most readable English translation—"middle term"—carries with it a possibly misleading nuance. We might have chosen "middle," "midpoint," or "mid-point." With great hesitation we have sometimes rendered *die Mitte* as "middle term," aware of the risk that the language will tend to reduce the tension and movement in Hegel's thought of *"die Mitte"* to a logical nexus—thereby covering over the experiential character of the phenomenology of spirit that Hegel's work undertakes and that Heidegger's reading of Hegel's work invites us the reader to participate in.

rein. We hope that translating *rein* as "sheer" rather than "pure" will allow us to get closer to what Hegel has in mind. It seems to us that the English word *sheer* better reflects the absolute character of the process which Hegel has in mind.

wahrnehmen and *die Wahrnehmung.* These words are usually translated as "perceiving" and "perception" respectively. We have also done that. But in some crucial places we have used the more literal phrase "taking for true," in order to keep visible the root meaning of *wahr-nehmen.* This meaning is implied in the English word *perception,* but it is not explicit. *Wahr-nehmen* as "taking-for-true" is of central *philosophical* concern for Hegel as well as for Heidegger reading Hegel.

wissen. This term in Hegel refers at times to the process of knowing and at times to knowledge itself. Thus, we have translated *wissen* sometimes as "knowing" and sometimes as "knowledge." Again, this occasionally became a matter of interpretation, something that the German edition—and perhaps Heidegger himself—did not need to make so explicitly. (Note: We have translated the German word *die Erkenntnis* as "cognition," precisely to reserve the English words *knowing* and *knowledge* for *wissen.*)

zugrundegehen. We found that Heidegger's word *zugrundegehen* is as diverse as Hegel's *aufheben*. Thus, we have translated it variously as "running aground," "going under," and "being annihilated."

Technical Aspects of the Text in Translation. All additions to the German text by the translators are within square brackets [ ], including information that was added in the footnotes. Significant and problematical German words that we chose to carry along in the body of the text are also in square brackets. The symbols { } are used to distinguish Heidegger's additions or comments within quotations.

Footnotes from the German edition are at the bottom of the page and are numbered consecutively from the beginning of each major section—following the German text. Translators' footnotes are at the bottom of the page, in brackets, and are designated by asterisks. Footnotes designated by asterisks without brackets contain information that appears in the text itself in the German edition. The numbers in the running heads refer to the pagination of the German edition.

References to Hegel Texts. In an attempt to clarify which texts by Hegel (and which editions) are being referred to in Heidegger's text and to make proper and adequate reference to English translations of these Hegel texts, we have proceeded in the following way in all footnote references:

1. We have reproduced the references that appear in the German edition as they appear there. When there is simply a Roman numeral and page number, it refers to the volumes of Hegel's *Gesamtausgabe* of 1832ff., which Heidegger refers to most of the time. The later and more accessible *Jubiläumsausgabe* reproduces in its margins the volume and page number of the 1832 edition.

2. References that are added in this translation and identified as "GW" refer to the *Gesammelte Werke* of Hegel published by the *Hegel-Archiv* through Felix Meiner Verlag.

3. For Hegel's *Phenomenology of Spirit*, abbreviations in the footnote references mean as follows:

II   *Gesamtausgabe* or *Jubiläumsausgabe*

GW IX   *Phänomenologie des Geistes*, hrsg. Wolfgang Bonsieger und Reinhard Heede, Gesammelte Werke, Band 9 (Hamburg: Felix Meiner Verlag, 1980)

Hoff.   *Phänomenologie des Geistes*, hrsg. Johannes Hoffmeister, Philosophische Bibliothek, Band 114 (Hamburg: Felix Meiner Verlag, 1952)

E.T.   *Phenomenology of Spirit*, trans. A. V. Miller (Oxford: Oxford University Press, 1977)

4. Besides the *Phenomenology of Spirit*, the English translations of two other Hegel texts are referred to in the footnotes simply as "E.T." These are:

The Difference between the Fichtean and Schellingian Systems of Philosophy, trans. J. P. Surber (Atascadero, Calif.: Ridgeview Publishing, 1978) (*Jubiläumsausgabe* I; GW IV)

Hegel's Science of Logic, trans. A. Miller (Atlantic Highlands, N.J.: Humanities Press, 1976) (*Jubiläumsausgabe* III; GW XI–XII and XXI–XXII)

5. All other references to English translations appear in brackets in the respective footnotes.

This translation owes an immeasurable amount to the generous help that it has received from Robert Bernasconi, both in terms of the preparation of references to the various editions of Hegel's works and in terms of a careful and concern-filled reading of our text. We express our deepest gratitude to him, even as we assume full and final responsibility for this work of translation. We also thank John Sallis for his careful reading of the text of this translation.

We are grateful to the National Endowment for the Humanities for partial support of this project. Our gratitude is also due to the Faculty Research and Development Committee of the College of Liberal Arts and Sciences of DePaul University, the Research Council of DePaul University, the University Research Committee of the University of Wisconsin-La Crosse, and the College of Arts, Letters and Sciences of the University of Wisconsin-La Crosse.

Parvis Emad
Kenneth Maly

Notes

1. Cf. Martin Heidegger, *Holzwege*, Gesamtausgabe, Band 5 (Frankfurt: Vittorio Klostermann Verlag, 1977), pp. 115–208; trans. *Hegel's Concept of Experience* (New York: Harper and Row, 1970).

2. Cf. Martin Heidegger, *Wegmarken*, Gesamtausgabe, Band 9 (Frankfurt: Vittorio Klostermann Verlag, 1976), pp. 427–44.

3. Heidegger focuses on these sections because it is precisely in them that the further development and overcoming of Kant's position in the *Critique of Pure Reason* take place. Cf. in this regard the Editor's Epilogue to this present volume.

4. R. G. Collingwood makes some interesting remarks on the fundamental inadequacy of merely reading a text, in his *Autobiography* (Oxford: Oxford University Press, 1970), pp. 40f.

5. Cf. Walter Biemel, *Martin Heidegger* (Hamburg: Rowohlt Verlag, 1975), pp. 14ff.

6. Martin Heidegger, Lettre à J. M. Palmier (1969), in M. Haar (ed.), *Martin Heidegger* (Paris: Cahier de l'Herne, 1983), p. 117.

7. Martin Heidegger, *La "Phénoménologie de l'esprit" de Hegel*, trans. E. Martineau (Paris: Éditions Gallimard, 1984).

HEGEL'S
PHENOMENOLOGY
OF SPIRIT

Introduction

The Task of the *Phenomenology of Spirit* as the First Part of the System of Science

The following lecture course is an interpretation of Hegel's *Phenomenology of Spirit*. By discussing the title of this work in its various versions, we shall provide ourselves with a necessarily preliminary understanding of the work. Then, bypassing the lengthy preface and introduction, we shall begin with the interpretation at that place where the matter itself begins.

Phenomenology of Spirit, the current title of the work, is certainly not the original title. It became the definitive title for the work only after it was used in the complete edition of Hegel's works, published by his friends from 1832 onward, following immediately after his death. *Phenomenology of Spirit* is the second volume of the *Complete Works* and was published in 1832. Johannes Schulze, the editor, reports in his foreword that at the time of his sudden death, Hegel was himself preparing a new edition. For what purpose and in what manner this was a new edition can be gleaned from that foreword.[1]

The *Phenomenology of Spirit* appeared for the first time in 1807 with the title *System of Science: Part One, The Phenomenology of Spirit*. The work is thereby given a principal and comprehensive title: *System of Science*. The *Phenomenology* is attached to this system and ordered under it. Thus, the content of the work can be grasped only by considering this inner task, which—on the surface—consisted in being the first item in and for the system.

---

1. Hegel's philosophical works will be cited by volume and page number from the *Complete Edition* of 1832ff., insofar as they have appeared there. In its reissue as the *Jubilee Edition*, these page numbers appear in the margin. [For information on how references to Hegel's work are made in this translation, see Translators' Introduction.]

§1. The system of the phenomenology and of the encyclopedia

To what extent does the system of science require the *Phenomenology of Spirit* as its first part? What does this subtitle mean? Before we answer this question, we must recall that this subtitle, which later became the only title of the work, is not the complete title. Rather, the complete title of the work initially read: *System of Science: Part One, Science of the Experience of Consciousness*. The subtitle *Science of the Experience of Consciousness* was then turned into *Science of the Phenomenology of Spirit*, out of which grew the abbreviated and familiar title *Phenomenology of Spirit*.

In discussing the title, we must obviously stay with the most complete version of it, which appeared in two forms, both of which say the same thing in different ways. From the most complete title, it can be inferred that the first part of the system of science is itself science: it makes up "the *first* part of science."[1] What is peculiar about this first part should become clearer when we compare it with the second part. But aside from this first part, no other part of the system of science ever appeared.

However, soon after the appearance of the *Phenomenology of Spirit* in 1807, Hegel began publishing a work known as the *Logic*. The first volume of this work appeared in 1812/13, and the second volume in 1816. But the *Logic* did not appear *as the second* part of the system of science. Or is this *Logic*, in accord with the matter at issue therein, the remaining second part of the system? Yes and no. Yes, insofar as the complete title of the *Logic* also indicates a connection with the System of Science. The actual title of this work reads: *Science of Logic*—unusual and strange, for us as well as for Hegel's time. But this title loses its strangeness when we recall the complete subtitle of the *first* part: *Science of the Phenomenology of Spirit*. The system of *the* science is thus 1. science of the phenomenology of spirit and 2. science of logic. That is to say: as system of *the* science it is 1. system *as* phenomenology and 2. system *as* logic. Thus, the system appears necessarily in two shapes. Inasmuch as they mutually support each other and are interconnected, the *Logic* and the *Phenomenology* together form the entirety of the system in the fullness of its actuality.

In addition to and apart from the inner, essential relation which the *Phenomenology* has to the *Logic*, Hegel refers explicitly to the *Logic* in many passages of the *Phenomenology of Spirit*.[2] Not only do we find anticipatory references to the *Logic* in the *Phenomenology*, but also the reverse: references back from the *Logic* to the *Phenomenology*.[3] But most important, Hegel writes explicitly in the preface to the first volume of the *Logic*, first edition,

---

1. Preface, II, 28 [GW IX, 29; Hoff., 31; E.T., 20].
2. Cf. II, 29, 37, 227 [GW IX, 30, 35, 168; Hoff., 33, 40, 223; E.T., 22, 28, 181].
3. Cf., for example, III, 33–34, 35, 41, 61 [GW XI, 20, 20–21, 24, 33; GW XXI, 32, 33, 37–38, 54; E.T., 20, 20–21, 24, 68].

1812: "As regards the external relation {of the *Logic* to the *Phenomenology of Spirit*} it was {!} intended that the first part of the *System of Science*, which contains the *Phenomenology*, should be followed by a second part, which would contain the logic and the two concrete [*realen*] sciences of philosophy, the philosophy of nature and the philosophy of spirit, and which would have completed the system of science."[4]

Now it is clear that with the appearance of the *Phenomenology* in 1807, the entire system was originally thought to have two parts. However, the second part was to contain not only the logic, but the logic together with the concrete sciences of philosophy. The entirety of what should be the second part of the system is nothing other than the transformed concept of traditional metaphysics, whose systematic content likewise thoroughly determined the Kantian inquiry: *Metaphysica generalis* (ontology) and *Metaphysica specialis* (speculative psychology, speculative cosmology, and speculative theology).

This second part, which was to follow, would have contained the entirety of general and special metaphysics, that is, traditional metaphysics—transformed, of course, to fit Hegel's basic position. That transformation can be briefly characterized as follows. Hegel divides the entirety of general and special metaphysics into two parts: I. logic and II. philosophy of the concrete [*reale Philosophie*]. However, he divides the philosophy of the concrete into philosophy of nature (cosmology) and philosophy of spirit (psychology). Speculative theology (the third part of special metaphysics and for traditional philosophy the decisive part) is missing from the philosophy of the concrete, but not from Hegel's metaphysics, where we find speculative theology in an original unity with *ontology*. This unity of speculative theology and ontology is the proper concept of Hegelian logic.

Speculative theology is not the same as philosophy of religion, nor is it identical with theology in the sense of dogmatics. Rather, speculative theology is the ontology of the *ens realissimum*, the highest actuality as such. For Hegel this is inseparable from the question of the being of beings. Why this is the case should become clear in the course of the interpretation.

However, if the second part of the system that Hegel planned was to represent metaphysics, then the first part of the system, the *Phenomenology of Spirit*, was to be the foundation of metaphysics, its grounding. But this grounding is not an epistemology (which was as foreign to Hegel as it was to Kant), nor does it involve empty reflections on method prior to its actual implementation in the work. It is, rather, the preparation of the basis, the "demonstration of the truth of the standpoint,"[5] which metaphysics occupies.

---

4. III, 8 [GW XI, 8; GW XXI, 8–9; E.T., 28–29].
5. III, 61 [GW XXI, 55; E.T., 68].

But why did the *Science of Logic* not appear explicitly under the title of the second part of the system of science? Hegel says: "But the necessary expansion which logic itself has demanded has led me to have this part published separately; it thus forms the first sequel to the *Phenomenology of Spirit* in an expanded arrangement of the system. It will later be followed by a treatment of the two concrete philosophical sciences mentioned."[6]

But does this justify the omission of the main title *System of Science*? By no means. Precisely *when* the system is given a larger plan, it becomes more necessary to identify all the detailed parts in their relation to the system. It would not have been contrary to the original or to the enlarged plan of the system if its entirety had been arranged something like this: System of Science: Part I, Science of the Phenomenology of the Spirit; Part II, First Sequel: Science of Logic; Second Sequel: Science of the Philosophy of the Concrete.*

Why is the title *System* omitted as early as 1812? Because between 1807 and 1812, a transformation was already underway. The sign of the initial transformation in the idea of the system can be seen in the fact that the *Logic* not only loses the main heading but also stands separately, by itself—not because it turned out to be too detailed, but because the *Phenomenology* is to take on a different function and position in the fluctuating arrangement of the system. Because the *Phenomenology* is no longer the first part of the system, the *Logic* is no longer its second part. The *Logic* was separated in order to remain free to assume another place in another arrangement of the system which was then unfolding.

We gain an insight into the time between the appearance of the *Phenomenology* in 1807 and the publication of the first volume of the *Logic* in 1812 (and the second volume in 1816) if we bear in mind, if only in a rough manner, Hegel's "Philosophical Propaedeutic."

When the *Phenomenology of Spirit* appeared in 1807, Hegel was no longer in Jena, where he had settled in 1801 (having relinquished his tutorship in Frankfurt) in order to qualify for lecturing under Schelling. Hegel indeed became a university lecturer in 1805. But his salary was so insufficient that he did not need the catastrophe which happened in Prussia in 1806 to persuade him to seek support for himself in a different manner and elsewhere. As early as 1805 he applied without success for a professorship in Heidelberg. It was in Bavaria—which was where many others, including Schelling, had moved—that Hegel found employment as the editor of a

---

6. III, 8f. [GW XXI, 9; E.T., 28].
*Cf. Jena Lectures of Winter Semester of 1802/3: *Logica et Metaphysica secundum librum nundinis instantibus proditorum* (to appear at the annual fair). [This reference appears in the text itself in the German edition. The word *nundinis* appears erroneously as *mundinis* in the German text. This was brought to the translators' attention by F.-W von Herrmann.]

newspaper in Bamberg. In 1808 he was able to exchange this position for a more appropriate one as headmaster of the secondary school in Nürnberg, where he stayed until 1816, when the second part of the *Logic* appeared and the call to Heidelberg University came. It was in Heidelberg on October 28, 1816, that Hegel delivered his inaugural lecture,* which is well-known especially for its conclusion, which is characteristic of Hegel's basic position. That conclusion reads as follows:

> We elders, who have grown to adulthood in the storms of the age, consider you fortunate, because your youth falls in these times in which you may devote yourselves to science and truth with less curtailment. I have dedicated my life to science; and it is a true joy for me to find myself again in this place where I may work to a greater degree with others and with a wider effectiveness, in the interests of the higher sciences, and help to direct your way therein. I hope that I may succeed in earning and gaining your confidence. But at first I wish to make a single request: that you bring with you, above all, a trust in science and a trust in yourselves. The love of truth, faith in the power of spirit, is the first condition for philosophy. Man, because he is spirit, may and should deem himself worthy of the highest; he cannot think too highly of the greatness and the power of his spirit; and with this faith, nothing will be so difficult and hard that it will not reveal itself to him. The essence of the universe, at first hidden and concealed, has no power to offer resistance to the courageous search for knowledge; it must open itself up before the seeker, set its riches and its depths before his eyes to give him pleasure.[7]

Already at the end of 1817, the offer from the University of Berlin for Fichte's chair, first made to Hegel in 1816, was repeated. What prompted Hegel to accept the call this time was certainly not the prospect of getting involved in all the sundry activities of a professor of philosophy, but exactly the opposite. For in the letter of resignation that he had sent to the government of Baden, Hegel expressed the hope that "with his advancing age he might be able to give up the precarious function of teaching philosophy at a university, in order to be of use in another activity {today we would say a politico-cultural activity}."[8] This is an indication that already in his Heidelberg period, Hegel had made up his mind about philosophy and was done with it: The system was established. On October 22, 1818, Hegel began his lectureship in Berlin. And he remained professor of philosophy to the end of his life, thirteen years later in 1831.

Apart from his *Philosophy of Right* (1821) and a few book reviews, Hegel published nothing in his Berlin period that was of great significance for his

---

*Cf. XIII, 3.

7. XIII, 5f. [*Lectures on the History of Philosophy*, trans. E. S. Haldane and F. H. Simon, I, xiii.]

8. Haym, *Hegel und seine Zeit* [Berlin: Verlag von Rudolph Gaertner, 1857], p. 356.

philosophy. In his lectures, Hegel worked out the system which was given its decisive and final form in 1817 in the Heidelberg *Encyclopedia*. (According to their volume, the lectures of the Berlin period constitute the major part of Hegel's complete works.) But it was between 1807 and 1816, when he was a newspaper editor and a secondary-school teacher, that Hegel prepared the *Encyclopedia* and produced his essential philosophical work, the *Logic*.

As I said earlier, it is through Hegel's "Philosophical Propaedeutic" as presented to the senior classes of the secondary school that we gain an insight into the work of Hegel between 1807 and 1812. It was not published by Hegel himself. In 1838, seven years after the philosopher's death, Karl Rosenkranz, one of his students, found the manuscript among Hegel's literary remains, as he was passing through Berlin. Subsequently, in 1840, Rosenkranz published the manuscript as Volume XVIII of the *Complete Edition*.

Philosophy instruction at the secondary school was divided into three courses. The first course was for the lower grade and included instructions in law, morality, and religion. The second course was for the middle grade and was made up of phenomenology of spirit and logic. The last course was for the upper grade and was made up of logic in the sense of the Doctrine of the Concept [*Begriffslehre*] and the philosophical encyclopedia. It is important to note that logic appears here in two different places. In the second course logic follows phenomenology, which is in keeping with the plan of the system in which the *Phenomenology* belongs and for which it was written. In the last course, however, logic is the foundation for the philosophical encyclopedia, precedes everything else, and is followed by the science of nature and science of spirit.

Then in 1817, while in Heidelberg, Hegel elaborated further on the encyclopedia, in which logic is now the first significant part, and published it under the title *Encyclopedia der philosophischen Wissenschaften im Grundrisse* [*The Encyclopedia of the Philosophical Sciences in Outline*]. This *Encyclopedia* presents the new and final form of the System, having three parts:

A. Science of logic

B. Philosophy of nature

C. Philosophy of spirit.

Thus, following what we have said so far, the encyclopedia contains the whole of metaphysics.

But then what became of phenomenology? It became a segment of a segment of the third part of the system, namely, the philosophy of spirit. This is again divided into three parts:

1. Subjective spirit
2. Objective spirit
3. Absolute spirit.

The second section of the first part (subjective spirit) contains the phenomenology, which has now lost its fundamental position and function in the transformed system of philosophy.

In the last years of his life, around 1830, Hegel had to prepare a new edition of both the *Phenomenology of Spirit*, which had been out of print for a long time, and the *Logic*. While preparing the second edition of the *Logic* in 1831, and while editing the preface to the first edition, Hegel added a footnote to the passage mentioned above, where he speaks about the external relationship of the *Phenomenology* (the first part of the system) to the *Logic*. This footnote reads, "This title {namely, the initial main title of *Phenomenology of Spirit: System of Science*} will not be repeated in the second edition, to be published next Easter. In place of the projected second part, mentioned here, which was to contain all the other philosophical sciences, I have since brought out the *Encyclopedia of the Philosophical Sciences*, the third edition of which appeared last year."[9]

This remark by Hegel needs clarification. What does it mean to say that the encyclopedia has taken the place of the second part of the system as projected from the vantage point of the phenomenology? However accurate this may be, it does not truly reflect the facts pertaining to the new form of the system. It is correct to say that the encyclopedia corresponds to the second part of the system and was planned to follow the phenomenology as the first part. However, the encyclopedia functions neither *as the second part* of the old system, nor as part of the new system. Rather, the encyclopedia presents the whole of the new system. It recognizes the phenomenology neither as an independent nor as a foundational part of the system, but only as a segment of a segment of the third part. Therefore, we shall from now on call the system which has two parts and is defined in terms of the phenomenology, but is not exhausted by it, simply the *phenomenology-system*. We shall distinguish this system from that presented in the encyclopedia, which we shall call the *encyclopedia-system*. In each case logic takes a different position and fulfills a different function. The following diagram offers a representation of what has been said so far:

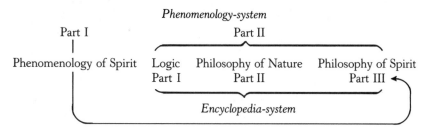

9. III, 8 Anm. [GW XXI, 9; E.T., 29n].

The change in the position of logic is nothing less than the transformation of the idea of the system. But this transformation is not a rejection of the previous standpoint as untenable, which is the judgment that the professional pen-pushers like to record in their history of philosophy. Rather, it is the transformation of the system enforced by the initial realization of the phenomenology-system. It is thus that the *Phenomenology of Spirit* itself comes to be regarded as superfluous.

If we do not differentiate both systems as first and second, it is because another system, the so-called Jena-system, precedes the phenomenology-system. This is, of course, only a general designation. The various indications are that it was precisely in the Jena period that the specifically Hegelian idea of system matured; and accordingly the drafts took many forms. Although the sources are still insufficient, there is reason to believe that already prior to his Jena period in Frankfurt, Hegel projected his entire philosophy—the system. This took place in close connection with a systematic and penetrating confrontation with Hellenism, with which Hegel had familiarized himself at that time, especially because of his friendship with and close proximity to Hölderlin. The effect of the confrontation with Hellenism—and philosophically with Plato and Aristotle—is so fundamental and lasting for the Jena-system that no one who has ever made a similar attempt would imagine that anything like it could be accomplished in one semester, even if he could apply the full force of Hegel's mind to it. That confrontation must have begun and developed its essential clarity already in Frankfurt. Therefore, one can with some justification speak of a Frankfurt-system. One can also assume, in judging Hegel's philosophical existence as we must, that he left Frankfurt for Jena for more than simply becoming a university lecturer and embarking upon an academic career. When he left Frankfurt, Hegel *knew* what he as a philosopher sought in Jena; he knew it as any 31-year-old can know what philosophy intends to do with him, if he happens to be Hegel.

Thus, in summary we have the following sequence of systems and plans for systems: the Frankfurt-system, the Jena-system, the phenomenology-system, and the encyclopedia-system. Hegel's final and proper system, the encyclopedia-system, shows much more strongly a relationship to the earlier plans for system than to the phenomenology-system. The phenomenology-system has a singular place in the whole of Hegel's philosophy, and yet it belongs necessarily to its inner form. This is so because, to repeat what was said earlier, the *Phenomenology of Spirit* remains the work and the way that not only once but always, and in a definite and indispensable manner, prepares the ground—better: the space, the dimensionality, the realm of expansion—for the encyclopedia-system. The fact that the phenomenology is left out of the encyclopedia-system as a fundamental part of it is not a deficiency of this system. Rather, the omission of the phenomenology—after it inaugurated the system—marks the beginning of the system which has the logic as its only appropriate beginning. This is so because the system of absolute knowing, if it understands itself correctly, must have an absolute beginning. Now, since on the one hand the phenomenology does not begin as absolutely as the logic does and thus must be left out of the beginning of the system, while on the other hand the phenomenology prepares the domain for a possible absolute beginning, the omission of the phenomenology from the encyclopedia-system articulates its indispensable affiliation with and relationship to this system. But sufficient justice is not done to this affiliation when the phenomenology shrinks into a segment of a segment of the third part of the encyclopedia-system, although the system for its part also requires such shrinking. Therefore, the *Phenomenology of Spirit* occupies a double position in the encyclopedia-system: In a certain way the phenomenology is a foundational part *for* the system while being at the same time an affiliated component *within* the system.

This double position of the *Phenomenology of Spirit* is not the result of Hegel's failure to gain clarity about this work and its role, but is the outcome of the system. Thus, in the course of our interpretation from now on, we shall have to ask:

1. How is the double position of the *Phenomenology of Spirit* systematically grounded?

2. To what extent can Hegel accomplish this grounding on the basis he provides?

3. Which fundamental problem of philosophy comes to light in the double position of the *Phenomenology of Spirit*?

We cannot avoid these questions. But we can formulate them and respond to them only after we have first grasped clearly the *primary* character and the essential dimensions of the *Phenomenology of Spirit*.

§2. Hegel's conception of a system of science

a) Philosophy as "the science"

The foremost character of the *Phenomenology* can be determined only by considering the intrinsic mission that is initially and properly assigned to this work as a whole, as it stands at the service of the Hegelian philosophy and begins its exposition. But this intrinsic mission for the whole of Hegel's philosophy is announced in the complete title of the work, which reads: *System of Science: Part I, Science of the Experience of Consciousness. (Science of the Phenomenology of Spirit)*. A preparatory discussion of this title offers a rough and ready understanding of that task and so allows a glimpse of what actually takes place in that work.

Thus, we repeat our initial question: To what extent does the system of science require the science of the experience of consciousness, respectively the science of the phenomenology of spirit, as its first part?

What does *System of Science* mean? Let us note that the main title is not *System of Sciences*. This expression has nothing to do with the compilation and classification of various existing sciences of, say, nature or history. The system is by no means aiming at such things. Here we are dealing with *the* science and *its* system. *The* science also does not mean scientific research in general, in the sense that we have in mind when we say: "Barbarism threatens the continued existence of *the* science." *The* science, whose system is at issue, is the totality of the highest and most essential knowledge. This knowledge is philosophy. Science is taken here in the same sense as in Fichte's notion of the "doctrine of science." That doctrine is not concerned with sciences—it is not logic or theory of knowledge—but deals with *the* science, i.e., with the way in which philosophy unfolds itself as absolute knowledge.

But why is philosophy called *the* science? We are inclined—because of custom—to answer this question by saying that philosophy provides the existing or possible sciences with their foundations, i.e., with a determination and possibility of their fields (e.g., nature and history), as well as with the justification of their procedures. By providing *all* sciences with their foundation, philosophy must certainly be science. For philosophy cannot be less than what originates from it—the sciences. If we add to the field of that for which it is the task of philosophy to give a foundation, not only knowing in the manner of the theoretical knowledge of the sciences but also other forms of knowing—practical knowledge, both technical and moral—then it will be clear that the foundation of all these sciences must be called "science."

This view of philosophy, which has flourished since Descartes, has been more or less clearly and thoroughly developed. It attempted to justify itself with recourse to ancient philosophy, which also conceived of itself as a knowing, indeed as the highest knowledge. This concept of philosophy as *the* science became increasingly dominant from the nineteenth century to the present. This took place, not on the basis of the inner wealth and original impulses of philosophizing, but rather—as in neo-Kantianism—out of perplexity over the proper task of philosophy. It appears to have been deprived of this perplexity because the sciences have occupied all fields of reality. Thus, nothing was left for philosophy except to become the science of these sciences, a task which was taken up with increasing confidence, since it seemed to have the support of Kant, Descartes, and even Plato.

But it is only with Husserl that this conception of the essence of philoso-phy—"in the spirit of the most radical scientificality"[1]—takes on a positive, independent, and radical shape: With this conception of philosophy, "I am restoring the most original idea of philosophy, which has been the founda-tion for our European philosophy and science ever since its first concrete formulation by Plato, and which names an inalienable task for philosophy."[2]

And yet if we proceed from this connection between philosophy and the sciences and from philosophy conceived as science, we do not comprehend why for German Idealism philosophy is *the* science. From this vantage point we also do not comprehend the ancient determination of the essence of philosophy. Granted that the tradition of modern philosophy was alive for Fichte, for Schelling, and for German Idealism generally, philosophy for them and especially for Hegel does not become *the* science because it should supply the ultimate justification for all sciences and for all ways of knowing. The real reason lies in impulses more radical than that of grounding knowledge: they are concerned with *overcoming finite knowledge and attain-ing infinite knowledge*. For it is possible to meet the task of laying the foundation for the sciences, of realizing the idea of a rigorous scientificality of knowing and cognition, without regard for this specific problematic peculiar to German Idealism, namely, how philosophy unfolds of itself as absolute knowledge. If the task of founding the sciences—grasping its own intention more or less clearly—presses in the direction of absolute knowl-edge, then the above-named task would cease to exist and would lose its own distinctive mark. For then it is not absolute knowledge because it lays the foundation for the sciences, but rather it can be this foundation-laying in this sense only insofar as it tries to found itself as absolute knowledge. But founding absolute knowledge is a task which has nothing to do with founding sciences. In the course of our interpretation of the *Phenomenology of Spirit*, we shall see and understand what is positively required and what decisions must be made from the very beginning for the founding of absolute knowledge.

In any case, we must from the very beginning confront the confusion that today very easily emerges if one connects current attempts to found philoso-phy as the first and essential science with Hegel and to regard him as confirming them. When we read in the preface to the *Phenomenology* that "the true shape in which truth exists can only be the scientific system of such truth" and "to help bring philosophy closer to the form of science, to the goal where it can lay aside the title *love of knowing* and be *actual knowing*—

---

1. *Jahrbuch für Philosophie und phänomenologische Forschung* XI, Epilogue to "*Ideen zu einer reinen Phänomenologie und phänomenologischen Philosophie*," p. 549.
2. Ibid.

that is what I have set myself to do,"³ and when Hegel states similar things elsewhere, then the word *science* has a different ring altogether, and its concept an entirely different meaning. And in fact, this meaning of the concept of science arises from and is the final development of that approach which Western philosophy already adopted in antiquity as its guiding question. In contrast to this very intrinsic intention of *bringing the guiding problem of ancient Western philosophy* to its completion, the propensity toward laying the foundation of the sciences and toward the thus oriented formation of philosophy as rigorous science is of lesser significance.

But the guiding problem of Western philosophy is the question, "What is a being?" The shaping of this question stands in an inner, de facto relation to λόγος, νοῦς, *ratio*, thinking, reason, and knowledge. This does not mean primarily and simply that the question, "What is a being?" is dealt with by an intellectual *procedure* and is known theoretically. Rather, the thesis according to which the inquiry into beings is related to λόγος says something about the *factual content* of this question, namely, that a being as a being, i.e., regarding its being [*Sein*], is grasped *from* the λόγος and *as* λόγος. It maintains that fixing an interconnection between a being, ὄν, and λόγος already represents a decisive (not a random) *answer* to the guiding question of philosophy.

This answer, which was of necessity prepared at the start of ancient philosophy, was brought to completion in a radical way by Hegel. That is, *by really carrying through* the answer, he brought to real completion the task which was implied in ancient philosophy. (Accordingly, a *being as such*, the actual in its genuine and whole reality, is the idea, or the *concept*. The concept, however, is the power of time, i.e., *the pure concept annuls time*.⁴ In other words, the problem of *being* is properly conceived only when *time is made to disappear*.) The Hegelian philosophy expresses this disappearance of time by conceiving philosophy as *the* science or as absolute knowledge.

Now, in claiming that philosophy is *not* science, I am saying that, considering the actual content of philosophy, its guiding question cannot be left in the form that it had for the ancients, nor, consequently, can it be left to stand on the foundation provided by Hegel's problematic. Thus, I am suggesting parenthetically that philosophy can find its way back into its fundamental problems less than ever as long as it is primarily conceived on the model of the idea of a rigorous scientificality and in terms of the founding of knowledge and of the sciences.

By seeing the task of philosophy as lying in the thesis that "philosophy is not a science" (a thesis which sounds negative but whose positive character comes clearly to the fore in the title of my book *Being and Time*), I am not

---

3. II, 6 [GW IX, 11; Hoff., 12; E.T., 3].
4. Cf. II, 604 [GW IX, 429; Hoff., 558; E.T., 487].

suggesting that philosophy should be delivered over to fanaticism and to the proclamation of any opinions about the world whatsoever (in other words, what currently carries the eminent title of "existential philosophy"). In this view, all strict conceptuality and every genuine problem are reduced to the level of mere technique and schematic. It was never my idea to preach an "existential philosophy." Rather, I have been concerned with renewing the question of *ontology*—the most central problem of Western philosophy— the question of being, which relates to λόγος not only in terms of *method* [*Mittel*] but also in terms of *content*. One cannot decide whether or not philosophy is *the* science by considering some epistemological criterion or other. This decision can be made only from out of the actual content and the inner necessities of the first and last problem of philosophy—*the question of being*. If we suggest that philosophy cannot and should not be *the* science, then we are also not saying that philosophy should be made a matter of whim. Instead we are saying that philosophy is to be *freed* for the task which always confronts it whenever philosophy decides to turn into work and become actuality: It has become free to be what it is: philosophy.

Philosophy should strike an alliance neither with the scientific nor with the unscientific, but rather simply with the matter itself, which remains one and the same from Parmenides to Hegel. And what about Kierkegaard and Nietzsche? We should not say offhand that they are not philosophers; much less should we hurriedly say that they are philosophers and thus are part of the genuine history of philosophy. Perhaps in both Kierkegaard and Nietz- sche—and we cannot take them seriously enough—something has been realized which in fact is *not* philosophy, something for which we as yet have no concept. Therefore, in order to understand them and their influence, it is crucial that we search for that concept instead of pitting them against philosophy. We must keep the possibility open that the time to come, as well as our own time, remains with no real philosophy. Such a lack would not be at all bad.

In these preliminary observations, it had to be said that the goings-on of contemporary philosophy are confused and vacuous in terms of genuine relations to the philosophical tradition and to the actual presence of its spirit. This must be mentioned only to suggest that, no matter how much this activity interferes with us at every step, we must push it aside if we wish to understand anything at all regarding the problematic of Hegel's *Phenome- nology of Spirit*.

b) Absolute and relative knowledge. Philosophy as the system of science

The preceding clarifies, at least in a negative way, the overall sense of the *System of Science*, which is the main title of the *Phenomenology of Spirit*. In a positive way the title means: system of absolute knowledge. But what does "absolute knowledge" mean? We shall find that answer only by interpreting the *Phenomenology of Spirit*. However, even at this stage we can—and must—illustrate the expression "absolute knowledge" by offering a preliminary concept of it.

The term *absolute* means initially "not relative." And what does the expression *relative* mean when it is applied to knowledge? Knowledge is first of all obviously relative if it is a knowledge of this *or* that thing while *not* being the knowledge of something else. This knowledge is relative because it is related to something and *not* related to something else. Knowledge is said to be merely relative (without being aware of its own relativity) when there is still something else about which that knowledge *knows nothing*. Relative knowledge is that which does *not* know *everything* there is to know. However, such a concept of relative knowledge would be only quantitatively relative, since it means not knowing everything that there is to know. Correspondingly, the idea of an absolute knowledge would also be quantitatively absolute, since it would mean *knowing everything that there is to know*. But for Hegel the concepts of relative and absolute, as characters of knowledge, are to be understood not quantitatively but qualitatively. It is possible that a quantitatively absolute knowledge, which knows everything so far as range is concerned, could nevertheless be relative in accordance with the *character* (*quale*, *qualitas*) of knowing involved. In what way? What then does the term *relative* mean when it designates the *how*, the character and manner of knowing? Is not every kind of knowing, in its own way, a relative knowing, in the sense of being in itself a relation to that which is known? Is not knowledge as such a knowledge of something? This is precisely what Hegel denies and must deny when he claims that there is a knowledge which is qualitatively *not* relative, but absolute. To be sure, we fail to grasp the Hegelian notion of the *relativity* of knowledge if we understand it to be *in itself* a relation to something. I shall attempt to clarify, if only provisionally, exactly what Hegel always means by the terms *absolute* and *relative* as qualitative characters of knowledge; and I shall do so by drawing upon the lexical meaning of these designations.

A *scientia* is *relativa* as *scientia relata*. It is relative not simply as *related to* something but as a knowledge which in its knowing attitude is a *relatum*, in the sense of being carried over to that which it knows. Carried over and across, this knowledge *remains knowingly in what is known*. It knows it precisely so as to be *held fast* by what is known. Thus, as a knowing of that which is known, this knowledge *is consumed* by it, surrenders to it, and is knowingly lost in it. Even if such a knowledge is a knowledge of *everything*, lacks nothing quantitatively, and is therefore absolute, it is still relative according to the kind of knowing involved. For example, if we think of all the beings which exist and think of them as created by a God who also exists, then the totality of beings known in this way would still only be relatively known. Such a relative knowledge would be caught up in and imprisoned by what it knows. Hegel calls such knowing "consciousness."

But we must ask if there is a possibility of knowing which is qualitatively different from this. It is obvious that we can come to a proper decision about this only if we take it up in terms of the quality of knowing. This means that we have to ask whether the quality of relative knowledge as such allows for something qualitatively other than relative knowledge. For knowledge to be qualitatively other than relative knowledge, for it to be other than a knowledge which is carried over to what is known and bound there, it must not remain bound but must liberate and ab-solve itself from what it knows and yet as so ab-solved, as absolute, still be a knowledge. To be ab-solved from what is known does not mean "abandoning" it, but "preserving it by elevating it."[5] This elevation is an absolving which *knows*; that is, what is known is still known, but in being known it is now *changed*.

Obviously such an absolving presupposes the *attachment* of relative knowledge. And absolving as a *detaching which is aware of itself* must first of all be a knowledge in the sense of relative knowledge. The possibility, as it were, to free the so-called relative knowledge is given in our capacity to know it again, to become conscious of that which is extant in the broadest sense. In the process of its unfolding alongside things, consciousness absolves itself in a certain way from them as soon as it becomes aware of itself *as* consciousness. Becoming aware of itself, this consciousness turns into what we may accordingly designate *self-consciousness*. Here in the nature of relative knowledge lies a possibility for detachment; and herein lies the question—and it is one of Hegel's most decisive questions in his confrontation with the philosophy of his time and with Kant—whether in relative knowledge this detachment actually takes place or whether relative knowledge is still *consciousness*, albeit *self-consciousness*.

Is not this knowledge, which knowingly absolves itself from consciousness and knows it (consciousness), in turn also a relative knowledge, bound now, of course, not simply by what is known in consciousness, but by consciousness as the known? Thus, we quite appropriately grasp the knowledge which absolves itself from consciousness as self-*consciousness*. Yes indeed, but the first consequence of this is that although *self-consciousness* is absolved, it is still relative, and therefore *not absolute knowledge*. What is known through such absolving is that that knowledge itself is a way of knowing, is aware of itself, and is a self-consciousness. Thus, in self-

---

5. Cf. *Enzyklopädie*, III. Teil-*Die Philosophie des Geistes*, Einleitung VII, 2, 21 [*Hegel's Philosophy of Mind* (Oxford University Press, 1971), p. 12].

consciousness we realize two things: (1) that knowledge can be detached, and (2) that there is a new form of knowledge which can only be consciousness—such that now knowing insists on the *I* and remains entangled with itself, such that it gets tied to the *self and the I*. Thus, this knowledge is relative and bound in two ways: (1) This knowledge knows itself as self, and (2) it distinguishes this self from existing things. In this way self-consciousness remains relative in spite of the detachment that has asserted itself.

Nevertheless, it is just this self-consciousness, relative in one respect and not relative in another, that reveals the possibility of a detachment or liberation. This liberation is indeed such that it does not discard that from which it liberates itself; but in knowingly absolving itself—knowing it—it takes and binds to itself, as that which frees itself. This self-conscious knowledge of consciousness is, so to speak, a relative knowledge which is free; but as relative it is still not absolute, still not genuinely free.

Obviously the *pure* kind of non-relative knowledge will be primarily that which absolves itself even from self-consciousness, which is not fettered to self-consciousness and yet is aware of it—not as existing *for itself*, *next to* which there is still simple consciousness, but as self-consciousness of consciousness. *The unbounded origin of the unity of both* self-consciousness and consciousness, as they *belong together*, *is a knowledge that is aware of itself as the purely unbounded, purely absolved absolute knowledge*, which provisionally we call reason. This knowledge, absolute and absolved as it is, is a knowledge which, while not relative, holds onto, possesses, and retains that which it knows relatively.

Hegel designates all three—consciousness, self-consciousness, and reason—as consciousness. Thus, *consciousness* means three things:

1. Any kind of knowledge
2. A knowledge which is related to things without being aware of itself as knowledge
3. Consciousness in the sense of self-consciousness.

Whatever is known relatively—in the qualitative sense, not merely quantitatively—is known as something limited. But whatever is limited is, in its multiplicity, related to the absolute, as that which has no limit. That is why Hegel, in his essay of 1801 on the difference between the systems of Fichte and Schelling, writes:

> But because the relation of the limited to the absolute is, like the limited, manifold, philosophizing must aim at relating to this manifold. The need necessarily arises for producing a totality of knowledge, a system of science. By this means the manifold of those relations will first be released from being accidental, in that they will preserve their places in the context of the objective totality of knowledge, and their objective completeness will be brought about. The philosophizing which fails to construct a system represents a continuous

escape from limitations. It is more like reason's struggle for freedom than reason's attaining pure knowledge of itself, in its certainty and clarity about itself. Liberated reason is identical with its action, and its activity is a pure presentation of reason itself.[6]

Absolute knowledge is genuine knowledge, *the* science. That science which knows in an absolute way "knows the absolute."[7] Science as absolute knowledge is *in itself system*, according to its most essential character. The system is not an optional framework or an ordering of absolute knowledge by way of addition. Rather, absolute knowledge is conceived and is exclusively aware of itself only when it unfolds and presents itself in and as system. Thus, we must not rewrite the main title of the *Phenomenology of Spirit*—"System of Science"—to read "System of Philosophy." Rather, *philosophy* itself means nothing but the *science in system* or *system of science* (as absolute knowledge). (Hence it becomes clear how absurd it would be to say, with regard to this Hegelian concept of philosophy, that it expresses a striving for a "scientific philosophy" in the conventional sense of this word.)

§3. The significance of the first part of the system with regard to the designation of both of its titles

What does it mean to say that the first part of the system of science requires the science of the experience of consciousness, or the science of the phenomenology of spirit?

To begin with, we must not lose sight of the fact that the first part is science, which cannot now mean some scientific discipline or other. Rather, science means absolute knowledge, and this in turn means the system. The first part of the system of science, as science, is itself the system, the system in its initial presentation.

What must this initial presentation of science be like? The answer is provided by both titles used for designating the first part of the system of science. These titles are worded differently, say something different, and yet they mean the same. We shall first try to elucidate each of these titles separately, in order then to determine what unites them in sameness. Subsequently we can grasp the specific character of the first part of science.[1] But this calls for a preliminary look at what is peculiar to the second part of the phenomenology-system; and in accord with what was said earlier, that in turn means taking a look at the first constitutive part of the final encyclopedia-system.

---

6. I, 199 [GW IV, 30; E.T., 113].
7. Introduction, II, 61 [GW IX, 54; Hoff., 65; E.T., 47].
1. Cf. Preface, II, 28 [GW IX, 29; Hoff., 31; E.T., 20].

a) "Science of the Experience of Consciousness"

The first title used for distinguishing the first part of the system of science reads: "Science of the Experience of Consciousness." The words which make up the title are familiar to us as long as we take the title in its outward appearance, and particularly if we know the philosophical terminology. And yet this familiarity does not help us; on the contrary, it misleads us. If we do not keep in mind, both from the outset and subsequently, that "science" here means "absolute knowledge," then we are already hopelessly led astray. Only by keeping that meaning in mind can we grasp what is meant by "experience," "consciousness," "experience of consciousness," and finally by "Science of the Experience of Consciousness."

To be sure, a real title, which does not stem from out of perplexity or with a view to appeal and the like, can be understood only on the basis of a thoroughgoing appropriation of the work so entitled. Such an appropriation is also necessary for understanding the introduction of that work. Therefore, even if in discussing the titles we now refer above all to the introduction[2] to the *Phenomenology*, and to its important preface,[3] then we gain a limited and provisional understanding of the titles. But above all we must do without a complete interpretation of the pieces just mentioned.

Insofar as we have provisionally explained what the concepts of "science" and "consciousness" mean in Hegel's sense, we can now inquire what the expression "experience" in "Science of the Experience of Consciousness" means. We are familiar with this expression as a technical term in Kant's *Critique of Pure Reason*. One of the formulations of the problem of the first *Critique* is the question concerning the possibility of experience. Here experience means the totality of the theoretical knowledge of existing beings (nature). In this sense even today the natural sciences are called experimental sciences.* It is this kind of experience which, in terms of its essence, is the object and theme of philosophical knowledge. That is why the *Critique of Pure Reason* could be taken as a science or theory of experience, a theory about what experience is.

But if Hegel characterizes the *Phenomenology of Spirit* as the science of the experience of consciousness, then (1) experience is not taken in the Kantian sense, and (2) phenomenology as *the* science as such does not mean a knowledge *of* or *about* experience. This holds particularly true when we grasp experience as Hegel does. What does experience mean *for* Hegel? Is there any *connection* at all between Hegel's concept of experience and that of

---

2. II, 59–72 [GW IX, 53–62; Hoff., 63–75; E.T., 46–57].
3. II, 3–58 [GW IX, 9–49; Hoff., 9–59; E.T., 1–45].
*[*Erfahrungswissenschaften*: literally, "experiential sciences."]

Kant and his problem? If the answer is in the negative, *from where* does Hegel get what is then obviously his own concept of experience?

We must ponder what the word *experience* means generally, prior to its terminological use in philosophy, in order to see that it is not arbitrarily and without reason that Hegel uses the word in this central place.

For example, we say: I have learned or experienced [*erfahren*] that such and such has happened, for example, that lightning has struck a house. "I have learned or experienced" means that I have not merely heard something about it, but rather that I heard it from someone who knows it and *was there*, or who heard it from those who were there. I have heard, I have learned. Again, someone is sent out to inquire about something—e.g., the condition of a patient—and returns with the response that "there was just nothing *to find out* [*erfahren*]." Here the term *erfahren* means to find out, *to establish how certain things are*. In this and in similar cases, *erfahren* means to learn and to establish how things are, what is happening and what has happened. *Experiencing* [*in Erfahrung bringen*] means to pursue *the matter itself* in a certain way and to see whether what has been said or believed can be confirmed. *Experiencing* means to let an opinion be confirmed by the matter itself. Accordingly, experiencing is a knowledge which is confirmed by someone who goes directly to things and sees them. Such knowledge makes a person who lets himself be guided by it an *experienced* human being. Because he is experienced, he can be regarded as one who has been *proved* to be, for example, an experienced physician. To say that someone is experienced is to say that he knows what he is doing, observes how things must be going if they are to take the right and not the wrong course.

The issue for us is not to list and explain all of the differences, nuances, gradations, and interrelations of meaning in the term *experience*. Rather, we would like only to find out in which direction Hegel's use of the word goes. And in this respect it should be pointed out that the use of this term by Hegel is not in line with the meanings we have mentioned so far. If we bring these meanings into a first group, then *experience* means the immediate demonstration of an opinion or a knowledge by way of returning to things in the broad sense of the term, i.e., by seeking recourse in the intuition of some thing as the means of its confirmation. There is a second group of meanings which does not focus exclusively on the element of seeing for oneself or on taking a view of one's own in order to confirm an opinion and to be guided by it. Rather, in this group of meanings *experience* connotes the process of undergoing experiences in the course of which the experienced matter itself will be confirmed and its comportment verified by determining whether or not the matter is what it is, or how the matter is joined to something else. Experiencing here means testing the matter itself in and for the context to which it belongs. Expressions such as "to undergo experiences with something," "to have to undergo experiences with something," "to have become richer by certain experiences," always convey two senses: First, they indicate a certain sense of having been disappointed and surprised because things turned out other than expected. Second, they suggest an additional learning of something new that is increasingly verified.

Let us briefly distinguish both groups or concepts of experience. 1. Experimenting in the sense of demonstrating and proving an opinion about something with recourse to sense perception *of that* thing itself. 2. Undergoing an experience in the sense of letting the matter itself demonstrate *itself* and so be verified as it is in truth.*

According to the first group of meanings, we speak of the sciences of experience as *"experimental sciences."* Depending on whether we conceive the notion of a *demonstrating-intuition* in a narrow or a broad sense, we change the concept of experience. If we do not limit demonstrating-intuition to what is sensible—and is obtained primarily through the sense organs—but conceive of this intuition simply as the manner of confirming an opinion on the matter at hand, then the concept of an *intuition of essences* may emerge. For example, such an intuition is required in determining the structural relation of a subject and a predicate in a proposition, a relation which can neither be seen by the eyes nor heard by the ears. Even less will we invent something arbitrary about it. Instead, we must demonstrate the structural relation in a living proposition as such. We must render this relation evident for what it is, we must render its essence "evident" as it *emerges out of the relationship itself.* The intuition which delivers the essence in this first sense, is the *phenomenological intuition.* Because such an intuiting can be confirmed in terms of the things themselves, as they are in themselves, the phenomenological intuition can also be called experience. It was in this fundamentally extended sense that Scheler used the expression "phenomenological experience" in his early important works over twenty years ago. Recently Husserl too seems to have taken up this extended concept of experience whenever he uses that word—a practice which is in keeping with his conviction, held by him for a long time now and mentioned often, that phenomenology represents empiricism and positivism, properly understood.[4]

The *Hegelian concept of experience* as it appears in the title of his *Phenomenology,* "Science of the Experience of Consciousness," does not go in the same direction as the aforementioned contemporary phenomenological concept of experience. In Hegel the emphasis *is not on the moment of*

---

*[In both sentences Heidegger uses the phrase *eine Erfahrung machen.* However, we translate the first one as "experimenting," since it refers to the natural sciences.]

4. Cf. *Formale und Transzendentale Logik,* 1929.

significance in confirmation by intuition. Saying this, I am saying at the same time something whose mention is really superfluous from the first, namely, that "science of experience" has nothing at all to do with the "experimental sciences" in the current sense, e.g., biology or history. With the expression "science of experience," Hegel does not want to emphasize that this science should be confirmed and proved in the experience of either a sensible or an intelligible intuition. Therefore, it is quite misleading to try, from this point of view or in general, to establish a connection between contemporary phenomenology and that of Hegel—as Nicolai Hartmann does, as if Hegel were concerned with the analysis of the acts and experience of consciousness.

The Hegelian concept of experience moves much more in the direction of the second group of meanings which the term *experience* has, namely, experience as denoting, both negatively and positively, *undergoing an experience with something in such a way that this something is verified,* experiencing it as not being what it first seemed to be, but being truly otherwise. However, what proves to be different will not be thrown aside. Rather, the appearance in such and such a way [*das So-Scheinen*] belongs precisely to that which is experienced and is included in that which renders the experience richer. For Hegel this way of undergoing an experience is certainly not related to events, tools, or people. So to what is it related? The answer is given in the title of the *Phenomenology*: Science of the experience of consciousness. If this means that the experiences are experiences of consciousness, then this consciousness is the object of experiencing. But it is questionable whether the term "of" in the expression "experience *of consciousness*" is to be interpreted as an objective genitive, however much the ordinary meaning of the title may suggest such an interpretation. "Experience of consciousness" does not mean primarily experiences that are in and about consciousness. Rather, this expression suggests that it is consciousness itself that undergoes these experiences. Consciousness, as Hegel says, is "comprehended in the experience itself."[5] If we ask in what consciousness undergoes its experiences or with what it must undergo its experiences, the answer is: In and with itself [*an ihm selbst, mit sich selbst*]. So maybe consciousness *is* the object of experience, and the above interpretation is correct? By no means. On the contrary, only because consciousness in the quite specific sense of absolute knowledge is the subject of experience is consciousness the object of experience and can undergo an experience with itself—not the other way around. To the extent that consciousness as subject undergoes the experience (consciousness and experience understood in the Hegelian sense), it cannot do this other than in itself. If, on the contrary, we take

---

5. II, 72 [GW IX, 61; Hoff., 74; E.T., 56].

consciousness initially as an object, then it is indeed possible that consciousness can be experienced and described differently, e.g., as phenomenological experiences *with* [am] consciousness, which have nothing to do with what Hegel means by the "experience of consciousness."

Experience of consciousness is, therefore, "the experience of itself which consciousness goes through."[6] What sort of experience must consciousness undergo with itself? We have already delineated the basic features of such an experience. Initially consciousness is relative knowledge to such an extent that it knows nothing about *itself*, about what it is. Consciousness knows only about its own *object*, and only insofar as it is in consciousness. It does not even know the object *as such*, where the object stands opposite the knowing of it. As soon as knowledge knows its object, it already knows that the in-itself is object *for* consciousness. This is to say, *being-for-consciousness* is a being-known [*Gewußtsein*]. This being for . . . is *knowledge*. To the extent that consciousness is aware of itself as a knowledge of . . . that allows the object to take a position opposite consciousness, to that extent the object loses its character as in itself and becomes something else, turns into something *for consciousness*, into a knowledge. And as a knowledge that is known, this knowledge becomes something other than what it formerly was when consciousness was simply absorbed in the knowledge of the object. There emerges now another mode of knowledge; and what was known formerly, the being in itself of the object, becomes different.

When consciousness *undergoes its experience* of itself as knowledge of the object and thus also undergoes its experience in terms of the object, then consciousness must experience that it becomes something other for itself. Consciousness *verifies* to itself what it really is, in the immediate knowledge of the object, which is not further known. In this verification consciousness loses its initial truth, what it at first thought of itself. However, in this verification consciousness not only loses its initial truth but also undergoes an experience and becomes richer by it, in that consciousness obtains a truth about itself. Thus, "*the new true object*"[7] issues forth for consciousness. And inasmuch as consciousness and its knowledge are the sole object of this experience, consciousness becomes richer by a knowledge of *knowledge*, a knowledge of what knowledge is. Through this experience knowledge increasingly discovers the way to itself and to its ownmost essence.

Thus, the experience which consciousness undergoes with itself has a negative and positive aspect, corresponding to the second concept of experience we discussed earlier. Through the experience which consciousness undergoes with itself, consciousness becomes other to itself. But this becoming-different-to-itself is exactly a coming-to-itself. As Hegel puts it:

---

6. Ibid.
7. II, 70 [GW IX, 60; Hoff., 73; E.T., 55].

"And experience is precisely the name we give to this movement, in which the immediate, the unexperienced, i.e., the abstract {relative}, whether it be of sensuous (but still unsensed) being or is only thought of as simple, becomes alienated from itself and then returns to itself from out of this alienation, is only then revealed for the first time in its actuality and truth, and becomes also a property of consciousness."[8] Hegel calls experience a "movement," and in the introduction to the *Phenomenology* he says explicitly that *consciousness* undergoes this experience, that "consciousness exercises . . . this movement on itself. . . ."[9] This experience is the experience of consciousness which is possible only when consciousness is the *subject* of experience.

In the experience which consciousness undergoes with *itself*, consciousness must undergo its *experience* with itself. Thus, consciousness experiences itself as that which *must* undergo such experience with itself, i.e., consciousness experiences the inevitability of its own essential character. Because consciousness as knowledge is essentially absolute and not relative, it must undergo the experience that the relative knowledge exists only because it is absolute. Absolute knowledge which is aware of itself purely as knowledge and knows of its self—and through this selfhood knows itself as *true* knowledge—is *spirit*. For spirit is nothing but being-alongside-itself which comes back to itself in becoming something other than itself. Spirit is this "*absolute restlessness*,"[10] but understood properly as *absolute* restlessness to which nothing more can "happen" in principle. Later Hegel calls this restlessness "absolute negativity," and "infinite affirmation."[11]

Thus, what emerges out of the experience which consciousness has of itself—what shines forth or *appears*—is spirit. In experience as the movement of consciousness that has been characterized as becoming-other by coming to itself, there takes place *the coming-to-appearance* of spirit, or the *phenomenology of spirit*.

Thus, by elucidating the *first* subtitle of the work, "Science of the Experience of Consciousness," we are unexpectedly led to the *second* subtitle: "Science of the Phenomenology of Spirit." In this way the inner connection of both subtitles becomes clear.

b) "Science of the Phenomenology of Spirit"

To understand the second subtitle and thus the entire work, it is crucial that once again we determine correctly what the genitive means in the

---

8. II, 28f. [GW IX, 29; Hoff., 32; E.T., 21].
9. II, 70 [GW IX, 60; Hoff., 73; E.T., 55].
10. II, 127 [GW IX, 100; Hoff., 126; E.T., 101].
11. VII, 2, 20 [*Philosophy of Mind*, p. 12].

expression "phenomenology of spirit." This genitive must not be interpreted as a *genitivus objectivus*. Easily misled by current phenomenology,
one might take this genitive to be object-related, as though here we are
dealing with phenomenological investigation of spirit that is somehow
distinguished from a phenomenology of nature or that of economics. Hegel
uses the term *phenomenology exclusively* in reference to spirit or consciousness. But he does so without conceiving spirit or consciousness as the
exclusive themes of phenomenology. It is Husserl who speaks this way
about phenomenology as "transcendental phenomenology of consciousness," which investigates consciousness in its quintessential self-constitu-
tion and in the constitution of the totality of consciousness of objects—an
investigation whose agenda would be set up for decades and centuries to
come. In Hegel's conception of the phenomenology of spirit, on the contrary, spirit is not the *object* of a phenomenology. Here "phenomenology" is
by no means a title for an investigation of or a science *about* something like
spirit. Rather, phenomenology is not one way among many but *the* manner
in which spirit itself exists. The phenomenology of spirit is the genuine and
total coming-out of spirit. But before whom does it come out? Before spirit
itself. To be a phenomenon, to appear means coming forward in such a way
that something shows itself which is other than what previously showed
itself, in such a way that what comes forward does so *in opposition to* what
previously appeared, and what previously appeared is reduced to *mere
illusion* [*Schein*].

Experience, properly understood in Hegel's sense, as *having-to-undergo-
an-experience-with-oneself*, means appearing as a self-showing of knowledge
which comes forward as what *becomes-other-than-itself* by coming to itself.
To appear means to come out in the twofold sense of something's *showing*
itself and thus showing itself in *opposition to* what has already shown itself by
showing it to be *a mere illusion*. To appear means that consciousness in its
knowledge becomes something other to itself.[12] Accordingly, six years
before the publication of the *Phenomenology*, Hegel writes in the essay of
1801 entitled "The Difference between the Systems of Fichte and Schelling"
(in connection with the question as to how the absolute should be posited
and conceived): "Appearing and separating are one."[13] By separating Hegel
means becoming other than oneself in the sense of moving apart and
standing in opposition.

In Hegel, appearing and appearance are also primarily and exclusively
related to that which already emerged in his concept of experience: the
emergence of something negative, in its contradiction to something posi-

---

12. Cf. below, pp. 107f.
13. I, 263 [GW IV, 71; E.T., 166].

tive. The *contradiction is what appears*, a no *and* yes with regard to the same thing. Spirit or the absolute appears in the history of appearance. Hence, Hegel states quite clearly in the *Differenzschrift* of 1801: " . . . the purely formal appearance of the absolute is the contradiction."[14] In that the absolute becomes something else, something simultaneously arises and passes away. That is why Hegel states in the preface to the *Phenomenology of Spirit*: "Appearance is the arising and passing away that does not itself arise and pass away, but is in itself [*an sich*] and constitutes the actuality and the movement of the life of truth."[15] But truth—if we add what was said earlier about the concept of experience—verifies itself only in the experience of consciousness as absolute knowledge, as spirit. Appearing in the sense of manifesting itself is not something fortuitous and accidental which happens to spirit, but is its essential character.

Now we see that the complete subtitle—"Science of the Phenomenology of Spirit"—is by no means the tautological expression which one tends to take it to be nowadays. For according to current notions, phenomenology means the science of consciousness, and the Hegelian title means only science of the science of spirit. Such a view is out of the question. In expressions such as science *of* experience and science *of* phenomenology, the term "of" is not to be taken as a *genitivus objectivus* but as an explicative genitive and means: science is absolute knowledge, i.e., the movement which consciousness exercises on itself. This movement is the self-verification of consciousness, of finite knowledge, as spirit. This self-verifying is nothing but the appearance of spirit, or phenomenology. Experience, phenomenology, is the way in which absolute knowledge brings itself to itself. For this reason this experience is called *the* science. This science is not a science *of* experience. Rather, it is *the experience, phenomenology as absolute knowledge in its movement*.

We have now said explicitly how both subtitles of the first part of the system of science complement each other. The first subtitle indicates *what* it is that verifies and represents itself in its truth: consciousness—in that *it* undergoes the experience. The second subtitle indicates *as what* consciousness verifies itself: as spirit. The manner of verification is experience in the sense of *undergoing-an-experience-with-itself*, which is what happens in phenomenology. The experience which consciousness undergoes in science—by bringing itself to absolute knowledge—is the experience according to which consciousness is spirit and spirit is the absolute. "The best definition of the absolute is that *it is spirit*. One can say that finding this definition and grasping its meaning and content was the absolute direction of all education

14. I, 194 [GW IV, 27; E.T., 109].
15. II, 36 [GW IX, 35; Hoff., 39; E.T., 27].

and philosophy, that it was toward this end that all religion and science was driven, and that it is only out of this drive that world-history can be grasped."[16]

Thus, we have clarified the complete title of the work: *System of Science: Part I: Science of the Experience of Consciousness*, or *Science of the Phenomenology of Spirit*. We see now that the proper concept of science is decisive for understanding the title. We arrived at this concept by defining what "consciousness," "relative knowledge," and "absolute knowledge" mean. Absolute knowledge and only absolute knowledge is in itself system. Then we had to clarify what "experience," "spirit," and "phenomenology" mean. The outcome of all of this was that we had to understand the genitive in the subtitle as *subjective*—an understanding which at the same time shows the connection of both subtitles. In the preface to his work, Hegel once used a title which connected the decisive terms of the titles we discussed so far. He took the term *system* (from the major title *System of Science*) and the term *experience* (from the subtitle *Science of the Experience of Consciousness*), and the term *spirit* (from the subtitle *Science of the Phenomenology of Spirit*) and formulated a new title, which read: *System of the Experience of Spirit*.[17] This means that the work represents the absolute whole of experience which knowledge must undergo with itself and in which knowledge becomes manifest to itself as spirit, as absolute knowledge, which fundamentally undergoes the experience.

§4. The inner mission of the phenomenology of spirit as the first part of the system

Our clarification of the complete title of the work has still not provided us with an answer to the question: To what extent does the system of science require as its first part the science of the experience of consciousness, or the science of the phenomenology of spirit? As long as this question is not answered, we have, strictly speaking, not explained the full title, for we have left unexplained the meaning of the phrase "first part." Or to put it differently, as long as this question is unanswered, it remains unexplained *why* "Phenomenology of Spirit" stands simultaneously as a main title and a subtitle.

a) Absolute knowledge coming to itself

We mentioned already that the function of the first part can really be grasped only by considering the second part. And yet if the discussion of the

---

16. Enz. III. Teil, Phil. d. Geistes VII, 2, 29 [*Philosophy of Mind*, p. 18].
17. II, 30 [GW IX, 30; Hoff., 33; E.T., 22].

title brings to light the inner thrust of the work, then the inner mission assigned to the first part of the system must also become intelligible. In its first exposition, science allows absolute knowledge (the absolute itself) to come out in its becoming-other-than-itself, in which it returns to itself, in order to grasp itself as absolute knowledge in its essence and nature. Hence, Hegel writes at the end of the introduction to the *Phenomenology* in one of his magnificent sentences in which language has become one with a mind which has been philosophically molded: "In pressing forward to its true existence, consciousness will arrive at a point at which it gets rid of its semblance of being burdened with something foreign to it, that is only for it and as some sort of other. Appearance becomes identical with essence and at just this point the exposition of consciousness will thereby coincide with the science of spirit proper. And finally, when consciousness itself grasps this its own essence, it will signify the nature of absolute knowledge itself."[1] Thus, the exposition of spirit as it appears in its character as movement itself reaches the point of becoming and of being actual, absolute knowledge. In and through its character as movement, the exposition becomes *itself what is to be exposed.* The exposition and what is to be exposed coincide, not by chance but necessarily. It should discover that absolute knowledge as the knowledge *that* it is, *exists*, and so itself knows itself absolutely. (Absolute self-knowledge is not a free-floating theoretical comportment, but the manner of *actuality* of absolute spirit; and as such it is *knowledge and will at the same time.*)

What does absolute knowledge gain by this? The gain for absolute knowledge is that it is *with itself*, i.e., it is in its own *element*, where it now unfolds itself absolutely as absolute knowledge for the purpose of knowing absolutely what it must know as such. But knowledge unfolded thus is presented in the second part of the system, i.e., in the second exposition of absolute knowledge. Accordingly, the first exposition has the inner mission of preparing itself for the element or "ether" in which absolute knowledge as such breathes. As Hegel says: "In it {the *Phenomenology*} it {spirit} prepares for itself the element of knowing."[2] Only in this way is consciousness transposed into its genuine element. "The spirit that has developed in this fashion and knows itself as spirit is *science*. Science is its actuality and the realm which it builds for itself in its own element."[3] Thus, the first part of the system has the inner mission of bringing absolute knowledge to itself and into its realm (element, ether); and in this realm it should unfold its supremacy as the second part.

What takes place in the first part is the coming of spirit to itself on the

---

1. II, 72 [GW IX, 61–62; Hoff., 75; E.T., 56–57].
2. II, 29 [GW IX, 30; Hoff., 33; E.T., 21–22].
3. II, 20 [GW IX, 22; Hoff., 24; E.T., 14].

path which is appropriate to the character of its own possibility of movement (experience, phenomenology). The *realm* of its kingdom unfolds out
of and in this kind of movement. But this realm is not an extrinsic enclosure
of spheres, sectors, and districts which would then have to be filled out.
Rather, this realm and its inner structure present the actuality of absolute
spirit itself; this actuality builds itself up and in so doing incorporates that
which comes to appearance on the way of spirit. Thus, what appears is not
shapes of consciousness that "pass by." Rather, it is the movement in which
spirit, in the form of the absolute history of absolute spirit, hands itself over
to itself and sublates the tradition. This sublating or *Aufhebung* must, of
course, be conceived, as always in Hegel, in terms of the resonance of its
threefold meaning: *tollere*, removing and eliminating the mere, initial illusion; *conservare*, preserving and including in the experience; but as an
elevare, a lifting up to a higher level of knowing itself and its known.

Science as system requires that as absolute knowledge it knows itself
absolutely in order to have its realm and its actuality in this absolute
knowing. Everything aims at absolute knowledge, and hence at absolute
knowledge knowing itself absolutely. The character and necessity of the
Phenomenology of Spirit is made intelligible only with reference to absolute
knowledge as *the* science, that is, with reference to the Hegelian concept of
spirit.

From this perspective—as something of an addendum, and more to
provide a negative orientation—we can cite the three main errors in current
interpretations of the *Phenomenology of Spirit*, as displayed from various
points of view. A formal critical debate with these views would be unpro-
ductive; and moreover, it is best taken care of by attempting to establish an
interpretation.

b) Misinterpretations of the intention of the *Phenomenology*

The *Phenomenology* has nothing to do with a phenomenology of consciousness as currently understood in Husserl's sense—either in its theme
or in the manner of its treatment, or above all in terms of its basic
questioning and intention. This is true not only if this phenomenology of
consciousness is given the task of universally grounding and justifying the
scientificality of every conceivable science, but also if the transcendental
phenomenology of consciousness is obliged to take on the task of exploring
and grounding the constitution of human culture universally, with reference
to consciousness. A clear differentiation is necessary in the interest of a real
understanding of both [the Hegelian and Husserlian] phenomenologies—
particularly today, when everything is called "phenomenology." Indeed,
according to Husserl's most recent publications, in which he emotionally

rejects those who worked with him so far, we would do better in the future to give the name of phenomenology only to that which Husserl himself has created and continues to produce. Granting that, it is still true that we have all learned from him and continue to do so.

In the phenomenology of spirit, as consciousness's becoming-other-to-itself and coming-to-itself, "forms" of consciousness emerge, as Hegel says; but this emergence of forms of consciousness has nothing to do with the procedure, now becoming routine and stemming from various motivations, of classifying the so-called *types* of world views and types of philosophical standpoints according to just any schema. These typologies and mor-phologies would be a harmless way of passing time, if at the same time the odd idea were not in play that, by placing a philosophy in the net of types, one has decided on the possible and of course relative truth of that philoso-phy. This urge toward classification and such like always begins at a time when the lack of power to do philosophy gets the upper hand, so that sophistry comes to dominate. But sophistry provides itself and its own barrenness with some respectability by first catching whatever ventures to emerge in philosophy in the net of standpoints, and then, having given each type a label, by leaving it with the people. This label sees to it that, regarding the philosophy in question, one will be interested in its label only so as to compare it with another label. Subsequently, the literary discussions about the label give rise to a literature which in its kind may be quite considerable. Consequently, the Kant literature is not only more important than Kant himself, but above all else it reaches the point where no one any longer gets to the matter itself. This procedure reflects the mysterious art of sophistry, which always and necessarily arises along with philosophy and controls the field. Nowadays the power of sophism has "organized" itself, one of the many indications of this being the popularity of typologies of philosophical standpoints—typologies which appear in various disguises (manuals and series). Philosophy becomes a managerial concern—a diabol-ical condition to which the younger scientific minds, rare enough as they are nowadays, fall prey in their prime. But the reason for mentioning these seemingly remote things at exactly this point is the fact that in their confusion these typologies appeal to Hegel's *Phenomenology of Spirit*, in the belief and pretense that in Hegel a similar typology is aimed at, although without the benefit of contemporary depth psychology and sociology.

Allied with these two misinterpretations, there is a third which takes the *Phenomenology of Spirit* as an introduction to philosophy in the sense that this phenomenology leads to a transition from the so-called natural con-sciousness of sensibility to a genuine speculative philosophical knowledge.

In summary, we maintain: Hegel's *Phenomenology of Spirit* is neither a phenomenology in the current sense, nor a typology of philosophical standpoints, nor an introduction to philosophy. *Phenomenology* is *none* of these. But what *is* it then? To the extent that we can answer this question now, we can say that phenomenology is the *absolute self-presentation of reason (ratio—λόγος),* whose essence and actuality Hegel finds in *absolute spirit.* This self-presentation of reason *is called for by the basic guiding problem of Western philosophy* and is forced into a definitive direction—not at all arbitrarily—by German Idealism.

But is it not the case today that Hegel's conception is already completely overcome, in that from various points of view it is said that it is not just *ratio* and rationalism that dominate in Hegel, but rather that the most acute irrationalism positively obtains in his work? To be sure, because one has seen absolute rationalism at work in Hegel, one can correctly find irrational-ism in this interpretation, too—indeed must do so. But this is only one more proof that as little is gained from an explication of Hegel in terms of rationalism as from one in terms of irrationalism. Both rationalism and irrationalism represent an external labeling of the standpoint of the Hegel-ian philosophy, which does not succeed in unfolding this philosophy in terms of the fundamental issue in question.

c) Conditions for a critical debate with Hegel

According to its intention and inner mission—and from the begin-ning—the *Phenomenology* moves *within* the element of absolute knowledge; and only because of this is it capable of venturing to "prepare for" this element.

But should one not say then that Hegel already at the beginning of his work presupposes and anticipates what he wants to achieve only at the end? Certainly this *must* be said. Indeed, whoever wishes to understand anything of this work must say that again and again. The attempts to diminish this "fact"—as we would like to call it—show, furthermore, how little this work has been understood. We *must* repeat again and again that *Hegel presupposes already at the beginning what he achieves at the end.* But we ought not to bring this up as an objection to the work. It should not be brought up as an objection, not because it does not touch Hegel, but because it completely misses the point of philosophy. For it pertains to the essential character of philosophy that wherever philosophy sets to work in terms of its basic question and becomes a work, it already anticipates precisely that which it says later. But that is not to be taken as a surreptitious proof or as a sham procedure; for philosophy is not concerned with proving anything in the usual sense of following a formal principle of proof in a logic which is not that of philosophy itself.

Thus, we are once again confronted with a truth which remains inaccessible to sophistry and which can and should never be demonstrated to it. For such a demonstration would require that sophistry renounce itself and enter into philosophy, which would automatically render all proofs superfluous.

But what does it mean to enter into philosophy? It means that we yield to what is essential in philosophy, so that, in view of the tasks shown there, we may gain clarity *about ourselves*—whether we still have or can have essential tasks, and, if so, what kind of tasks. This entering into what is essential forms the core of a true confrontation, without which every interpretation remains a blind and pointless exercise.

However, the will for a true confrontation finds itself up against a requirement which cannot be adequately met by intellectual acumen, by diligence, or by philosophical accuracy. Hegel speaks of this requirement in the essay we have already and frequently mentioned, "The Difference between Fichte's and Schelling's Systems." He says there: "If the living spirit which dwells in a philosophy is to be revealed, it needs to be born through a kindred spirit. It slips by the historical approach—guided as it is by some interest or other in information about opinions—takes it as an alien phenomenon, and does not disclose its inner being. Spirit is indifferent to that fact, that it gets used for the purpose of increasing what is left of the collection of mummies and the general pile of contingencies. For during the process of gathering the information, spirit itself has slipped between the fingers of curiosity."[4]

If we wish to confront Hegel, then we are required to be "kindred" with him. And even if *on that account* we take the trouble to make the appropriate preparation in ourselves for such a confrontation, that is precisely when we must *above all hear the requirement* to be kindred with him. To be kindred means neither to be identical nor to be the same. Kinship is the identity of a so-called point of view; it is not here a question of belonging to a school, much less of agreement on propositions and concepts, and even less does it mean the leveling of a mutual agreement about the same so-called results and advancements of "research." To be kindred means to be *committed* to the first and last necessities of philosophical inquiry arising from the matter.

Is not the so-far concealed "living spirit" of Hegelian philosophy to be found at that place where Hegel himself tries to demonstrate the truth of the standpoint of philosophy, i.e., in the science of the experience of consciousness as the science of the phenomenology of spirit, in the first exposition of the system of science or system of philosophy?

When we speak like this, it sounds as if *we* are the ones who want to bring salvation now and provide humanity with the truth for all time. Although it sounds that way, something entirely different is intended. What we want is

---

4. I, 168 [GW IV, 9; E.T., 86].

simply to learn to understand that all of us today must first break through to that point where Dasein *gives us the freedom* to awaken in ourselves a readiness for philosophy. This would be freedom for a complete state of preparedness for the philosophical work of Hegel and of others before him, or, rather, of others *with* him. Thus, we must learn to understand that something like this does not take place through some kind of literary undertaking or by appealing to the supposed superiority of those who are more advanced. For in philosophy "there are neither predecessors nor successors."[5] This does not mean that philosophers are indifferent to one another; but on the contrary, every real philosopher is *contemporaneous* with every other philosopher, precisely by being, most intrinsically, the word of his time.

To awaken and to cultivate readiness and preparation for philosophy means to make an effort not to disregard the philosophy which has been at work all along. However, the most flagrant disregard takes place when one mentions the earlier philosophies in casual quotations and distortions and leaves the rest to the historians of philosophy. For we are not dealing with the history of philosophy as something that has ceased to exist and has been left behind, but with the actuality from which we of today were long ago *expelled*, such that—afflicted with blindness and vanity—we waste away with our own little intrigues. *We have no regard for the fact that much too much is happening, and very little of it has an effect.*

Preliminary Consideration

§5. *The presupposition of the* Phenomenology: *Its absolute beginning with the absolute*

Our aim is to comprehend the *Phenomenology of Spirit*, that is to say, actualize it in ourselves as science. Science here means *the science*, the system itself as *absolute knowledge*. This knowledge must come to *itself*. Hence, the work ends with the short section DD, which is entitled "Abso-

---

5. I, 169 [GW IV, 10; E.T., 87].

lute Knowledge."[1] If absolute knowledge as a knowing knowledge is wholly itself only at the end, and if absolute knowledge *is* a knowing knowledge by *becoming* it, by *coming* to itself, and is that by becoming other to itself, then absolute knowledge must at the beginning of its movement toward itself be *not yet* with itself. Absolute knowledge must still be other, and indeed without *having become* other *to itself*. It must be something different at the beginning of the experience that consciousness undergoes with itself, an experience which is nothing other than the movement or the history in which *coming to itself* takes place as *becoming other to itself*.

At the beginning of its history, absolute knowledge must be different from what it is at the end. Certainly. But this otherness does not mean that knowledge is at the beginning *not yet and in no way* absolute knowledge. On the contrary, this knowledge *is* right at the beginning already absolute knowledge, but has not yet come to itself, not yet *become* other. Rather, it is simply other. The absolute is other and so is *not absolute*, but relative. The not-absolute *is* not yet absolute. But this "not-yet" is the not-yet *of the absolute*. In other words, the not-absolute is absolute, not in spite of, but precisely because of its being *not*-absolute. The "not" on the basis of which the absolute can be relative pertains to the absolute itself. It is not *different* from the absolute. It is not finished and *lying* dead *next to* the absolute. The "not" in "not-absolute" does not express something which exists in itself and lies *next* to the absolute, but expresses a mode of the absolute.

Now, if knowledge in its phenomenology is to undergo the experience with *itself* wherein it learns both what it is *not* and what belongs *to it*, then knowledge can do that only when the knowledge which undergoes (fulfills) experience is itself already somehow absolute knowledge.

This is decisive for a clear and reliable understanding of the work. To put it negatively, we understand nothing at all if we do not already from the beginning know in the mode of absolute knowledge. We must have already from the beginning given up the common-sense approach and the so-called natural attitude, not just partially, but totally. Only then will we be completely able to follow how relative knowledge gives itself up and truly comes to itself as absolute knowledge. It follows from this that we must be always already one step ahead of *what* is presented and of *how* it is presented; and it must be that very step which will be taken by the presentation itself. But according to Hegel, this being ahead is possible only because it is being a step ahead in the direction of absolute knowledge, which already from the beginning is the properly knowing knowledge and the one which completes the phenomenology.

---

1. II, 594–612 [GW IX, 422–34; Hoff., 549–65; E.T., 479–93].

a) The stages of spirit's coming-to-itself

Relative knowledge is also absolute knowledge, although in a concealed way. The most relative relative knowledge is consciousness as that which is not yet revealed to itself as spirit, a knowing which is without spirit. For this reason the *Phenomenology of Spirit*, as the coming-to-itself of absolute knowledge, begins with the knowing that knows itself initially as *consciousness* and has for its knowledge what is thereby given to it. Correspondingly, the first major section is entitled: "A. Consciousness."[2]

When knowing gets to know *itself* as consciousness, this knowing *knows* of itself; and it comes to experience, through various stages, that it is *self-consciousness*. For this reason the second major section is entitled: "B. Self-consciousness."[3]

However, self-consciousness, taken for itself within the relationship of consciousness, as the entirety of the self-relatedness of an I (self) to an object, is initially only one aspect. To the extent that self-consciousness undergoes the experience with itself of being not only one aspect but *the* aspect *in* which and *for* which *the other* aspect *also* manifests itself as what *it* is, to that extent there arises a knowing which knows itself as both self-consciousness and consciousness, i.e., as the essential ground which unifies both. Self-consciousness relinquishes its one-sidedness and becomes reason. Hence the third section: "C. Reason."[4]

In Hegel's statement that "reason is the certainty of consciousness that it is all reality,"[5] the term *all* already contains—in a qualitative sense—the announcement that absolute knowledge has somehow arrived at itself in reason. Nevertheless, the work does not end with this section, and phenomenology has not yet reached its goal. For spirit, which is the essence of the absolute, does not appear yet *as such*. And yet with Section C we are already at the end because the absolute has already come *to itself*, although not yet explicitly and in its truth. This double whereby the end is both confirmed and denied is expressed in the way the third section (C) is designated: "C(AA) Reason." Because the phenomenology begins again with reason as the being-with-itself of absolute knowledge, this section is further subdivided. This first form of being-with-itself has not yet truly come to itself; it has not yet genuinely undergone the experience that the absolute (reason) is *spirit*. That is why Section C(AA) is followed by Section (BB): "Spirit."[6]

---

2. II, 73–130 [GW IX, 63–102; Hoff., 79–129; E.T., 58–103].
3. II, 131–73 [GW IX, 103–31; Hoff., 133–71; E.T., 104–138].
4. II, 174–326 [GW IX, 132–237; Hoff., 175–312; E.T., 139f.–262].
5. II, 175 [GW IX, 133; Hoff., 176; E.T., 140].
6. II, 327–508 [GW IX, 238–362; Hoff., 313–472; E.T., 263–409].

"Reason is spirit when its certainty of being all reality has been raised to truth and is conscious of itself as its own world and of the world as itself."[7]

With Section (BB) the explicit, absolute history of absolute spirit *begins*: Section (BB) is the beginning. The subsequent experience of spirit with itself is presented in Section (CC): "Religion."[8] "In religion the self-knowing spirit is immediately its own pure *self-consciousness*."[9] But what we know already about the transition of consciousness to self-consciousness repeats itself here in the history of spirit, namely, self-consciousness again initially takes up a position over against consciousness as its other and thus *next to itself* as independent. Only when spirit also brings this other to itself as what belongs to it, only when spirit knows itself as the truth of the other, only then does spirit know itself absolutely. Only then is it spirit which knows itself as spirit, and so is *actual* as absolute knowledge, *the will which knows itself absolutely* and which is itself the actual power *for* itself as what alone has been willed. Only then does the *Phenomenology of Spirit* reach its goal. Hence, the last section is called: "(DD) Absolute Knowledge."

From Section C on, the three subsequent sections—spirit, religion, and absolute knowledge—are designated as subsections. But as is shown by the title on the first page of each subsection, these may also be marked consecutively. In that case C is simply C and not C(AA); the following section is not C(BB) but D; C(CC) is E; and C(DD) is F.

These considerations seem to be external and technical issues related only to the printing arrangement. And yet the determination of the inner mission of the work and the conception of its fundamental content intimately depend on them. Hegel himself hesitates here—with the kind of hesitation that is not the result of a merely provisional penetration of the issues, but pertains to genuine understanding as it approaches what is ultimate. Our short-sighted comprehension should not find fault with this hesitation. Instead we should know how richly and how rarely such hesitation is given to man. For *this* hesitation characterizes philosophical thinking when it is "ultimate."

This hesitation about how the explicit, absolute history of the appearing of spirit belongs to the phenomenology of spirit, and thus about how one conceives phenomenology itself, is clearly shown in Hegel in that, in the later presentation of the phenomenology of spirit in the third part of the encyclopedia-system, the phenomenology ends with the section on reason. It is the height of superficiality to say that the *Encyclopedia* presents only a short version of the earlier *Phenomenology*. The account of spirit in the

---

7. II, 327 [GW IX, 238; Hoff., 313; E.T., 263].
8. II, 509–593 [GW IX, 363–421; Hoff., 473–548; E.T., 410–478].
9. II, 511 [GW IX, 364; Hoff., 474; E.T., 411].

Encyclopedia (from Section 440 on) does not belong to phenomenology at all anymore, but to psychology. In the *Encyclopedia*, phenomenology of spirit has the *exclusive* significance of being a part of *one* discipline within the philosophy of spirit. Phenomenology takes its place there between anthropology and psychology.

b) Philosophy as the unfolding of its presupposition. The question concerning finitude and the problematic of infinitude in Hegel

The survey of the structure of the work that we have just offered provides little more than a sequence of empty titles. Nonetheless, the division of the work must always be present to us. From this division we conclude once again that the end of the work does not escape its beginning, but presents a return to this beginning. *The end is the beginning which has only become other and thus come to itself.* And this means that the standpoint of one who grasps it and thinks it through is, from the beginning to the end and from the end already in the beginning, one and the same standpoint, namely, that of absolute knowledge, knowledge which sees the absolute in front of itself. What Hegel already stated in the *Differenzschrift* corresponds to this: "The absolute itself is . . . the goal which is sought. The absolute already exists—how else could it be sought? Reason only produces the absolute by freeing consciousness from its limitations. This sublating of the limitations is conditioned by the limitlessness which is presupposed."[10]

Therefore, we can begin to understand the work only if we have already reached its end. In this lecture course I presuppose such a first reading of the entire work. If such a reading has not taken place or does not take place in the next few weeks, there is no sense in sitting here: You cheat not only me but yourselves. However, the first reading is not a guarantee that with the second reading we really understand the work. Perhaps the first reading must be frequently repeated, which is only to say that the first reading is utterly indispensable.

I say "utterly" because this way of reading is demanded by every *philosophical* work and indeed in a *fundamental* sense, based on the fact that all philosophy from first to last merely unfolds its *presupposition*. These presuppositions are not psychological preconditions or biographical gossip, but rather the *inherent content* and *inherent form of the basic problem* [*of philosophy*]. Philosophy's presupposition is not something which lies ahead and outside of philosophy, only occasionally playing a role, and then as covertly as possible. Rather, the presupposition of philosophy is the opening of the whole itself and is precisely that which is there *from the first continuously to*

---

10. I, 177 [GW IV, 15].

the end, waiting to be unfolded. The presupposition of philosophy is not an assumption with whose help we tentatively experiment, only to exchange it hastily for some other assumption. Rather, its pre-supposition is the history of the manifestation of beings as a whole, which is already taking place and where we find ourselves already situated. This presupposition is *the* actuality and can wait, whether *we* take it seriously or whether we are reduced to ridicule in it. Whoever understands this the most intrinsic distress of Dasein's decision, which is simultaneously given with the manifestation of beings, will also understand that everything here *has changed*, including that *distress* itself. Everything *becomes* necessary in the sense of that necessity wherein we have to look for the essence of *freedom.**

Therefore, everything depends on how philosophy entertains the presupposition and whether this presupposition is adhered to and sustained within its beginning. Only someone who adheres to this matter can really hesitate over it. By contrast, take someone who never settles anywhere but wants always to know everything better and to have always known better, and who has invented a principle for his barrenness in the form of a supposed superiority over against all viewpoints. Such a person merely staggers from one opinion to another without ever knowing whether it is his own or someone else's opinion which he has just heard.

But an understanding of the end is *plainly* indispensable in the case of Hegel and for understanding *his* basic intention and inquiry, which begins and must begin with absolute knowledge. This is so because the end is already plainly the beginning and because the *way in which* the end *is* the beginning (and vice versa) has already been decided. The meaning of *this way of being* is determined precisely from and with absolute knowledge itself.

This is what we mean when we say that the *Phenomenology of Spirit begins absolutely with the absolute.* That this *takes place* and really must take place, rather than having to rely on extensive promises and pretentious assurances, provides the necessity which drives Hegel's philosophy forward. And this is not a private opinion. It is for this same necessity that Fichte and Schelling also relentlessly struggle so that the whole would come to language through it.

What is meant when we say the *Phenomenology of Spirit begins absolutely with the absolute* is something that cannot be shown in a formal discussion. One should simply keep in mind that the absolute presents itself differently, in accordance with the heterogeneity of the inner openness of the system. The variety of the systematic presentations of the absolute is grounded in

---

*[The German text draws on the inherent connection between the "distress" that "has changed" (*Not gewendet*) and necessity (*Notwendigkeit*).]

the absolute itself and in the *way* in which it is grasped. What Hegel and like-minded people basically demand is stated in his short critical essay entitled "How Philosophy Is Viewed According to Man's Common Understanding" (1802). There Hegel speaks of "what at the present time constitutes the primary interest of philosophy, namely, to place God absolutely at the beginning once again on the pinnacle of philosophy as the sole ground of everything, as the only *principium essendi* and *cognoscendi*, after he has been placed long enough *alongside* other finite things, or after he has been put right at the end as a postulate which proceeds from an absolute finitude."[11] Hegel states the same thing in the treatise entitled "Faith and Knowledge," published at the same time as the above-mentioned essay, when he says: "But the first task of philosophy is to know the *absolute nothingness*."[12]

It is in this spirit and on its basis that Hegel lets the *Phenomenology of Spirit* emerge. The problem is that of *infinitude*. But how can in-finitude become a more radical problem than that of finitude? It is a question of the *not* and the *negation* whereby the not-finite must, if it can, come to truth. In our obligation to the first and last inherent necessities of philosophy, we shall try to *encounter* Hegel on *the problematic of finitude*. This means, according to what we said earlier, that through a confrontation with *Hegel's* problematic of infinitude we shall try to create, on the basis of our own inquiry into finitude, *the* kinship needed in order to reveal the spirit of Hegel's philosophy. But in this context, infinitude and finitude are not two different-sized blocks of wood which may be rubbed against each other or which one could carelessly throw around in verbal gymnastics. Rather, infinitude and finitude *say* something only insofar as they draw their meaning from the guiding and basic question of philosophy—*the question of being*.

Infinitude and finitude are not answers but rather pre-suppositions in the sense defined earlier. They name tasks or questions.

But one may ask whether setting up a confrontation with Hegel like this is not superfluous. Was it not Hegel, in fact, who ousted finitude from philosophy in the sense that he *sublated* it or overcame it by *putting it in its proper place*? Certainly. But the question is whether the finitude that was determinant in philosophy before Hegel was the *original and effective finitude installed* in philosophy, or whether it was only an incidental finitude that philosophy was constrained to take up and transmit. The question must be asked whether *Hegel's conception of infinitude* did not arise from that *incidental* finitude, in order to reach back and absorb it.

---

11. XVI, 57f. [GW IV, 179; tr. H. S. Harris in *Between Kant and Hegel*, ed. G. di Giovanni and H. S. Harris (Albany: SUNY Press, 1985), p. 299].

12. I, 133 [GW IV, 398].

The question is whether finitude, as the innermost distress at the heart of the matter in question, determines the necessity of questioning. If not, then the confrontation with Hegel is not *in opposition to him*, in the form of a defense of the finitude which *he has surmounted*, but is concerned rather with *what* he has surmounted and the *way* in which he did so.

But if finitude as the innermost distress forces the basic question of philosophy to become worthy of questioning, then this finitude is in the final analysis not a sign under which dubious antiquities may be peddled any more than it is like a hairstyle which would fashion another new look for the tradition.

This distress, which is that of being itself (and not only of our own human being), should not be judged too hurriedly according to our usual and quite inadequate standards, to be either a deficiency or a privilege. And supposing the distress of being is real, would we be able simply to state it, in the same way that we say that the sun shines or that we are in a good mood? Or will this distress [Not] of being become manifest only when we ourselves are *compelled* [genötigt]?

In this compulsion we no longer have a choice whether to commit ourselves or not. But the necessity of commitment for the philosopher—if, as is the case, philosophy is actual and remains only as work—is simultaneously the necessity of exposure [Aus-satz], of being exposed to the fact that the distress will be fought over as a subjective standpoint and perverted into a form of sentimentality and so lose its essence and not compel at all. That the distress compels does not mean that it should be reproduced and felt, but that it gives a hint into the distress of being itself so that it becomes, in the face of this distress, *thoroughly inessential*, publicly and so far as others are concerned.

The most tangible witness of how far the business of philosophy is removed from philosophy itself is to be found in the fact that people believe that philosophy is a matter of talent and the like and that in all that gets written, no one meditates on the way philosophy ultimately has its own original demands, standards, and decrees, which cannot be learned like prescriptions for setting up experiments or for settling legal disputes.

c) Brief preliminary remarks on the literature, on the terminology of the words *being* and *beings*, and on the inner comportment in reading

The *Phenomenology of Spirit* begins absolutely with the absolute. This alone makes it sufficiently clear that it is no accident that access to the work is so difficult. From its first sentence, and without any concessions by way of introduction, guidance, or the like, the work moves on the level attained by philosophy in its passage from Parmenides to Hegel. Kant, and after him Fichte and Schelling, have progressively secured and clarified this level in the sense that it no longer vaguely represents a position outside and distinct from the matter of philosophy, but belongs to philosophy itself and constitutes the structure of philosophy's own inner realm. This level is *effective* and is simply concealed from us. People speak of a collapse of Hegel's philosophy after his death and see in that collapse the collapse of previous philosophy generally, which, presumed to be finished, is awarded the consolation prize of being condescendingly called "classical" philosophy. However, it is not that Hegel's philosophy has broken down. Rather, his contemporaries and successors have not ever yet stood up so that they can be measured against his greatness. People managed to "stand up" to him only by staging a mutiny.

Instead of constantly complaining about the difficulty of the work, we should first take seriously what the work demands. We do not need to discuss this demand extensively. We must try *to begin* with Hegel himself, but in such a way as not to disregard the seemingly external difficulties and the tools needed to overcome them. In this respect we shall draw attention to a few things which deal with an attempt to penetrate the work—the *literature*, the *terminology*, and the *approach* to reading.

Depending on one's capacity for passing judgment and one's inner philosophical security, everyone is free to read everything or nothing in the fast-growing literature on Hegel. For explicating the *Phenomenology of Spirit* in particular, only the works of the secondary-school teacher Wilhelm Purpus are to be considered: *Die Dialektik der sinnlichen Gewissheit bei Hegel, dargestellt in ihrem Zusammenhang mit der Logik und der antiken Dialektik* [*The Dialectic of Sense Certainty in Hegel, Presented in Its Relation to Logic and Ancient Dialectic*] (Nürnberg, 1905) and his *Die Dialektik der Wahrnehmung bei Hegel* [*The Dialectic of Perception in Hegel*], Part One (Schweinfurt, 1908), both published together as a whole under the title *Zur Dialektik des Bewusstseins nach Hegel* [*On Dialectic of Consciousness According to Hegel*] (Berlin, 1908).

These extremely careful and unassuming works were undertaken at a time when one was laughed at if one took Hegel seriously philosophically. They are arranged so as to bring together passages from all of Hegel's works and lectures, corresponding to each section of the *Phenomenology*, thus explaining Hegel through Hegel. Of course, in terms of grasping the *Phenomenology in its actual design*, great care should be taken in using the explanatory quotations whenever they are taken—as they mostly are— from later works such as the *Logic* and the *Encyclopedia*. Explaining Hegel through his own works does not, of course, amount to a philosophical penetration in the sense of bringing to life a closed problematic. However, these limitations and the warning that I have introduced regarding Purpus's use of quotations should not be taken as diminishing the value of these writings, since what matters today is to develop again a taste for such helpful works that have been accomplished without fanfare. By contrast, any halfway useful professor or university lecturer can nowadays write a "brilliant" total exposition of Hegel without much effort.

Two brief remarks on Hegel's terminology. It was stated earlier—and for the moment only as a claim—that the *Phenomenology* presents the self-exposition of reason, which is recognized in German Idealism as absolute and is explicated by Hegel as spirit, an exposition which is called for by the fundamental problem guiding Western philosophy. But the guiding problem of ancient philosophy is the question τὶ τὸ ὄν? *What is a being?* And we can then transform this guiding question into the prior shape of the fundamental question, namely, *What is being?* Our interpretation will be carried out on the basis of a presupposition regarding the realm of inquiry for the already mentioned fundamental question of being. Following the external characterization of the meaning of the word *being*, we use it both for what something is and for its manner, *how* it is, the manner of its actuality. We use this term *being* in this double (by no means self-evident) sense for whatever is not nothing and even as a moment of the nothing itself.

By contrast, Hegel uses the terms *being* and *beings* terminologically only for a certain region of beings as we understand this term and only for a certain mode of being in our sense. What Hegel calls *beings* and *being* we designate with the terms *extant* and *extantness*.* That Hegel uses the term *beings* and *being* in this specifically limited sense is nothing arbitrary, like an accidental choice of words. Nor is it the obstinacy of forming one's terminology, as the philosophical mob imagines. Rather, it is a *response* to the *inherent* problem of being as broached by ancient philosophy.

On the other hand—so far as such a juxtaposition may be allowed—if *we* use the terms *being* and *beings* in their greatest possible extension, then this does not mean that we are forcing the problematic back to the formulation of the question in ancient philosophy and leaving it there or merely extending the inquiry of ancient philosophy to the present day. Rather, the point is that the question concerning beings and the way in which this question was and must have been raised, and so led to its sublation in Hegel—that this history of the question must be renewed, and that necessarily means set in motion *more originally*. Not in order to correct something or to hold ancient philosophy in esteem as a matter of preference, and not because it simply occurred to me as a possible pursuit, but rather on the basis of the necessities of *our* Dasein itself, in which that history of the problem of being is *actuality*.

Thus, from first to last being means something radically different for

---

*[Or: "What Hegel calls *das Seiende* and *das Sein* we designate with the terms *das Vorhandene* and *seine Vorhandenheit*."]

Hegel than it does for us. But this is not a difference between two points of view that are side by side but indifferent. Nor is it a severed and dead difference which could now be treated as a lifeless distinction. Rather, it is difference *itself*, which is possible only by being removed equally from what is insignificant as well as from what is discussed in isolation. And it is possible only through commitment to what is simple, unique, one, and essential.

My second remark concerns the general character of Hegel's terminology in the *Phenomenology*. This terminology has not yet assumed the stability which is achieved in the *Logic* and which later received its sovereign expression in the *Encyclopedia*. If we issued a general warning against an unrestrained explication of the *Phenomenology* on the basis of the later works, then this warning applies above all and especially to its terminology. The fact that the terminology is somewhat loose in the *Phenomenology* does not stem from Hegel's uncertainty, but belongs to the essence of the matter itself.

In conclusion, a brief remark on the approach to reading required by the *Phenomenology*. To speak negatively at first: Do not be in a hurry to criticize and to raise objections as they come to mind piecemeal. Instead go along with Hegel, go along at length, with patience, and with labor. Hegel says how he wants that to be understood, in the preface to the *Phenomenology*: "Everyone is convinced that in the case of all the sciences, arts, skills, and crafts, a multiple effort of learning and practice is necessary to achieve competence. Yet when it comes to philosophy, the prejudice seems now to dominate that, whereas not everyone who has eyes and fingers and is given the leather and the tools is immediately able to make shoes, everyone nevertheless understands immediately how to philosophize and how to evaluate philosophy, since he possesses the measure for doing so in his natural reason—as if he did not equally possess the measure for a shoe in his foot."[13]

Only if we go along with this work with patience—understood in the sense of really working with it—will it show its actuality and its inner form. However, the form of this work—here as everywhere else in genuine philosophy—is not an addition which is meant for the literary connoisseur. Nor is the question that of literary decoration or of stylistic talent. Rather, its inner form is the inner necessity of the issue itself. For philosophy is, like art and religion, a human-superhuman affair of primary and ultimate significance. Clearly separated from both art and religion and yet *equally primary* with both of them, philosophy necessarily stands in the radiance of what is beautiful and in the throes of the holy.

---

13. II, 53 [GW IX, 46; Hoff., 54; E.T., 41].

FIRST PART

Consciousness

•

Chapter One

Sense Certainty

The history of spirit happens in a movement characterized as coming to itself, a movement which shows a remarkable monotony and uniformity, often to the point of the constant application of certain specific formulae. But we should not fail to see, over against precisely such a monotony, that each stage of that history always has its *own* actuality. Our interpretation cannot therefore follow a rigid schema into which we would force the individual chapters each in its turn. Rather, each section demands to be thought through, interpreted, and clarified in its *own* way. This is so not only because each section has its own content in itself, but also because this content is in each case different, depending on the already transmitted history of the absolute spirit.

According to what we have said so far, it is clear that the first section of the *Phenomenology of Spirit*—"A. Consciousness"—and particularly its first part—"Sense Certainty"—demands an interpretation which is entirely peculiar to it but in which it nevertheless must then avoid losing itself. Here we must try to see whether we can succeed in awakening the *inner law* of the work, enabling us to attain the depth and fullness of the whole. It would be easy—or at least it is not the most difficult thing—to drag a whole profusion of historical and systematic issues into individual sentences and concepts and so shape the interpretation in such a way that the lawfulness *proper* to the work and its problem would disappear from view.

The first long section of the work is entitled: "A. Consciousness" and has three parts: "I. Sense certainty; or the this and intending/meaning,"* "II.

---

*[*Das Meinen* (intending/meaning) and *das Meine* (mine) are intimately tied together in the *Phenomenology of Spirit;* in the following pages the connection that these two words have in German is impossible to maintain in translation.]

Perception; or the thing and deception," "III. Force and Understanding, appearance and the supersensible world."

§6. Sense certainty and the immediacy

a) Immediate knowledge as the first necessary object for us who know absolutely

Hegel begins by saying: "The knowledge which is at first or is immediately our object cannot be anything else but immediate knowledge itself, a *knowledge* of the *immediate* or of a *being*. Our approach to the object must also be *immediate* or *receptive*; we must alter nothing in the object as it presents itself. In apprehending it, we must refrain from trying to comprehend it."[1]

Hegel begins with this short passage, which succinctly outlines what "our object" is "at first"—and not just *is* our object, for this or that reason, but what our object *must* be at first (it "cannot be anything else . . . "). This already assigns the task of saying *how* this object must be our object. We are in general clear about what the overall pervasive object presented by the unfolding of the *Phenomenology of Spirit* is: it is *knowing*. That is why Hegel begins by saying: "The knowledge which is at first. . . . " But which knowledge? What does knowledge mean when taken formally? We "know" something when this something exists *for* a consciousness. For this reason Hegel says in the introduction: knowledge is the relation "of the *being* of something *for a consciousness*."[2] That knowledge and not something else is our object is not discussed further. Rather, question and answer aim at once at *that* knowing which "at first" must be "our object."

In which sequence within which progression should this "at first" be understood? What the "at first" means can be determined only on the basis of this question. But Hegel himself already gives an explanation: he says, "at first or immediately." This "or immediately" is not idly written down to crowd out the foregoing expression, but is rather its interpretation. However, what does "immediate" mean? Does it mean simply what we have before us accidentally without further ado? At times that can be a different knowing. One person is in the midst of an ethical decision, another is involved in a religious debate. One person is immersed in a work of art, the other philosophizes. One person keeps a head count, the other observes the stars in a telescope, and another drives a car. In every such case each person

---

1. II, 73 [GW IX, 63; Hoff., 79; E.T., 58].
2. II, 67 [GW IX, 58; Hoff., 70; E.T., 52].

finds himself in a different knowing. How can one say which knowing is immediately our object? Obviously this question can never be settled in a way which is valid for everyone. But does "immediate" here mean what anyone would simply hit upon if he wanted to pinpoint knowledge in himself? The question is not about a knowing which suggests and presents itself simply to anyone. Rather, the question is about "the knowing" which must be "immediately our object." "Our"? Who are the "we" for whom this "our" is meant—"our object," object for us? Does the "we" refer to us who sit here and think about this or that, who now read the *Phenomenology of Spirit*, just as earlier we were reading a text in middle high German or a medical textbook, just as later we shall be reading Pindar or a newspaper? No. Rather, the "we" refers to those who already from the outset know *absolutely* and who apprehend and determine things in the manner of *this* knowing. The manner of this knowing is not to know relatively, not to know merely by constantly fastening precisely on what is known, but rather detaching oneself from *what* is known, to know the knowing of this known. It means, not to be absorbed in what is known, but to transmit it *as such*, as *what is known* to where it belongs as known and from where it stems, i.e., *to transmit* the known to the knowledge of it and so *to know* the *mediation* between what is known and knowledge. This is to say that this mediating knowledge itself now takes in its turn what it knows only as a means, so that with its help the mediating knowledge knows what is known more originally as such. Mediation is in its turn transmitted into the means by which the mediation knows what is its known, etc.

The object for us, our object, is the object for those who from the outset know *in such a way* as to comport ourselves *mediatingly*, in the manner of sublating that has already been characterized, a sublating which is itself the way absolute knowledge occurs and is the character of that restlessness which is the absolute and which Hegel also calls "absolute negativity" or "infinite affirmation."[3] What this means is shown in the *Phenomenology of Spirit*. It suffices for now to say that so far as this knowledge is concerned, the knowing attitude is never a simple affirmation or a simple obstinate denial. It is not the denial of an affirmation, or the affirmation of a denial. Rather, this attitude is what serves as the inner law of the negation of the negation.

According to what has been said, what is im-mediate for us, *the media-tors*, is for *our* mediation *not yet* mediated. To the extent that from the outset we basically and constantly comport ourselves *mediatingly*, to the extent that we in principle and actually know everything as mediated or *mediatable*, we come across what is im-mediate only when we, who know absolutely, fail

---

3. VII, 2, 20 [*Philosophy of Mind*, 12].

to take ourselves seriously enough, when we as it were condescend only to immediate knowledge. We do not surrender ourselves and our way of knowing by this condescension. The immediate to which we, the mediators, condescend always already stands under the dominion of mediation and sublation. The latter in turn can of course be what it is only when it condescends to what is *un*-mediated, precisely in order to *mediate* it. The *im*-mediate is already the im-*mediated* of mediation.

It thus becomes clear who the "we" are who right at the beginning say "for us." "We" are those who know in terms of the science of absolute knowledge. From the beginning the "we" has lost the option of being this or that person and thus of being, randomly, an ego.

It is only from this perspective that we can and must ask which knowledge *must* at first be our object. In order to mediate absolutely, we must comport ourselves immediately, in keeping with the character of our mediation. Our non-mediation at the beginning amounts to our postponing all sublating and mediating; we comport ourselves toward knowledge absolutely relatively—receptively only—in that we do not as yet "get thought moving in manifold ways."[4] "Getting thought moving in manifold ways" does not mean thinking back and forth, but means rather the movement of absolute restlessness. To some extent this movement rests for a moment in knowing what is immediate. But it should be noted how the character and necessity of the possible first object is determined in terms of the knowledge of the *knowers*. It is not at all as if one were seeking some vague immediacy. Rather, the sense of the immediacy is determined from the very beginning, thus circumscribing the scope for what can and must be the first object of this knowledge. We the mediators must necessarily take as our first object that knowledge which as such is knowable *in such a way* as to demand on its own basis nothing else but pure apprehension. That is why the first object for us—which is knowledge as such—must be "knowledge of the immediate."

A being is what Hegel calls this immediate as the object *of* that knowledge which is the immediate object for us who know absolutely. Accordingly, we have in our knowledge *two* objects, or one object twice. This is the case necessarily and throughout the entire *Phenomenology*, because *for us* the object is basically and always *knowing*, which in itself and according to its formal essence already in its turn has its object which it brings along with it. Hegel expresses this relation exactly by distinguishing the "object for us" from the "object for it"—for it, namely, for that knowing which is in each case the object for us. Insofar as the knowing which is our object is only a knowing because something is known for it, the object for this knowing belongs precisely to the object for us.

---

4. II, 74 [GW IX, 63; Hoff., 79; E.T., 58].

Now, the experience which consciousness undergoes with itself in the *Phenomenology* is just that it comes to know that the object for it is not the true object. It learns that the truth of its object lies precisely in what this object is for us—for us who know knowledge and its known already in its character as sublated, knowing it this way fundamentally although it is still under wraps. The object for it must develop through us into the object for us. Through us does not mean that as random subjects we would arbitrarily set to work on that object, but rather that from out of knowledge itself (for which it is always an object) the possibility is given to the object for it to become what it *is*, namely, absolute knowledge. Thus, knowledge reveals itself as that which at the time it is not and as that which in this not-being it simultaneously is in truth. Knowledge *itself* (as what is known in absolute knowledge) *brings to light the measure* by which it at any given time measures and finds its truth. But the respective measure itself then enters into knowledge as the truth for it.

However, we are still not yet entirely clear about the relations and how they become manifest, inasmuch as knowledge appears for *the* science and is presented by means of science, a presentation which constitutes the coming-to-itself of the science.

b) The being-in-and-for-itself of the subject-matter and the contemplation of absolute knowledge. "Absolvent" absolute knowledge

The object for us, who know the science, is always a *knowledge*. In this objectified knowledge lies knowledge's own relation to its known: the object for it. However, for it, for immediate knowledge, the object is at first and immediately not yet *for* it, but is *in itself*. For it, for totally immediate knowledge, the object simply *returns into itself*. Or more accurately stated: The object has not yet at all gone out of itself as what stands *opposed* [as *Gegen*-stand]. It has not gone to *oppose* knowledge of it in order to *stand* opposed to this knowledge. Remaining entirely *with itself*, this object is a *being-in-itself*. The object [Gegen-*stand*] "*stands*", but not as *opposed to* knowledge. Immediate knowledge in itself has just this feature and this character of knowing, that it *surrenders* the object *entirely to itself*. The object stands *in itself* as that which does not need to be for a consciousness. And consciousness grasps the object *immediately*, precisely as something invariable in itself. Thus, we have the object of the known knowledge in three ways:

1. The object *in itself*, as it is immediate for it (consciousness);
2. The being-for-it of the in-itself;
3. The being-for-us of what is a being-for-itself as such.

And yet what the object is as object for us is only the anticipated true *for-*

it of the in-itself. For being-for-it is already the first step of dissolution from immediate absorption in the in-itself; it is already the mode of mediating and no longer immediate knowledge. Immediate knowledge returns to this mediating absolute knowledge. Immediate knowledge begins the *return*, not to something *alien*, but to something which exists *for itself*. That is why the object is known absolutely only when it is not only in-itself and not only for it (that is, for consciousness that comes to know itself *in that way*), but also when the for-it becomes *for itself* and *the in-itself follows thereby*—in other words, when the object is known *in and for-itself*.

To put it differently and at the same time to anticipate an important aspect of Hegelian terminology, we can say that being-in-itself and being-for-another "fall within that knowledge which we are investigating."[5] They fall within that knowledge insofar as *we* who know absolutely know it. For *abstract* knowledge, by contrast, they fall apart, falling out of knowledge. Hegel likes to speak of the "falling out" and the "falling in" of what seemingly falls out into the truth of absolute knowledge, a knowledge which was previously still unevolved.

Regarding the difference between that which is in itself and that which is for another—in other words, for knowledge of the former—Hegel also uses the words *object*, *concept*, and *essence* as technical terms. Indeed, he interchanges these terms in a way which is characteristic of the entire problematic. That which is in itself can be called *object*, and what is for another—what is known or knowledge—can be called *concept*. But being-*for*-another is called object—in the sense of that which stands *against*—and accordingly, what the object is in itself, is called its *essence* or its *concept*. In both instances we are to experience, in the *Phenomenology*, whether and how the object corresponds to its concept or the concept corresponds to its object. As Hegel states: "It is evident that the two cases are the same. But the essential point to retain throughout the whole investigation is that these two moments, *concept* and *object*, *being-for-another* and *being-in-itself*, both fall within that knowledge which we are investigating. Consequently, we do not need to import standards, or to make use of *our* ideas and thoughts during the investigation; it is precisely when we let these go that we succeed in contemplating the subject matter as it is *in and for itself*."[6]

We let our ideas and thoughts go: we who know *absolutely* do not become so by taking *up* and taking on what is one-sided or what has been omitted. Rather, we will know absolutely when we *let go*. Basically, we *know absolutely* already and have already let go what is ours in the sense of what is relative to human beings. We are already those who know absolutely; otherwise we

---

5. II, 68 [GW IX, 59; Hoff., 71; E.T., 53].
6. II, 68 [GW IX, 59; Hoff., 71; E.T., 53–54].

could never begin. We can bring the subject matter into view only if we, the contemplators, are those who know absolutely.

But, of course, this way of talking can be misunderstood. One could think that what is required here is for absolute knowledge to be present in its unfolded and developed absolute fullness. It is not the absolute fullness and its absolute presence which is required but rather *the character and way in which* the absolute *is*, the *absolute restlessness* of mediation, which alone can be *absolutely* immediate, can be *relative* in an *absolute* manner, so absolute that it *is* relative and, *being relative*, brings about its dissolution. It is precisely in showing *how* as absolute it *is* absolute, that the absolute comes to light in the *Phenomenology*. But in the absolute this *how* of *being* absolute is at the same time its *what*—the distinction between what and how (or *essentia* and *existentia*) has basically no place in the absolute. But in order to characterize the absolute *specifically* with regard to its *being absolute*, as an absolute knowing, we would like to introduce a term which expresses more precisely this manner of knowing absolutely. We shall be speaking of restless absolute knowledge as *absolvent* (in the sense of absolution). Then we can say that the essence of the absolute is the in-finite absolving, and therein negativity and positivity are at the same time absolute or in-finite.

We shall now try to read again the short introductory paragraph of the first part of the first major section: "The knowledge which is at first or is immediately our object cannot be anything else but immediate knowledge itself, a *knowledge* of the *immediate* or of a *being*. Our approach to the object must also be *immediate* or *receptive*; we must alter nothing in the object as it presents itself. In apprehending it, we must refrain from trying to comprehend it."[7]

Now it is clear that if we were to try to interpret the individual sentences and paragraphs of the entire work in this manner, we would perhaps reach the end only after many years. However, we refrain from this form of interpretation, not only because we want to reach the end faster, but also because it is not necessary. On the contrary, with the step-by-step coming to itself of science, its own knowing grows and unfolds, and its inner light becomes clearer and more luminous. Of course, this does not mean that the appropriation of the work becomes increasingly easier and more evident. Just the opposite! This growing difficulty arises not from the formal aspect of the work, but from the way in which that which is to be known becomes more concrete in the manner of its being known. What does this mean? It means that the collectivity of those who know, which has been opened up, will be required to become increasingly more exacting. The commitment of the philosopher in and to philosophy can less and less be held back and obliterated by a pseudotruth.

---

7. II, 73 [GW IX, 63; Hoff., 79; E.T., 58].

The first object to submit to the absolvent knowing of science must *of necessity* do so as *that* knowledge which in its turn is in fact the most immediate knowledge. And this in spite of what Hegel states in the second part of A, which deals with knowing as "perception": "the way we take in perception" (as object of absolute knowledge) "is no longer a taking in which just appears, as in sense certainty, but is a necessary one."[8] We have to understand this remark to mean in the first instance that the taking in of the first object which is exhibited in the *Phenomenology* is *not* a necessary one. On the other hand, sense certainty as the most immediate knowledge is not accidentally and arbitrarily the first object; rather, Hegel states explicitly that this knowledge "cannot be anything else" but immediate; consequently, the sense certainty *must* be the *first* object.

Thus, the taking in of sense certainty as an object is not a necessary one (cf. II, 84 [GW IX, 71; Hoff., 89; E.T., 67]), while at the same time sense certainty is necessarily the first object (cf. II, 73 [GW IX, 63; Hoff., 79; E.T., 58]). Sense certainty, in its character as an object for absolute knowledge, is necessary and yet not necessary! Or is the non-necessity which pertains to sense certainty only a non-necessity in the distinction from the *specific* necessity of perception? Sense certainty would not then be necessary in the manner of perception but would be necessary in *its* own way. In that case we would have a twofold necessity. That is indeed the way it is. But this twofold necessity is basically one and the same, by being required by absolute knowledge itself. For if this knowledge is really *absolute*, then in no way—not even at the beginning—can it be dependent upon the surrender of an object which is independent of this knowledge. Rather, even when it is a matter of "taking in," this *taking in* must be one which *takes* the object absolutely and *surrenders itself* to the object absolutely. *Perception as what necessarily comes forward*—in that it emerges from out of the first sublating mediation of sense certainty—emerges from out of absolute knowledge, insofar as it is absolvent in movement. But this same necessity applies to mediation in the direction of its *return* to immediate knowledge, which *is given over to* the previously and, in retrospect, necessary mediation. The taking-in which appears is no less necessary than the transition from sense certainty to perception, only necessary in a different way. The necessity of *coming forward* and the necessity of *taking in* stem in like manner from mediation, which, *mediating* the immediate, allows something else to come forward necessarily which for its part, as a mediation which mediates the *immediate*, must have taken in something immediate with equal necessity.

Hegel begins with immediate knowledge. He must begin with it. But this beginning with the immediate is already no longer an immediate beginning. It is not only for Hegel that the beginning is not an immediate one;

---

8. II, 84 [GW IX, 71; Hoff., 89; E.T., 67].

philosophy itself can never begin immediately, but always begins with mediation. We leave it open here what meaning the word *mediation* has in each case.

It has been our intention to develop extensively the problematic of the beginning with regard to Hegel, because it is otherwise impossible to find one's way already in the first, brief part on immediate knowledge: sense certainty. For this discussion of immediate knowledge, in which we comfort ourselves purely "receptively"—receptively in Hegel's sense—is anything but an immediate description of *what is given*. This discussion is not a description of that kind, not because Hegel would have been unable to offer such a description or because for some reason he would suddenly have become unfaithful to his own task, but rather because there is generally nothing like pure immediate description in philosophy. This is not to say, however, that it is impossible for philosophy to grasp *the matter itself*. This is quite possible. But the matter itself is not of a kind like things and living beings, which one can describe *immediately*. Such a seeing is immediate in that the horizon in which seeing takes place is not known *but is simply there*. But when what is at stake is the matter of philosophy—in this case, spirit, or absolute actuality—then it would require a *most original* adherence to the matter. If the matter itself in philosophy is not evident to those who just happen to run into it, that is no objection against philosophy. Indeed, we read again and again in Hegel that, in following and following up the phenomenology of spirit, we should only "look on," not adding anything, but only taking and receiving what we find there. This is indeed the way it is. But the question is: What is this "looking on"? This looking on is not an indeterminate, arbitrary, unprepared staring, guided by whims, but is a looking on *within the attitude of undergoing an experience*, the way *this experience* sees. This looking on is a looking with the eyes of absolute knowledge.

The structure of each part—and particularly the structure of the first part—shows how little it is a matter of immediate description. With what does Hegel begin the real presentation of sense certainty? With two paragraphs up to II, 74 [Hoff., 80; GW IX, 63; E.T., 59], which anticipate the entire problematic and the result. This happens not only because it is proper to give an arrangement of the thought sequence to come, but also because *the* disposition should explicitly be created in which *we* are disposed to the openness of the gaze, which should subsequently *look on*.

c) The immediacy of the object and of the knowing of sense certainty. "Pure being" and extantness

What along with Hegel we call sense certainty appears as a *cognition*. We are not told further what this cognition is, but what is understood thereby is the way in which something becomes manifest according to some specific point of view as to what it is and how it is. Every cognition—and that includes sense certainty—has its *truth*. It follows from this that Hegel does not use the expression "certainty" in order to designate its character as somehow equivalent to the truth of cognition. Rather, in every instance certainty means the entirety of the relation, in knowing, of a knower to what is known, the unity of knowing and what is known, the manner of being known and consciousness in the broadest sense of knowing and cognition.

Furthermore, it is worth noting right at the beginning that with regard to *sense* certainty, Hegel offers a short essay on *sense* certainty without even mentioning anything about the senses, let alone the sense organs. He does speak about seeing and hearing,[9] but not about the eyes, not to mention the retina, and the nervous system. He says nothing about ears and the labyrinth of the ears—none of that is there. We do not even learn anything about visual and auditory sensations, about the data of smell and touch (the very least that today's phenomenologists would demand). And yet Hegel offers an interpretation of sensibility which is unequaled in the history of philosophy. We could of course cut this short essay into pieces and for each piece quote something analogous and similar-sounding from somewhere in the history of philosophy, from Kant to Plato. But doing so, we would only provide proof that, as long as we subscribe to such exact principles of interpretation, (1) we do not *want* to understand anything of Hegel himself, and (2) we *cannot* do so. What is unprecedented about Hegel's interpretation of sensibility is that he *understands it entirely in terms of spirit and in spirit*—as shown in the very posing of the problem. It is *in* spirit and *for* spirit that sensibility appears. Thus, this is the only way to grasp how Hegel captures the appearance of sense certainty.

Sense certainty appears—as the *"richest"* as well as the *"truest"* cognition. It has the greatest richness and the highest truth. This is the way sense certainty appears. And yet we know in advance that, basically, this sense certainty is the poorest and is that which has the least truth. But sense certainty appears initially as the richest and the truest—and we must pursue this appearing. This twofold designation pertains to *what* is known in sense certainty, the content, as well as to *how* this certainty, in knowing, *has its* known.

According to its content, sense certainty appears to be the richest, so rich that its fullness has no end—a richness without end. (*How* this richness belongs to sense certainty and *whether* this richness belongs *to it* at all are questions which are left open.) This richness is "extended." The dimensions of its extension are *space and time*. I, like everyone else, see this lectern, this

---

9. II, 77 [GW IX, 66; Hoff., 83; E.T., 61].

bench, this window, this blackboard, and so on through the whole university building, out on the streets, in individual houses, even throughout the whole city, the environment; I see this tree and this blade of grass and this and that without end "out there" among the whole range of what is extant. And at the same time I see this lectern, this section covered by the notebook, this edge and from this edge again a short span, then I see a finger breadth and so on all the way to the smallest—so again everything else which is stretched out in the whole range of space—by "going into" the narrowness of what gets increasingly narrowed. Correspondingly, that is the way it is with time.

Going beyond every point in time and space, sense certainty follows the broadening of breadth and the narrowing of the narrow. Sense certainty is always situated somewhere in breadth and narrowness—not fixed, but with the possibility of broadening and narrowing. Nevertheless, it is always situated such that, wherever sense certainty turns its gaze, it has *this here* and *this now* before itself.

Likewise, space itself wherein this thing stands here is this space; time itself wherein this tone now sounds is this time. That is how it stands with what is known, with the *content* of sense certainty.

And what about the *mode* of knowing of sense certainty? This is the mode of pure *having something before itself*. In what sense? Not as if we would all at once place ourselves before the whole richness of the broad and narrow and would mean *that richness*, but rather that this is always before me in that I *encounter this and nothing else; this and only this*, with regard to which it is always so as if *it* is *everything there is*—this, that I would only need to encounter in order for me to have it right in front of me in its total "completeness." I *only meet with it*; I do not trouble myself with it at all, not even so that I would *leave out* something thereby. I take this in its entirety as it is, as it lies in full meeting view and as it is first tangibly extant before the hand in the meeting. This is this, and that means: *it* is and *is* just *it*, and nothing further.

Sense certainty has thereby expressed itself—whether in actual utterance or in that silent speaking which inheres in sensuous knowing—when I intend a this. Sense certainty has expressed *itself*—itself! This means that the knowing of what is known is expressed—*how* it is something which is known—as well as what is known itself. But—and it is decisive to pay heed to that, here already—sense certainty expresses itself by *stating* something *about* what is its known. *What* is is stated, just as it is in truth. What is stated is the truth, and vice versa. It is not as if truth is stated only in passing. Rather, truth is in itself what is stated: the proposition. The truth of sense certainty is always this being [*dieses Seiende*] which sense certainty means; and sense certainty means it, this, as what is extant; it means it, *this, which is*. The *"is"* is the statement and the truth of sense certainty. Sense certainty states the extantness of what is extant, or to put it in Hegel's terminology, it states being [*Sein*]. That is why Hegel says "the truth {of sense certainty} contains nothing but the *being* of the matter."[10] Hegel does not say that the truth of sense certainty contains the being of the matter, but rather "*nothing but* the being of the matter." Sense certainty expresses *itself* by expressing itself regarding its matter, this extant thing. Doing so, sense certainty does not state anything further about itself, a knower and its knowing. For the *truth* of sense certainty is not concerned with the knower, "consciousness," or the "I." It is in sense certainty's own interest that by always meaning this, which *is*, sense certainty *does not take*—and also does not need to take—an interest *in itself*. For sense certainty this is *because it is*, and for this knowing there is nowhere an authority which could be asked *why* this being is. Rather, it is only because it is. The being is what is extant and nothing more.

Sense certainty is as little interested in itself as knowing as it is in the this *as object*. Being *oblivious of the object*, sense certainty means only the *this*. As the knower I am certain only of being the knower who knows: I, this knower. But this knower does not mean anything more regarding this knowing. In sense knowledge I who know am nothing more than the pure knowing of its known, of the this that is. Therefore, here, too, Hegel says: "Consciousness for its part is in this certainty only as a pure *I*; or *I* am therein only as a pure this, . . . "[11] Hegel does not say that consciousness is the I, but "only" I, this, just as earlier he had said about the object; what is, and "nothing but" that.

By trying to grasp sense certainty as it appears in its appearing, Hegel speaks in *restrictive* terms—in this "nothing but" and "only"—thus setting everything else outside the limit. And what is "everything else" which sense certainty is not yet? Taken as a mode of knowing, sense certainty is not yet something that moves thought in various ways and that unfolds itself. Knowing is not involved in any movement appropriate to knowing. Nothing further transpires in it, and it still has no history. In terms of its subject matter, sense certainty is nothing that is known, which as such has an abundance of "various properties." This means that in both respects sense certainty does not yet show any mediation; this is still disregarded. That is why sense certainty is only what is not mediated, what is im-mediate. Sense certainty does *itself* appear when it so appears. But it appears in the light of a gaze which takes sense certainty *only* immediately, *disregarding* all mediating sight, which already belongs to that gaze. Otherwise this gaze could not look on and observe and see only what is immediate in its immediacy.

---

10. II, 73 [GW IX, 63; Hoff., 79; E.T., 58].
11. Ibid.

Therefore, our way of looking on up until now was *a looking on which disregards* [*absehendes Zusehen*].

This is in keeping with the characterization which Hegel, and we with him, offer of the truth of sense certainty: "But this {sense} *certainty* proves itself indeed to be the most abstract and the poorest *truth*."[12] But here Hegel specifically stresses that it is sense certainty which proves *itself* as this kind of truth. To be sure, sense certainty says what is true for it: it is the extant, precisely as extant. But what sense certainty here lays out as its truth is not what shows sense certainty *as such* to be the most abstract and poorest truth. Sense certainty itself is not at all capable of grasping itself as abstract knowing. But that sense certainty is the "most abstract" and "poorest" truth is what *we* are saying as those who are in and for absolute knowledge, which "indeed" and "in truth" is true knowledge. For this knowledge (absolvent knowledge) what is known by the senses is altogether a one-sided knowing, stuck one-sidedly in a single relation, most relative, most abstract, and most one-sided. But what such a knowing is is known least of all by abstract knowing, which knows the least about itself as *such*. In his later period in Berlin, Hegel wrote a short essay entitled "Who Thinks Abstractly?"[13] "Who thinks abstractly? The uneducated, not the educated man."[14]

We have already emphasized that the truth which sense certainty states about its *object* is *the* truth which it articulates *itself*. Consequently, this truth is also the truth which certainty as knowledge (as a knowing relation to . . .) is. In truth this relation is also only one of pure being-extant, its merely extant character: "pure being, which constitutes the essence of this certainty and which this certainty pronounces as its truth"[15]—its truth, what this certainty in its entirety is. Sensuous knowledge as self-relation is also only being-extant, because this knowledge, merely let loose toward the extant and absorbed in it, is only extant—and not even as extant as its object itself is.

The object of sense certainty and the knowledge of this object have now been characterized. The result of this characterization is that, according to both moments, the essence of sense certainty is *immediacy*.

However, with this result the presentation of sense certainty is not at an end—so far from it that it can only now begin. For the presentation must be carried out *from the experience* which absolvent knowledge undergoes with consciousness. This absolvent knowledge has in the above characterization of its immediate object—namely, of sense certainty—not yet gone beyond

---

12. Ibid.
13. XVII, 400ff. [trans. W. Kaufmann, *Hegel: Reinterpretation, Texts, and Commentary* (London: Weidenfield and Nicolson, 1966), pp. 461–65].
14. XVII, 402; cf. the piece on p. 404 about the market woman [trans., p. 464].
15. II, 74 [GW IX, 64; Hoff., 80; E.T., 59].

the initial reception of what appears. Our primary task now is to examine how things stand with sense certainty. Have we actually surveyed the pure immediacy of sense certainty—have we remained in it—in order to grasp it in what it knows and how it knows it? It will become apparent that several approaches are necessary for that—one approach preparing the way for the other.

d) Distinctions and mediation in the pure being of what is immediate in sense certainty. The multiplicity of examples of the this and the this as I and as object

"When we look on," we see at once that we cannot stop at "pure being," the extant character of the sensible object and its knowledge. For "with this *pure being* . . . much more is in play besides."[16] What is "in play besides" shows itself when we actually turn an actual sense certainty into an object. Let us try it. Each one of us should do it and should place himself in what he has immediately before himself, a this. Let us say "this," the lectern here. I discover that I mean this here as something extant and that—as the one who knows about it in a knowledge of it—I, this, am. What else is in play? Each one of us has before himself a this. Of course, that is nothing different from what was said earlier, namely, that the object of sense certainty is the this. The *this*? But our object is *this lectern*, and if we look further, this blackboard, this door. Thus, each time we have another this, and each time we have looked in this or in that direction. Each time the this is a lectern, a door, a tree, its branch, a twig, a leaf. Each time there is an *actual* this, and "*the this*" itself is precisely not the object of sensible knowing. When we generally intend the this, we find that "this" *sends* our intention *away*. It sends our intention away, not generally, but rather in the definite direction of something which has the character of *a* being *this*: a lectern, a window, a piece of chalk. Because the particular this, in accord with its own import, has in itself the character of being a this, therefore the particular this is *not* the immediate object.

Hence, it follows that actual sense certainty is never merely this sheer immediacy that we take it to be, but rather each actual sense certainty *is an example*—is indeed an example in an essential sense. In what way? If, for example, we imagine a tree in a general way, then a fir, a beech, an oak, or a linden—and any other tree—is an example of it. But actual sense certainty is not only in this sense an example [*Beispiel*] for that which we initially determine as its *essence*; there are no isolated cases each of which could be brought at random as an example and then "subsumed" under the general

---

16. Ibid.

concept. Rather, the actual sense certainty as *actual* is *in each case in itself* an example. For to the extent that sense certainty refers to and means this and to the extent that the this has the character of being a this, to that extent every act of "meaning this" is in itself exemplifying. Every actual sense certainty as such is an example, a by-play [*Bei-spiel*]. The act of intending [*meinen*], which refers to the this, lets its character as being a this be exemplified in and through the this in each instance. Here we must take into consideration that the lectern, the blackboard, and the door are as such not examples of the this, but examples of objects of use: Only as having the possibility of being a this are they all in each instance a this. But what do we mean by having the possibility of being a this? We cannot yet answer this question. At this point we can only say that meaning is in itself exemplifying. By contrast, the lectern in its being a lectern is not an example.

Pure being, the true immediacy, is therefore a sense certainty which in each case exemplifies. The "I" too is in each case exemplified just as the this, which has the character of being a this [*das Diesige*].* Thus, we see that what we took earlier to be already the essence of sense certainty—the this as object *and* a this as I—both have already fallen out of pure being. Both are differentiated, and both constitute a difference which has to be addressed as a "principal difference." As long as we are guided by what has fallen out of pure being, we do not have the immediate in its immediacy. It is also just as obvious that this falling out has happened to us. It is clear that the this as object *and* the this as I could fall out of pure being only because as the principal difference they are in the end already *in* the essence of sense certainty, in immediacy. Furthermore, if we not only look at this difference but also reflect on it, then we come to the conclusion that both—the differentiated—are not *simply extant* in *essence*, but the one is *through* the other and vice versa. I have certainty through the matter at hand [*Sache*], and the matter at hand is certain only through the I who knows. Both of the differentiated are mediated and reside *with* this mediation *in* the essence of what is immediate. But the question to which our observations have come so far has not been asked: Can we stop at *immediacy* as the truth of sense certainty? Are we not stating exactly what sense certainty is *not*? Are we not *contradicting* the essence of sense certainty when we address it thus?

Let us keep in mind that, after the initial determination of the essence of sense certainty, we have now looked closely.** We have reflected on what came to light through this looking; we have reflected on the difference

---

*[According to F. W. von Herrmann, *das Diesige* means *in der Art des Dies-seins*: having the character of being a this.]

**[The German word used here (*Zusehen*) normally has an object. Here it does not. This lack of object seems deliberate on Heidegger's part. It may be intended to keep our focus on the process, rather than taking us immediately to an *object* of that activity.]

between the "this" and the "I intend," the difference between pure being and what is in play besides. At the same time and by means of this distinction, there arises explicitly the difference between essence and example.

e) The experience of the difference between immediacy and mediation. What is essential and not essential in sense certainty itself. The this as the essence, its significance as now and here, and the universal as the essence of the this

We make the distinction between the essence and the example, between immediacy and mediation. But Hegel says explicitly: "It is not just we who make this distinction . . . rather, we find it within sense certainty itself."[17] It is not that we do not make this distinction at all, merely finding it, as we might find a knife in the street, something which we certainly did not make. Hegel is not saying that we do not make this distinction, merely finding it. Rather, he says: "It is *not just* we who make the distinction. . . . " Certainly we make this distinction, we must make this distinction, nay we must have already made this distinction in order to be able to find it. Indeed, we have already made the distinction between immediacy and mediation, because this distinction and its making is nothing else than the basic character of our comportment in absolvent knowing. Whatever is to encounter us there is from the beginning seen by us in the brightness of the light of this difference. It should *encounter* us; we should look carefully to see how that which encounters us shows itself in this light, how it itself carries this difference in itself. That is why Hegel says: "It {the distinction between immediacy and mediation} is to be taken up in the form in which it is present {in sense certainty} not as we have just defined it."[18] It is already quite clear here how in the process of absolution we go—explicitly, though not with complete specificity—one step beyond the phenomenon in Hegel's sense and, as it were, bring the phenomenon to light in order then first and foremost in the light to go to and to go back to the phenomenon. If we have already illuminated this light in the right way, then this way must lead us to what is true. That means that the elucidation of sense certainty as it is in itself must confirm what we said about it by way of anticipation. Our anticipatory and absolvent knowing must prove itself by coming to its own truth [bewahrheiten]. In this manner consciousness itself must come one step closer to its truth. Now our absolvent gaze is enlightened—with reference to what appears—in order to see.

---

17. II, 74–75 [GW IX, 64; Hoff., 80; E.T., 59].
18. II, 75 [GW IX, 64; Hoff., 80; E.T., 59].

In what form do we find in sense certainty the difference between essence and instance, between immediacy and mediation?

Only now does phenomenology actually begin to happen. We are to undergo an experience with sense certainty. For this it is necessary to take sense certainty as it offers itself in itself. Sense certainty offers itself in general as certainty, as a knowledge of something known. If we wish to gather up this phenomenon in its entirety, we should *follow* this phenomenon as it is. Sense certainty is a knowing relation to. . . . Consequently, we dare not see "this relation to . . . " externally, as it were, like a band that entwines an I who knows and an object which is known. Rather, it is a matter of going along with knowledge and of gathering up that to which knowledge is knowingly related and how knowledge does so. In this respect, we already heard that for sense certainty, in accord with its manner of knowing, the object is what exists or *that which is*—what by itself remains extant even if it is not known. Knowing, and along with it the I who knows, is of no importance for the object as it is in itself. Sense certainty knows this and gives expression to it in that for and in sense certainty as a whole only the object is "what is true and the essence."[19] Knowing can also *not* be; both knowing and the I are all the same to the essence—they are un-essential. When there is knowledge, it is always in reference to the object. This is what sense certainty itself says. In this statement sense certainty says how, according to its saying, it carries in itself the difference between essence and what is un-essential.

Sense certainty lays out the object, the being in itself, as its truth. But is the object "in fact" extant in sense certainty as sense certainty announces it to be? Again the question emerges whether the object is "in fact" or in truth such. (In accordance with what truth? In accordance with the truth which from the beginning sets the measure for us who know absolutely.)

How are we to answer this question? How are we to decide whether the object of sense certainty, as this object is laid out to be by and for sense certainty, corresponds to the object which in truth is extant in sense certainty? Completely apart from how this question will be decided, with it the possibility is already indicated of a correspondence or a non-correspondence between the object as it is for sensible knowledge (the object for it) and the genuine truth of this object (the object for us).

The object for sense certainty is the this. So we ask sense certainty itself: What does the this mean to sense certainty? In what does the this-ness of the this consist for sense certainty? What does sense certainty say if it is interrogated, really interrogated in each actual case, as to what the "this" is? What does the this-ness of this window mean to sense certainty? That it is

---

19. II, 75 [GW IX, 64; Hoff., 81; E.T., 59].

the window *here*. Or the this-ness of this pulse-beat? That it is this now. Here and now make up the this-ness of a this. What is the now? What should sense certainty say about the now? What is there for sense certainty to say about the now other than to say what the now immediately is—with reference to the being which just now makes up the now? The now is just this afternoon, "now" it is afternoon.* Or considering the now, the now was, just as Hegel was interrogating sense certainty about the now, when he wrote the text: the now is night.

"Now" is afternoon. This is an incontestable truth. We preserve this truth by writing it in chalk on the blackboard. When the janitor comes to the lecture hall early tomorrow morning at eight o'clock, to see if everything is all right and if the blackboard is clean, and he reads the sentence "Now is afternoon," then he will not admit at any price that the sentence is true. Overnight the sentence has become false: The being which was the now, the now which from what was regarded as morning by the janitor was yesterday afternoon, is for a long time already no longer in being. It has no permanence. But "now," when the janitor reads the sentence, is also "now." However, "now" the now is morning. But since it does happen that professors make mistakes, and on the other hand the janitor also belongs to the university, he will in this case lend a hand and correct the sentence. *He* writes *"now"* the truth which he will defend at all cost: Now is morning. At one o'clock the janitor comes to the lecture hall and sees his truth standing there. Truth? "Now" is midday.

Which is then "now" actually true or in being? Each time it is "now," and each now is "now" already other, no longer what it was earlier. The now remains constant and is "now" each time in each given moment. But how does the now remain the now, and as what does it remain? The now remains the now in that what is the now in each case—morning, noon, afternoon, evening, night—*is* in each case *not*. The now is always not-this. This *not* always removes the immediate this—night, day—whatever happens to be the now. What is immediate is sublated, mediated. In order for the now to be able to remain the now that is, this constant negation belongs to the now. But how interesting that this constant sublation, this continuous change, does not disturb the now at all. It remains simply now and remains simply indifferent to what it is "now," be it day or night. As simple as this or as that, it is, however, never only this or exclusively that. This simple which is permanent in and through mediation is the *"universal."*

The question was: What is the this, or what constitutes this-ness? The answer: The now. And what is the essence of the now? The universal just

---

*[The word (*the*) *now* translates the German noun (*das*) *Jetzt*; the word "now" (in quotation marks) translates the German adverb *jetzt*.]

arrived at. This universal is the truth of the this, the truth of the object of sense certainty.

The same is true for the other "form" of the this: the here. To the question "What is here?" sense certainty, which we in each case interrogate about its object, replies by saying "Here, the lectern." "I turn around"[20] and the truth disappears: the here is not the lectern but the blackboard. It is invariably that way: wherever I turn and wherever I am, I see a here. I always take the here with me. Wherever I stand, the where is already turned into a here. To put it more exactly: the here first makes possible the where as the there which we interrogate from the here. The here remains, but what has the character of a here is in each case something else. And although the existing here requires each time something that definitely has the character of a here, yet it is at the same time entirely indifferent as to which one it is. The here is not troubled whether what has the character of a here is a tree, a bridge, the summit of a mountain, or the bottom of the sea. The here requires only that it is in each case something with the character of a here. But by requiring something like this, the here never turns directly to that which has the character of the this, which in each case is something with the character of the here. The here requires that which has the character of the here, while at the same time it discards it as this in each case. Just as with the now, the here *remains* the empty and indifferent here, mediated simplicity, i.e., universality. Thus, *this* determinateness of the this-ness also proves to be a universal.

f) Language as the expression of what is universal and the singular item which is intended—the ontological difference and dialectic

What is the this? What is it that is the object—the true and the being—for sense certainty? The this is a universal. But actual sense certainty does not mean the universal this. Of course not. Actual sense certainty means that which in each case has the character of the this, precisely that which sense certainty exemplifies: this tree, this house, this night. But what is exemplified is always and everywhere something else, *never* the same thing in every time and every place; it is something of the nature of a *nothing* [*Nichtiges*]. What sense certainty intends [*meint*] in exemplification, what sense certainty takes as a being by intending it, is a *non*-being, that which "does not continue existing."[21] The being is what *continues existing*, what is unaffected by change and disappearance, unaffected by the *not*. The being is *the true*.

---

20. II, 76 [GW IX, 65; Hoff., 82; E.T., 60].
21. II, 79 [GW IX, 67; Hoff., 84; E.T., 62].

By way of anticipation, we said at the beginning of this discussion that sense certainty expresses itself, sense certainty states *its truth*. Only now do we understand what that means. We say: This. What we *say* here is the universal this, and what we *intend* is what has the character of the this, namely, a tree. What we actually intend *by* the universal this we cannot say at all with the this. We say "this," and the result is the universal this. Language says the opposite of what we mean. We mean the singular item; language says the universal. But language not only says with obstinacy the opposite opinion, but also says what is true, because language always already says the universal. Language repudiates our intention. But language does not only repudiate us: language also turns into its opposite what is initially intended, what is supposedly true. Language allows us to experience that intention means nothing and to experience what really is true according to sense certainty. Language forces things into their opposites, sublates them, raises them to genuine truth. Language is in itself mediating; it prevents us from sinking into that which has the character of the this— that which is totally one-sided, relative, and abstract. By turning things into their opposites, language brings about the turning away from what is relative. That is why, at the crucial conclusion of the discussion on sense certainty, Hegel says that language has "the divine nature of immediately perverting the intention."[22] Language has a divine, absolute essence. Language has in it something of the essence of God, the absolute—what is non-relative—the absolute, or the absolvent. Language is divine because language is absolvent, because language detaches us from one-sidedness and allows us to state what is universal and true. Thus, man, to whose existence* language belongs, has access to what he means when he refers to "something this-like" only through the character of the this itself and *through the this*. More precisely: We *intend* "something this-like" only *because we have access to a this*. We can only intend because we "speak." This furthest externalization exists only in the nearest internalization [*Erinnerung*] of language. The definition of man from antiquity as ζῷον λογον ἔχον corresponds to this. In the *Phenomenology of Spirit* we shall again and again come across the basic essence of language as that which constitutes the existence of the self as self.[23]

What is stated about language is true precisely for *the* statement which sense certainty makes about its object when sense certainty states: The this *is*. We mean this particular individual entity and say of it, "it is"; thus, we

---

22. II, 84 [GW IX, 70; Hoff., 89; E.T., 66].
*[*Ek-sistenz*].
23. Cf. II, 382, 491, 533f. [GW IX, 276, 351, 380–81; Hoff., 362, 458, 496; E.T., 308, 395, 430].

state and articulate "being in general." Hegel explicitly emphasizes: "Of course, we do not *represent* the universal this or being in general, but we *express* the universal."[24] And yet we must say that we express the universal only because, although not thematized, being in general is stated by us; and being is stated by us only because being is already understood by us. When in sense certainty we *intend this being*, it is not as if being is understood in advance only in a general way. Rather, we could never intend a being if being were not already the true, that is: manifest. Only on the basis of this truth does there "emerge" in a specific sense *possible truth*, the manifestness of what is intended, insofar as we can speak at all of the truth of the latter—which is not at all the case for Hegel. Rather, the truth of the this *is* the universal, but this truth is not grasped and taken *in* itself by sense certainty. That is, this truth is not yet perception.

This brief reference to the understanding of being and its connection with the manifestness of beings (with ontic truth) is inserted here peripherally, in order to remember that in Hegel's problematic we are not confronted with an abstruse and arbitrary speculation. At the same time, in dealing with the problematic of the understanding of being, we are not dealing with a contrived amusement that might be taken as indicative of a particular point of view. In all of this there is only a simple and magnificent resonance of the question of philosophy: τί τὸ ὄν. But precisely on this account, our task is to grasp the most inner direction of the Hegelian problem by letting it take its own course and following it. And because following this direction involves a confrontation [with Hegel], the question arises as to whether this understanding and speaking of being, or language, is divine in the sense of being absolute. We can also put it this way: Is the understanding of being *absolvent*, and is the absolvent absolute? Or is what Hegel represents in the *Phenomenology of Spirit* as absolvence merely transcendence in disguise, i.e., finitude? Our confrontation with Hegel arrives at this crossing which is located between finitude and infinity, as crossroads, which is not the same as the opposition of two points of view.

However obvious and easy it is to bring up the problematic of the "ontological difference" in relation to Hegel's remarks on the expressing of the universal and the understanding of being (being in our broad sense, for Hegel no longer calls this "being") as one intends beings, the questions stand quite differently for Hegel. For Hegel, as the completion of Western metaphysics, the entire dimension of the problem of being is oriented toward the λόγος. But for Hegel λέγειν is not the simple proposition or one-sided general statement "S is P." Rather, λέγειν has already become διαλέγεσθαι. This means two things. (1) It means a διά, speaking

---

24. II, 76 [GW IX, 65; Hoff., 82; E.T., 60].

"through," a movement which lies specifically in speaking and knowing itself, the restlessness of the absolute, not a halting but rather sublating, the Platonic διαλέγεσθαι: a passing through. (2)* But it is not simply a passing through. Rather, there is a speaking to itself in διαλέγεσθαι as the medium. This is already the case with Plato, although dialectic is fundamentally different for Plato and for Hegel. What is spoken is oriented toward itself. The truth of what is spoken ultimately lies in the I, the subject, or spirit. This does not really become prominent in Western dialectic, but dialectic is nothing other than absolvence which is conceived on the basis of the logos, which is "logical" in the original sense. Hegel's philosophy (method) is dialectic: (1) the problem of being remains oriented to λόγος, and (2) this "logical" orientation is restlessness and is absolvent, understood in terms of in-finity.

Hegel and to a certain extent already Fichte see "the conflict of the form of a proposition"[25]: "What has already been said can be expressed formally: the nature of the judgment or proposition, which involves the distinction between subject and predicate, is destroyed by the speculative proposition; and the proposition of identity, which the former becomes, contains the counter-thrust against that subject-predicate relationship."[26] But in speculative "philosophical" propositions, the simple difference between subject and predicate is not abolished through identity, but rather is sublated. This is the absolvent proposition. In the proposition "is" is stated. Hegel brings the absolute restlessness of absolvence into this quiet "is" of the general proposition. The whole work of his philosophy is devoted solely to making this restlessness real.

§7. Mediatedness as the essence of what is immediate and the dialectical movement

a) Intention as the essence of sense certainty. The singularity and universality of intending

The course of the discussion so far has been the following: We interrogated sense certainty regarding what it says about its object and thereby about itself. Sense certainty states that the object is the being which exists in itself and is the true, the essential; for the object exists even if knowledge does not. And this knowledge, which does not need to exist, can exist only

---

*[Through a printer's error, the number 2 is missing in the German text.]
25. II, 49 [GW IX, 43; Hoff., 51; E.T., 38].
26. Ibid.

when the object exists. The object is what is essential; the knowledge of the object (intending the object) is inessential. A closer examination of what the "this" as object is reveals that this object, the singular "this," is not at all what lasts, but is what constantly changes. What thus changes is indifferent and inessential when compared with what lasts, with the now and the here. The object is not the true as the in-itself, but rather is in each case only the "intended" object *insofar* as the object is *my* object, insofar as the object is taken into meaning by *me*, by the I who knows—insofar as the object encounters the now and the here in the form of the this. The object *exists* because *I*, this I, know it. Thus, everything is reversed. What was formerly inessential and indifferent—knowledge and the I who knows—is now what is essential. The truth of sense certainty is detached from its object; this truth is expelled from that place and has settled itself in knowledge, in the "I know." This truth is indeed expelled and expellable from there because this truth was found and grasped in sense certainty only presumptuously, namely, in the presumption of sense certainty, in what sense certainty, lost to itself, is in its immediacy.

It is worth noting that this detachment and expulsion and forcing back into the "I know" did not happen because of our arbitrary machinations; they happened in that it was shown that and how sense certainty contradicts itself, because, in *saying* something about itself, sense certainty speaks against what it *intends*, and vice versa.

However, right at the beginning, in this first act of the expulsion of the truth of sense certainty from its object, we must see how sense certainty immediately takes the direction of the "I know," of the knower and knowledge. We must see in this first act an initial, as yet completely remote as well as short-lived, return of consciousness to itself—the first beginning of the phenomenology of spirit, as it were, on the most extreme margins of its aloofness [*Abseitigkeit*] and one-sidedness [*Einseitigkeit*], where the absolute restlessness startles the this and the intending, as it were, and now no longer leaves them at rest. For the matter cannot end with the truth of sense certainty's pulling itself back from its this to intending. That is why Hegel says: "Sense certainty, then, though indeed expelled from the object, is not yet thereby sublated, but only driven back into the I. We now have to see what experience shows us about this (its) reality."[1] This last sentence must be taken in its entire methodological bearing; and, according to what we said earlier, we do not have to deal with it extensively.

Experience is absolvent self-releasement into what appears in the light of absolute knowledge. This experience shows something to "us," but not as those who happen to be alive and are registered as students or employed as

---

1. II, 77 [GW IX, 66; Hoff., 83; E.T., 61].

teachers at this university. Rather, this experience shows something to us who know absolvently, who are actual *in spirit*. Experience is to show us something about the reality of sense certainty, about *what* sense certainty truly is. In experiencing the absolute, the question is always already about the essence. To undergo an experience means to look at and follow what remains in the presence of the grinding away of the absolvent. Here, then, one must initially inquire whether in truth the reality of sense certainty is the "intention" and not the "this."

"The force of its truth {the truth of sense certainty} thus lies now in the 'I,' in the immediacy of my *seeing, hearing,* and so on."[2] Is sense certainty true by virtue of the activity of intending, by virtue of the fact that I grasp as mine what is seen and heard in sensibility and take both into my seeing and hearing? For Hegel "intending" does not signify so much being directed at what is intended as "to take up into the intention," i.e., receiving, taking back into the receiver what is received—*recipere*. Since in seeing and hearing, each I "intends" and takes into its own only what it has seen, each I comports itself quite immediately, without letting itself be disturbed by anything other than what is seen. And that is what it should do: being immediately devoted to this, to intend only this [what is seen]. The immediacy of sense certainty, which we call immediate knowledge, lies in intending. Thus, we went astray when we sought the immediacy in the object of intending; for the object of intending is only what is intended. Each I *intends what is its own*, and what is intended is what is its this. I, this, affirm the lectern as the here; the engineer in the railway station affirms the engine as the here—and so does each person and every I affirm, with the same right and in the same manner of verification, namely, by appealing to the fact that, immediately and without further ado, the I takes only its own. The engineer would declare someone insane who would tell him that the here is the lectern; he would say that the fellow had lost his senses and has no sense for taking as his own what is immediate in intending. To an even lesser extent can I say that the here is the Feldberg; I cannot say it because in intending I do not come across the Feldberg at all—across this as little as across anything else. In the activity of intending [*im Meinen*], in the sense appropriate to it, I reflect only on what is mine [*des Meine*].

If we pay attention—as we did above—to what is the engineer's and to what is mine here, then we have already stepped out of intending. We are no longer in the activity of purely letting-it-be-for-it [*reines Für-es-sein-lassen*]. Insofar as we compare this intending with that intending, we see that each is true and that each is true in the same way and verified like any other. But precisely *because* each is true with the same right and in the same

---

2. Ibid.

manner as any other, none can claim a priority over the other. On the contrary, each intending denies the rights of the other with equal right. They mutually destroy each other and force each other to disappear. They do this by contributing—each intending for itself in each case—to the building of a manifold. If, as it happens, we look at this silent war of each intending against every other, then we find that in this war the intendings wipe each other out. But insofar as this disappearance *is* just what it is, something remains. What is manifold, the many of the singular intending and of the singular I's, this manifold is what disappears; and what is simple is what lasts. What is simple is that which does not let itself be pulled away into the manifold; what is simple is that which is the simple intending in each singular "I intend" and is the I in each singular "*I intend.*" When I say "I," I admittedly intend myself and only myself. But when I say "I," I say something which *everyone else* can say, because everyone else is an I. Everyone is that which I say when I say "I." That which everyone is, this simple thing, does not lie immediately in every intending. Rather, everyone is immediately in every case everyone—a manifold.

That which is simple exists *for us* only when we pull back from the manifold, when we look carefully to see what remains when the manifold forces itself to disappear. When we keep an eye on what disappears and look upon and follow what lasts, we comport ourselves as *mediating* between both: When we mediate, we find what is *simple.* The I and the intending—this universal, wherein we presumed the force of the truth of sense certainty to be—is also nothing immediate.

b) The immediacy of sense certainty as non-differentiation of I and object. The demonstrated singular now in its movement toward the universal

What is the outcome of the preceding discussion? The immediacy of sense certainty consists neither in the immediacy of the this nor in the immediacy of intending. Neither of these moments of sense certainty is exclusively and explicitly what is immediate: neither the object in itself nor intending for itself. The immediacy of sense certainty is the immediacy in *and* for itself. Both *together* make up what is immediate. What does this say about the right way to understand the essence of sense certainty?

Object and intending together mean that sense certainty as a whole knowing does not admit into itself any opposition between object and modes of knowing. In and for itself, sense certainty not only does not allow such opposition *to come forth*, but also has no inner motive for *evoking* such an opposition, much less a motive for placing its immediacy in one *or* the other. Sense certainty is totally immersed in immediacy and absorbs it completely into itself and itself into it. Sense certainty *as a whole* holds *on to itself* as immediacy. What sense certainty is *as a whole* must be taken as its essence. Sense certainty has already miscarried if we take the object to be essential and take intending to be inessential, and vice versa. For sense certainty this distinction does not exist at all. In itself sense certainty asserts itself to be the unchanging relation, admitting of no distinction, between I and object, wherein the poles of the relation as well as the relation itself are undifferentiated and not distinguished. Nothing is yet separated; nothing has moved beyond itself or toward itself. Rather, everything is completely ingrained in what in each case has the character of a this—to such an extent that the this is not yet differentiated *as* object in opposition to a mode of knowing and having.

According to its own inclination, sense certainty is only inclined in such a way that it reflects on its this. By intending what is mine, my "this," my this here, everything to which I am inclined is fulfilled. In this intending there is just no provocation for moving beyond it, in order to make it still better, as it were. Sense certainty has no motive at all for surrendering what it is for the time being. On the contrary, sense certainty is inclined to do only one thing, namely, to understand itself with regard to what is intended in sense certainty. I, this one for whom the lectern is the here—I, this one who intends—"do not turn around"[3] so that the here for me would become a not-lectern. Neither do I "take notice of"[4] the fact that the here can be an engine; I do not at all compare various heres and nows. Rather, this (my) intending is, in accord with its most proper inclination, *a staying with what I intend*. It is the same with the earlier example: the janitor who in the morning reads on the blackboard "Now is afternoon" simply insists that "now" is forenoon, if he is *really* intending—and he will insist that it is forenoon precisely when he is asked what is "now."

Thus, if *we* said, over against a sense certainty that was earlier shown to us, that "the now is not day but night," then sense certainty would not get involved at all with this question, provided that sense certainty is really taken as what is immediate, which it has now turned out to be. In the preceding case *our* observation did not allow sense certainty to stand in its immediacy, but rather forced it to become something which it is not. By forcing sense certainty into something that is for us, we have perverted it.

Thus, all that remains is to "step into" sense certainty and to let what the now and the here is be manifest and said only by sense certainty. We must retain the now that is at issue in the intending and not contrast it "after-

---

3. II, 79 [GW IX, 67; Hoff., 84; E.T., 62].
4. II, 79 [GW IX, 67; Hoff., 84; E.T., 63].

wards" with another now. To the same extent, we must not give up the here
and bring another one to the fore "at a distance from it."

It is precisely when our looking on is mediated and when we search for
immediacy that we are led to see that we have not yet taken full and
appropriate account of immediacy. What matters to us just now is to take
seriously the immediacy of what is immediate and to allow its *own truth* to
establish itself. We are called upon to turn wholly and solely to *this* I, to
remain wholly immersed in intending a this and in this immersion to let
ourselves be shown what the now itself is here. We undertake a final
approach in order to grasp immediately what is immediate.

"The *now* gets shown; *this now. Now.*"[5] It is noteworthy that we are no
longer concerned with whether the now is day or night; the now is not
meant as a point in time, but as the now itself in itself. "Now." What is the
now? In saying "now," it is already past. It belongs to the now no longer to
exist even as it exists. Thus, the now is what has already been. But as what
has been, the now does not have the truth of being: " . . . what essentially
has been is, in fact, *not an* essence that is"[6]; it has no constant presence. The
now is not, and yet it was with its *being* that we were concerned.

In this way we have taken the now just as it itself required. And what
happened thereby? We simply grasped the now, and unawares we grasped
the no-longer now and arrived at the truth that the now has been. In saying
that the now as something which has been is no longer, we sublated this
second truth, too—stating with this second sublation *what the now is,*
namely: the now is not what is immediately simple but rather something
that is reflected in itself. The now is something simple that remains what it
is in its being other. The now is what is absolutely many nows—it is
universal.

The experience that we undergo with the now, an experience about what
the now is not and what it then is, is an *exhibiting* [*Aufzeigen*]. The
exhibiting is thereby not an immediate knowing, but a *movement*, a mediation. In the same way what is known in sense certainty is not something
immediately simple but something mediately simple. Thus, what sense
certainty *is* as a whole, what remains in sense certainty itself when it is
exhibited, that is the movement, the history of this movement. In this
history that aspect of sense certainty is grasped and taken which is what is
true in it. In this history sense certainty itself unfolds to the point of taking
what is true in sense certainty: Sense certainty turns into perception. (Cf.
what Hegel says about "universal" experience over against experience that is
"undergone"—II, 81–82 [GW IX, 69; Hoff., 87; E.T., 65].)

---

5. II, 80 [GW IX, 67; Hoff., 85; E.T., 63].
6. Ibid.

c) The infinity of absolute knowledge as the being-sublated of the finite and as dialectic. The starting point of a confrontation with Hegel's dialectic—the infinitude or finitude of being

If we look back on the whole of Hegel's presentation of immediate knowledge and at our interpretation, then all of this certainly shows itself as a remarkable "history" and a constant movement back and forth. It was in this that sense certainty arrived at its truth for us. But this truth is not one truth among others—as if it were our opinion about this truth—but rather it is the only genuine truth which sense certainty can have, insofar as something *exists* in absolvence and for absolvence. The essence of the immediacy of immediate knowledge is mediation. What is shown again and again is the effort *to keep from* falling out of the immediacy, to avoid this falling out, in order to remain entirely *in* it. But it is worth noting that this has already always been our endeavor—the endeavor of those who know absolutely and who *want* to know absolutely. Thus, the effort was already in a certain way condemned to failing fundamentally. For as soon as we *inquire* at all into immediate knowledge and its essence, we are already beyond immediacy. What remains is only the one [*das Eine*], entirely immersed in immediacy, executing only an actual knowing of this kind—only intending, and *not posing questions*.

The fact that "intending" is in [Hegel's] title for this section says not only that we "intend" but also that we inquire into "intending"—and in such a way that it gets decided in advance wherein alone the truth and being (essence) of intending and of the this can and must consist. And yet in this way we have brought to consciousness immediacy itself as such; and thereby we have learned that nothing lets itself be immediately grasped so little or not at all as what is immediate, when it is to be grasped in immediacy. To put it positively, comprehension of the immediacy of what is immediate requires most of all the total energy of absolving mediation. Because this mediation can establish itself initially only in complete indeterminacy—considering that the beginning is with what is immediate—this first part of Section A and Section A as a whole has its special difficulties. Only because Hegel construes sense certainty (what is immediate in its *immediacy*) always already from within the horizon of absolvence—only by virtue of this construction does sense certainty become visible. Sense certainty becomes further visible only by means of a *reconstruction* that is carried out in the light of this construction, a reconstruction intended to regain what is already broken and lost and to let it be seen as entirely wholesome and untouched.

What makes the beginning difficult is just the fact that on the one hand we have to carry out a construction in which we are concerned with comprehending the immediate, while on the other hand we are not allowed to stop with this construction, by taking its outcome by itself and one-sidedly. Rather, returning from the construction, we are to undertake the reconstruction right away.

One immediately obviates all possibilities of understanding when, instead of getting involved in the entire movement, one cuts oneself off from the movement which goes back and forth in the absolvent construction which reconstructs. And it is now a matter, not of noting our interpretation, but of letting it disappear as we try anew simply to read the text with the help of that interpretation—a reading which is left to each individual.

Clearly no age has known so much, or had at its disposal such ready means for knowing everything swiftly and for cleverly persuading everyone, as our age. But clearly no age has understood so little of what is essential about things as our age. And there is so little understanding, not because this age has fallen victim to a general imbecility, but because this age—in spite of its greed for everything—resists what is simple and essential and what promotes involvement and *perseverance*. Furthermore, this emptiness can spread because in the man of today the virtue of *patience* has ceased to exist.

Patience—that is the quiet anticipation in our persevering attention to what we should want, namely, that it be. Patience is the care [*Sorge*] which has turned away from all that noisy procuring [*Besorgen*] and has turned to the whole of Dasein. Patience is the truly *human* way of being thoughtful about things. Genuine patience is one of the basic virtues of philosophiz-ing—a virtue which understands that we always have to build up the pile of kindling with properly selected wood so that it may at one point catch fire. Patience in the first and last instance—"patience"—this word has with-drawn from essential language. And we do not wish that this word become a slogan, but rather that we practice it and in practicing it gain a facility in it. It is in such practicing that we first attain to genuine measures of our Dasein and achieve the keen ability for differentiating what is offered to Dasein.

But the impatience of the many—who want to be finished already before they even begin, in order to be able to let go of their *abiding* impatience at the very first opportunity—this impatience might overtake us already with our first groping step into the work that we want to effect.

Right at the beginning of the *Phenomenology of Spirit* there is, as it were, a demand whose magnitude increases to the extent that it is not specifically and extensively dealt with. To speak concretely about the actual beginning, the demand is this: Just when we are concerned with comprehending immediate knowledge, precisely then we must carry out a construction in the light of absolute knowledge. At the same time we are not supposed to stop with this construction by taking its results one-sidedly for itself.

Rather, the construction should take over the reconstruction of immediate knowledge. Thus, to the strangeness of this reconstructing construction there is added a complexity which necessarily begins with this construction, the movement back and forth, which is called in short "dialectic."

In this distressing situation of initially not understanding or of finally misunderstanding the entire work—a situation from which no one can exclude himself—it is the lesser evil if at the beginning we lose courage and resign. The greater evil is to believe that the understanding of "dialectic" may eventually be attained by sheer cunning and imitated as a gimmick. This is, of course, in a certain respect possible, so much so that in the end nothing would resist such a detached thinking, to which all doors would open—but surely doors through which we pass from one vacuity into another, even believing that we have here a grasp of the fullness of actuality.

Even Hegel himself in his later period did not entirely overcome this danger of dialectic—not even Hegel himself, for whom dialectic grew out of a very definite problematic and from whom this problematic was realized by the original, substantial character of his philosophizing Dasein. That is why Hegel could and had to undergo the unequivocal experience of regarding dialectic as being productive in itself. For him it was no problem whether or not the principle of construction, whose unfolding is dialectic, is required by the actuality of the actual. It was required because Hegel understood being as absolute, in advance and without question; and this absoluteness and infinity never became a problem for him because they *could* never become a problem. This was the case, not because of a personal limitation of Hegel's mind or even because of an inflexibility of conviction, but rather because of the power of the *Weltgeist*, which goes its ways to the end, while we remain its small satellites.

Every genuine philosophy is unique and only as such has the power to be *repeated* and to be effective again in a particular time and in keeping with the spirit and power of that time. But never in such a way that—whether sooner or later—it becomes something that belongs immediately to everyone, as, for example, in the *Kantgesellschaft* and now in the "International Hegel Society." There are indeed many other opportunities than those provided by the names and works of philosophers for mutually securing for oneself a miserable importance. But Hegel is no longer to be protected from the fact that in this new year, which is the hundredth anniversary of his death, all kinds of incompetent enthusiasm prattles about him, and only because of the accidental and indifferent number of a "hundred."

We protect the uniqueness of Hegel's work only when we take the trouble to confront it thoroughly. This means that we introduce into the discussion the *question* whether and how this confrontation finds its necessity, that is to say, arises from the inner grounds of Dasein and thereby from the matter of philosophy itself.

We look for this intersecting of the confrontation in the *problem of being* as the guiding and fundamental question of philosophy. The question arises as to whether being in its essence is finite and whether and how this finitude is to be placed fundamentally within the problematic of philosophy, without finitude's becoming a property which, as it were, hangs around beings and is taken up only occasionally. Or—to put the same question in another way— does the infinity of absolute knowledge determine the truth of being, and in such a way that it has already sublated everything that is finite into itself, so that all philosophizing moves only *in* this sublation and *as* such a sublation in the sense of *dialectic?* This question arises—or more precisely put: the question has not hitherto arisen and is just now about to be raised—as the questionableness which, ungrasped, has motivated previous metaphysics, though more externally and only for short periods. For the fact that finite and infinite beings (*ens finitum* and *ens infinitum*) have for a long time been differentiated with more or less felicity proves precisely that the question concerning the essence of *being* remains in indifference.

A confrontation with Hegel which begins in this way is not only inherently and historically necessary, but is also at the same time productive. This is so because for Hegel the infinity of being does not remain a formal principle, but rather grows out of a basic experience of beings as a whole and preserves an inner union with the genuine tradition of Western philosophy.

d) Points of orientation regarding the problem of the infinity of being: The absolvence of spirit from what is relative. The logical and subjective justification of infinity

Before we take up the interpretation again, I would like to provide some points of orientation with regard to the problem of the infinity of being, listing them rather than developing them.

First we should recall what, in an attempt to clarify the general character of the work, was said about the title "Science of the Experience of Consciousness" and "Science of the Phenomenology of Spirit."[7] For Hegel, "to experience" means to learn or come to know what something is not, and thus simultaneously what it is. Likewise, "to appear" or "to be a phenomenon" means for him to disunite, to become other in remaining self-identical. This history of the experience of the appearing of spirit arises in the most extreme remoteness of the most immediate and one-sided relatedness of knowing to the this. And this history takes as its course spirit's finding its way back to itself from being lost. Spirit detaches itself (in the sense already characterized) from what is relative, in order to dissolve it in itself. Spirit's detachment or absolvence from the relative occupies a special place in the

---

7. Cf. above, pp. 18–26.

total design of the work, namely, the place which lies in the transition from Sections A and B, taken together, to Section C. We saw already in a very rough way that it is with Section C that we actually and explicitly enter the realm of the absolute and that from this point on two divisions are slid into each other.

The absolvence of spirit from what is relative is in itself an overcoming of the disunity and disruption of consciousness in its own one-sidedness. As such an overcoming, *absolvence* is thus a deliverance, as it were, from that disruption. As absolvence, the absolute becomes *absolution*. Therefore, it is no accident that the finitude to be overcome within the *Phenomenology of Spirit* comes forth precisely at that juncture where the disunity of consciousness is known by consciousness without being already overcome in this knowing. On the contrary, this knowing only intensifies the disruption. This consciousness, which is aware of its own disunity, Hegel calls the "unhappy consciousness." Hence, the final portion of the second part of the large Section B, which leads directly to Section C, deals with the unhappy consciousness.[8] The unhappiness, the consciously present disruption of consciousness, is now to be carried over into the unity of the happiness of the absolute. But this happiness is not just the bliss present for itself which has discarded all unhappiness. Rather, this happiness is the happiness which dominates unhappiness and precisely therein needs it for itself.

The intimate connection of unhappiness and happiness—not established in a third thing but in happiness itself, which comes to itself by allowing unhappiness to belong to it—this way in which what is split into two belongs together as one constitutes the *true infinity of the finite*.

Regarding the Hegelian concept of infinity, we now have to consider two things: (1) Already very early, as soon as he actually decided to go into philosophy—thus, right after his theological period—Hegel anchored infinity in a place where the problem of being is rooted as a matter of course in the λόγος, in accordance with the tradition and the starting point of Western philosophy. This is expressed in the conception of thinking and logic as speculative knowledge, or dialectic. Hence, dialectic—as has often been emphasized—is grounded in the *inherent content* of the *problem* of being, grasped specifically as such. Dialectic is not the quick witchcraft of "this as well as that," with whose help any mischief may be done and which one believes one must adopt, because for some reason dialectic is a powerful instrument that imposes an easy-going attitude on the matter of philosophy (the matter of being) or because dialectic goes so far as to bewitch one.

(2) The second point ties in quite closely with the logical grounding of infinity (which at the same time means the transformation of the logic of

---

8. II, 158–73 [GW IX, 122–31; Hoff., 158–71; E.T., 126–38].

understanding). To be sure, with Descartes metaphysics is not subjected to a development of its problem in terms of a new *content*. Nevertheless, with Descartes metaphysics is subjected to an explicit transposition, or an orientation that is in certain respects even more radical, of the λόγος, or of *ratio*, toward its nearest conceivable ground, the *ego*, the *cogitatio*, the I, consciousness. From this point on, the way opens up for a new shaping of the content of metaphysics as it comes to light in the Leibnizean monadology, as a radical theory of the substantiality of substance. In a certain pre-Kantian sense, this theory is a preliminary form of Hegel's fundamental thesis: Substance is in truth subject. But the work of Kant was needed first, in order to obtain in the "transcendental" a clear horizon for the metaphysical problematic. And then Fichte was needed, to take the absoluteness of the I into account for the first time—though incompletely—in the concrete labor of his doctrine of science.

Within the living presence of the works of Kant and Fichte, and conditioned by Schelling's doctrine of identity, it fell to Hegel to comprehend the subject as absolute spirit—by installing the essence of true infinity, logically conceived, in the essence of I-hood as subjectivity and by letting the essence of true infinity spring from out of the latter.

Both the "logical" and the "subjective" grounding of infinity—as we call them in short—are already carried out in the thoroughly concrete investigations which are handed down to us as manuscripts from the Jena lectures. But in these manuscripts everything is still at the beginning and is more within the scope of a confrontation with tradition; it has not yet found its own necessary shape. This happens for the first time in the *System of Science*, whose first part, the *Phenomenology*, presents the grounding we mentioned as our second point (the grounding of infinity in the subject and as subject), while the second part, the *Logic*, implements the first grounding that we mentioned above (the logical grounding), which is inherently and necessarily grounded in the second one.

In order to give merely an idea of the early logical grounding of infinity in Hegel, a grounding which is decisive for everything that follows, let me make a brief reference to the discussion of infinity in the manuscripts of the Jena period. We must forego actually working out the development of infinity which is accomplished there.

What immediately meets the eye is that infinity is developed in close connection with a speculative overcoming of—which is at the same time a grounding and determining of—the Kantian table of categories, and that there is just as decisively at work a new delimitation of the ancient metaphysics of Plato and Aristotle.[9] The essence of infinity "is the absolute

---

9. Cf. below, pp. 102ff.

sublation of determinateness, the contradiction that determinateness, so far as it is, is not, and so far as it is not, is."[10] Already here two things become clear: (1) the orientation of the determination of infinity to the "is" and (2) the determining (synthesis, simple) of the proposition, λόγος, but in the sense that the simple saying, speech, is in itself contradiction.

The "absolute opposition, infinity, is this absolute reflection {turning back} into itself of the determinate that is an other than itself (that is, not an other as such against which it would be indifferent on its own account, but rather its immediate opposite); and, as it is this, it is itself. This alone is the true nature of the finite: that it is infinite, that it sublates itself in its being. The determinate as such has no other essence than this absolute restlessness not to be what it is."[11] The "purely absolute movement, being outside itself while being in itself."[12] And accordingly: "To recall it provisionally, the true knowledge of the absolute is not that it will be merely demonstrated that the one and the many are one and this alone is absolute, but rather that in the one and the many itself the being-one [*Einssein*] of each one with the other is posited."[13]

This turning back of the determinate into itself, while precisely not escaping to another determinate outside itself, belongs to the essence of infinity. But this turning back of the other into the one, whereby the difference becomes a non-difference and wherein what is differentiated remains preserved and sublated, this reflection which marks the essence of infinity is genuinely actual in the I. For the I, by positing itself *as* I, differentiates itself from itself, so much so that what is differentiated does not fall out of the I, but rather becomes visible precisely as what is actually not differentiated and is the same. Herein is manifest the inner connection between the logical and the subjective I-like [*ichlich*] grounding of infinity. What is truly and really infinite in the declared logical sense is the subject and, what is more, the absolute subject as spirit—as is to be shown in the *Phenomenology*.

Conversely, for our confrontation we infer from this that the subject, the I, is conceived primarily as "I think," thus logically. But because what is logical is dialogical-dialectical, Hegel and German Idealism as a whole can grasp the totality of beings in their being from out of I-hood as infinity. This also comes to be expressed as follows: Infinity itself is the actual λόγος as concept.

---

10. *Jenenser Logik, Metaphysik und Naturphilosophie*, ed. Lasson, p. 27 [GW VII, 29; trans. J. W. Burbridge and G. di Giovanni, *The Jena System 1804–5: Logic and Metaphysics* (Kingston and Montreal: McGill-Queen's University Press, 1986), p. 32].
11. Ibid., pp. 30f. [GW VII, 33; *Logic and Metaphysics*, 35].
12. Ibid., p. 31 [GW VII, 34; *Logic and Metaphysics*, 35].
13. Ibid., p. 33 [GW VII, 39; *Logic and Metaphysics*, 37].

This should be enough to clarify the subsequent direction of our interpretive confrontation with Hegel.

The absolvent observation of sense certainty showed that, in keeping with its manner of knowing, sense certainty intends the *particular* this, but that the truth of sense certainty, which it itself already states in the word *this*, is a universal. While sense certainty intends the particular, it does not take what is true for it; sense certainty does not take what is true, is thus not taking for true [*Wahrnehmung*, perception];* and yet sense certainty is in a certain way already a taking of what is true—insofar as it has what is true with it, without, of course, grasping it explicitly. Sense certainty thus confirms already in advance the right and necessity of perception; the absolvent knowing of sense certainty is pushed beyond sense certainty to the knowing of knowing as perception.

Earlier we indicated the difficulty that exists in trying to understand the *Phenomenology of Spirit. That* this work is difficult hardly needs a lengthy demonstration. That it is *difficult* also does not of itself amount to anything about which a great deal has to be said. However, it is useful and necessary to point out the *reason* for the difficulty. This reason lies in the fact that the work begins at once in terms of the *absolute* and requires constant, absolvent, reconstructing construction. That the work begins *at once* absolutely is all right. For one can begin absolutely only all at once—or not at all; with the absolute one cannot begin gradually. The work confronts us with the demand that we continuously comport ourselves absolutely. And what may be more difficult for the most finite than to be infinite?

But will our comprehension of the work not be commensurate to it if we simply go along with it, without contributing anything to it? Going along, certainly; but merely repeating and reading and reporting—in short review-papers—does not help. If we only do this sort of thing, then we learn (either right away or later, it does not matter when) something remarkable, namely, that the work stays mute if we do not contribute anything to it. We have to bring to the work nothing less than a living question and its demands for an appropriate treatment. It is only thus that the content of the work gets *moving*; and the inner movement of the work, its transitions, are what is decisive—not so much the material which is graspable in detail. Transitions have to be entered into; and as long as we stay on one or the other shore and talk back and forth, transitions can never be achieved.

However, what presses us—and Hegel in the same way—to stay on

---

*[The words "taking for true" are used in translation here in order to keep visible the "literal" meaning of *Wahrnehmung*. This meaning is implied in the usual English rendering as *perception*. Our translation is also in keeping with what Hegel intends as he thinks through *Wahrnehmung*.]

course is the *question* concerning the essence of being. The ways of its questioning and answering cross one another.

Hegel does not raise the question, but he offers a response—prompted a long time ago by the inner constraint of the tradition—to the question concerning the essence of beings: He responds with the fundamental thesis that the essence of beings is infinity. We have discussed briefly what this means by observing (1) the logical and (2) the subjective grounding of infinity. We clarified how infinity stems from the "is" of the simple proposition as the determination of something as something. This infinity does not mean a continuous alignment of determinations, endlessly going forward from one to another, but the contrary; it means the return of something into itself, the reflection of the determinate back into itself, so that the determinate (as the other) returns to the one, and the other (as what is differentiated from the determinate) receives it; it means that the other (in unison with the determinate) becomes undifferentiated and remains preserved in sameness with it.

And now, when seen externally, what is astonishing is that this concept of infinity finds its proof and its concretion equally immediately in the *I*. For the I is that actual which, in positing itself as "I am I," differentiates itself from itself—but in such a way that what is differentiated does not fall away from what makes the differentiation but rather is taken back into what makes the differentiation and remains preserved therein. This peculiar difference of the non-differentiated is actual in the I. Thus, the logical difference, "the determinateness," and along with it the logical concept of infinity, are rooted in the I (logic as thinking is an *I* think). And a logic with such an orientation is not a doctrine of the proposition, detached from the I, but a logic which necessarily includes I-hood. In a Kantian sense it is a transcendental logic which has understood that, because λόγος is in itself infinite, the I-character is essential for thinking. This means that the actuality of the infinite is subject in the absolute sense of *spirit*.

Chapter Two

Perception

§8. Consciousness of perception and its object

a) Perception as mediation and transition from sense certainty to understanding

We now have a new object, which indeed arises necessarily from the previous one. Perception, the new object for us, who know in an absolvent manner, is again and for the first time legitimately a knowing, in accordance with its basic character. But the necessity of its objectivity for us is (as a necessity of mediation) different from the necessity of the objectivity of sense certainty. This latter necessity is mediated; and for the sake of that mediation sense certainty pretends, as it were, to be its possible victim.

However, since we are not merely going along with Hegel but rather following his text *interpretively*, it is important at this point to consider the following. Perception does arise for us; but as long as we are satisfied with the above-mentioned difference between perception as object and sense certainty as object, perception does *not* confront us as an absolvent object (as object held in absolvence). Perception as what is mediated is mediated not only in the sense of being inevitably *detected* in sense certainty, but also at the same time in the sense of being that which is placed in the *middle*. That means that, if we grasp perception's absolute objectivity only from the side of sense certainty and perception's absolvent *origin*, then we conceive it one-sidedly and thus not absolutely. It is exactly at this juncture that perception should be conceived as the middle term between . . . , so that we must here already look to the other side whither perception, as middle and between, is to be mediated further and beyond in the direction of its absolvent *future*. As the middle, perception is precisely a *transition toward* . . . ; in perception the movement of absolvence is, as it were, really and truly unsettled.

81

Perception knows no rest. Hence, that toward which perception moves must already emerge in perception itself. Perception *itself* is not to be taken as an inevitable *outcome*, as indeed it was with regard to sense certainty. What perception is *going to be* belongs already to perception. Perception *is* only *what* it is in its *having been and its future*.

If we here deliberately point to the *temporal* moments in the "being" [*Sein*] of what is to be known in an absolvent manner, we do so knowing full well that we are going beyond Hegel, and not simply in a direction that Hegel accidentally failed to take up as his own problem. We are, rather, taking a direction which would have turned *against* him, had he followed it. But this happens only if the fundamental problematic of time is *unfolded from out of the problem of being itself*. It is not enough—and indeed amounts to a complete misunderstanding of the problem—if we look into what Hegel or someone else said about time. Rather, we must see that *Hegel circumscribes time* in the same way *as he determines the I: logico-dialectically*, in accordance with a predetermined idea of being.

As we already saw, Hegel occasionally speaks about having been, but never about the future. This accords with his view of the past as the decisive character of time: It is a fading away, something transitory and always bygone. Consequently, we find here an orientation toward time and the past which reveals—in a different and indeed thoroughly radical way—a "crossroad."

Although Hegel's presentation of perception has an architectonic similar to that manifest in the treatment of sense certainty, its proper movement is different. This movement is different insofar as perception, in itself a detected middle, mediates a third moment: understanding. Just as perception is in a way the truth of sense certainty, so precisely as this truth perception is at the same time the untruth of understanding.

Accordingly, the title of the second part of "A. Consciousness" must be read in the right way. We are already prepared for such a reading in the treatment of the first part. Hegel discusses the title "Sense Certainty" through "the this and intending" and the title "Perception" through "thing and deception." The expressions "thing and deception" and "this and intending" look like a mere juxtaposition and enumeration of the two interpenetrating moments of consciousness (the known and the knowing of it). But we saw that "intending" has a double thrust. Intending says that the object is essentially one which is "intended," is mine, and that it is the object for sense knowledge; but it thereby also says that the truth of the object returns in a higher truth as perception. Correspondingly, the expression *deception* in the title of the second part says more than one may initially presume. Initially the expression *deception* could be taken to mean that, as we perceive things, we may be deceived or that perception may be sometimes true and sometimes false. But this view of deception would reflect only what occasionally "happens" to perception and would make no claim to be identified as necessarily belonging to the essence of perception, in the sense of that which is known in absolvence. What Hegel actually means by deception is that perception is *in itself* a deception, a continual self-deception, a talking oneself into something; and it "*is*" such insofar as the *being* of perception is conceived in absolvence, which is the only way to conceive perception if one follows Hegel. Perception already implies an intelligibility, an understanding; but this rendering intelligible is mere "sophistry."[1] It is not the intelligibility of pure understanding, but the intelligibility of perceptual understanding. Therefore, the absolvent presentation of perception is essentially concerned with showing how in perception itself a certain intelligibility and reflection takes on pretensions and thus emerges as a play of forces in the form of "empty abstractions."[2] This perceptual understanding is what is often called "sound common sense."[3]

Just as sophistry and sophistic illusion are defined in Plato, Aristotle, and Kant in accordance with the truth and the level of *their* basic philosophical quest in each case, so also in Hegel common understanding bears *his* mark. However, considering its roots, this is the same understanding which has been at work since philosophy became actual.

But even Hegel's explication of deception should not be taken one-sidedly, as if what matters to him is merely to demonstrate *that* common understanding appears in perception and does its mischief there. The task is to show that *precisely because* a perceptual understanding resides in perception, *thereby* perception perishes, all by itself. That means that perception is truly a middle term and a transition, one which has no permanence.

But this perishing should not be taken to mean a fluttering and scattering away into nothingness. If this were the case, then the middle term would not be conceived in its mediating character or as a transition toward something else. That is why we have to hear the positive in Hegel's negative, when he speaks of perishing: Perishing is returning to the ground [*Das Zugrundegehen ist das Zum-Grunde-Zurückgehen*]. Through the mediation of perception, sense certainty first reaches understanding and therein gets to its own ground as the true mode of consciousness. Thus, the *whole*, in which these three moments [sense certainty, perception, and understanding] are located—Consciousness (A)—comes into its own; the whole turns into *self-consciousness*.

At the present stage of discussion, we should not forget that perception, the second mode of knowledge which arises for us, is *consciousness* and that, in spite of the reflection that perception presumes to exercise, it is not *self-*

---

1. II, 97, 99 [GW IX, 79, 80; Hoff., 100, 101; E.T., 77, 78].
2. II, 98 [GW IX, 80; Hoff., 100; E.T., 77].
3. II, 98 [GW IX, 80; Hoff., 101; E.T., 77].

consciousness. To put it positively, perception, too, is and remains consciousness, a knowing that, in accordance with its manner of knowing, is always and initially directed toward the object as what is other and alien, and initially finds in the object the essence of itself and what is true. However, perception does not wish to have for its object the this which is merely an *intended particular*; perception as taking-for-true [*Wahrnehmung*] avails itself of the *true.* But that which is true is necessarily a universal. That means a simplicity [*ein Einfaches*], which exists through negation and is "neither this nor that," a not-this, such that through such negativity it is at the same time (positively) indifferent to being this as well as that (the dialectical and speculative concept of the universal).

Insofar as perception qua consciousness—as distinguished from self-consciousness—belongs to immediate knowing, perception no longer possesses what is immediate knowing; perception no longer possesses what is immediate in the particular, but rather in the universal. In its entirety, perception is "universal immediacy."[4] But precisely something like a "universal immediacy," or immediacy of the universal, is in itself already corroded by contradiction, inasmuch as the universal, as we saw, exists essentially in and as the negation of the particular, and consequently as mediation. This contradictory essence of perception cannot sustain itself at all: It destroys itself.

We must note again and again that this process is not described as a process of consciousness, but is seen from within the absolute. If one fails to keep this in view and proceeds naively, then one *has* to wonder how perception can ever destroy itself, because common understanding finds no occasion for this destruction, considering perception in reference to itself and as something extant.

The task is to show how perception breaks down and mediates something else. This is to be done by way of an exposition of the history of experience which *we* allow perception to undergo with itself. To this end it is necessary to begin with how perception qua consciousness appears.

b) The thing as what is essential in perception. Thingness as the unity of the "also" of properties

Perception, as a mode of knowing, initially shows its moments again in such a way that the perceived or the object is what is essential, whereas perceiving is the inessential. Hence, the apportionment of the difference between the essential and the inessential is one-sided and easily seen as such. The object of perception is the thing, this thing, "this salt,"[5] as this

---

4. II, 86 [GW IX, 72; Hoff., 90; E.T., 68].
5. Ibid.

simple one which exists entirely for itself in the immediate unity and gatheredness of the white, tart, cubically shaped, heavy salt. The moments which are gathered in this one thing and which are not separated in the thing as perceived are pulled apart and unfolded in the movement of perceiving. The way this happens is again shown by the statement in which perception articulates itself. Perception does not simply say, as in sense certainty, "this salt," whereby, as was shown, the said no longer says what was intended, because salt is something universal. Rather, perception says that this salt is white *and* tart *and* cubical *and* heavy, and so on. What sense certainty says, against its own intention, as it were—salt: something universal—perception expresses in such a way that it says *what* the salt here is. But this unfolding movement of perceiving is inconstant, against which the one simple object itself (the thing) is indifferent.

What matters in the first place, then, is to unfold in its essence the object as that which is the true in perception—doing this, of course, on the level and in the light in which the object now stands, as *originating* from sense certainty. Because it originates from sense certainty, the object is and remains in any case a *sensible* object. But its truth is the universal. However, we grasp universality as *mediated simplicity*. Perception itself expresses this: The object is "*the thing with many properties.*"[6] To unfold the true for perception means only to expound what constitutes the thingness of the thing. In other words, to show how thingness makes a thing a thing. Here again what matters is to carry out an absolvent construction of the object of perception or of the thing, a construction which should verify the full essence of perception.

Hegel thus proceeds from a comparison between the object of perception and the object of sense certainty. This is not an arbitrary comparative procedure, but lies in the nature of the matter itself, because the object of perception evolves from the object of sense certainty and therefore has a historical relation to the object of sense certainty—historical [*geschichtlich*] in the sense of the happening of the *Phenomenology* itself. The object of perception is no longer that object which was the object of sense certainty— the this, or, to stay with Hegel's example of perception, this salt which is here on the table. Perception does not mean simply and exclusively "this salt" and nothing else. Rather, perception takes for *true*; it is serious about grasping this salt as *what* the this is, and seeing that this what, the universal, is its object. And it is its object in that perception takes the object as what it is. But what *is* it? The object is that which can be taken by itself in the immediate saying of the "is," which can immediately be removed and thus enumerated.

This salt is white and tart and cubical and heavy, and so on. This salt is

---

6. II, 85 [GW IX, 71; Hoff., 89; E.T., 67].

that and that. Because the this is that and that, it is not simply this: The this is sublated in the not-this. Not-this in no way means nothing; but rather, being not only the this, the this is that and that. *What* the this is in being not-this, is a content; and the content emerges from out of the this, from out of what it is. What is it? White and tart—thus, not *this* white or *this* tart, with which I would mean only what has the character of a this in its whatness, without meaning the what itself. But now I grasp, not what has the character of the this, but its what. Thus, it is white and tart. What the this or the object is—its *whatness* [*Wassein*]—is a universal. But the immediacy of the this or the sensuous is preserved in this universal—white, tart. If we take the salt in this way—which is also how it is expressed in the proposition—if we thus neither simply intend the this nor do anything further about perception, then we are taking it as the white and the tart and the cubical and the heavy, etc. We differentiate these universals, take them apart, and thus regard them as many. In this way we take the many in such a way that, if we look closely, they are all indifferent to one another. In like manner the enumerated universals are all simply related to themselves— white, tart. . . . Indifferent to one another, they are not simply lined up in a row by means of a mere "and." Rather, these many are, each with the same validity as another, that which the salt is. The this in its whatness is white; and the same this is tart—it is not simply white and tart but white "and *also*" tart. In this "also" is expressed "just as it is white, it is also. . . . " In this "just as" the items that are indifferent to one another coincide and come together at the same time. The "and" indicates the mere side-by-side character of the indifferent items. But the "also" indicates the side-by-side character of these items within a simultaneous *subordination to the same*, which is not indicated by the "and."

The way in which the indifferently many items are together without being concerned with one another is expressed by the "*also*." The latter is the medium of thingness, the simple togetherness of the many. The possible ways of this togetherness in the "also" are already familiar to us: the here and the now (space and time). In its simple here, the salt is the *together*, as *what* the this is *positively*, or as the *mere* this is *not*. The "also" is the "indifferent unity,"[7] or more precisely: *the unity of what is indifferent*. Insofar as the thing is such that it exists for itself as a one, we have in the unity of the indifferent evidently obtained *one* of the characters of the one, a character which expresses that the particular, the simple "also," is *in itself* related to what is multiple. The "also" holds together what is multiple, although only in such a way that the universal "also" is indifferent to the multiple and thus allows the many *also* to remain indifferent to one another. Put more precisely: The "also" is thus the indifferent unity of the many that are indifferent to one another, but belong together.

---

7. II, 87 [GW IX, 73; Hoff., 92; E.T., 69].

Thus, we grasp something of the essence of the thing as the object of perception (as thinghood) without understanding *how* the thing can thereby be this thing that it is—or, as we said at the beginning: the thing with many properties. Insofar as we do not yet understand this in terms of the "also," the "also" is not capable of fully determining the essence of the thing, even though something already becomes manifest in the "also" that goes further and that belongs to the thing, namely, *having properties*. The unity of the "also" points to this "having of properties," because the "also" of the many shows the uniformity among them, and *indifferent belonging* to something, a certain *being-appropriated*—pro-perty.* Yet with this neither the essence of property nor the essence of the thing is achieved—both of which belong together. Only when thinghood is determined in such a way as to let us understand *how* thinghood becomes a thing—in the sense of how having properties belongs to it and what it itself is—only then is the essence of the thing (the true object of perception) achieved. For the time being it remains unresolved whether the essence of perception is achieved, where for perception what is essential is its *object*.

c) The exclusive unity of the thing as condition for having properties. The perceptual object's having of properties and the possibility of deception

If we stick to perception's proposition that "this salt is white, tart, and so on," then in this statement there is not only the enumeration of everything that the this *also* is, but in a certain sense it emphasizes that "this" is white and not black, tart and not mild, cubical and not round. In this emphasis there is an *exclusion* of the opposite; and in this exclusion—and in negation in general—there is that which in each case the this "also" is: *its determinateness*. But because this multiple "also" carries with it in each case an opposition, the unity which ties the opposites together cannot be a simple unity of indifference. Because multiplicities are in themselves oppositional, their unity is all the more an opposing unity. The unity of the "also," the unity of what is indifferent, does not exhaust thinghood. Rather, as the unity of opposing multiplicities, thinghood is itself the one which is so determined that, by opposing itself, it excludes the other. By means of this unity of exclusion, the unity includes itself in itself and becomes a unity for itself. Thus, thinghood (the "also") now becomes the thing, that which stands for itself and is independent.

Thus, the multiple first becomes subordinate to what stands-for-itself, and the many in the "also" first turns out to be *something which has properties*. The unity of indifference (the "also") and the unity of exclusion (the one and not the other) belong together in the full essence of thinghood.

---

*[*Zugehörigkeit*: belonging to; *Zugeeignetsein*: being appropriated; *Eigenschaft*: property.]

But insofar as this coupled unity is the simplicity of a manifold, the having of properties arises among the manifold. Thus, for the first time we are in a position to say something absolvent about what we encountered at the outset of sense certainty within its objectivity, namely, its "wealth."[8]

The wealth of sense certainty does not belong to sense certainty.[9] According to the manner of its knowing, sense certainty is incapable of having wealth *belong* to it as something it knows, because in each case meaning intends only the single this and not the what, the manifold, and the many in the one. But wealth can *belong* to perception—according to *its* essence—for it *takes* its object as the universal what, precisely as having properties. Something can belong only to a knowing which is in itself a taking [*ein Nehmen*]. Mere intending has no means for something like belonging to and belonging together.

Perception itself comes to recognize this manner of its knowing. Thereby perception does attain a specific consciousness. If the object of perception is necessarily the thing—as what has properties—then perceiving, if it wants to take what is true, must always take the this in its what, *as* that and *as* that and that. With this taking, which fundamentally takes from out of a multiplicity, perceiving can mistake the what by taking the object as that which the object is not: Perception *can* deceive itself. This possibility is not only present in perception as something that occasionally comes to pass, as something that befalls perception from somewhere else; rather, it is a possibility that belongs to taking itself, to having an object. This possibility belongs to the way in which the object is known and is thus a *conscious* possibility: "The percipient is conscious of the possibility of deception."[10]

All of this indicates that the taking in perceiving [*das Nehmen im Wahrnehmen*] is no mere apprehending. But perception is initially taken as such; and in this regard perception is alleged to be inessential to the object, and vis-à-vis the object, to be impermanent and untrue—thus attributing truth exclusively to the object. However, if taking is other than apprehending and if the grasping of apprehending can go awry, then taking as perceiving must in each case grasp in the *right* way. Taking as such must be intent upon being a true taking. "Taking" must deliberate, think, and must understand with the aim of not making a mistake. Thereby the possibility emerges that the truth of perception does not simply fall unilaterally in the object, but also and just as much in taking. But then the initial characterization of the object of perception and the allotment of what is essential and not essential contains a contradiction, although a hidden one. Whether and how this is the case must again be shown in this knowing itself. We must set in motion

---

8. II, 73 [GW IX, 63; Hoff., 79; E.T., 58].
9. II, 85 [GW IX, 71; Hoff., 90; E.T., 67].
10. II, 88 [GW IX, 74; Hoff., 93; E.T., 70].

a real act of perceiving and watch how it "takes" the true—the true which we have just now characterized for the essential determination of the thing with its many properties. Thereby the contradictions in the essence of perception must themselves come to light.

§9. The mediating and contradictory character of perception

Now we can say already in advance in what the contradiction of perception lies. This contradiction lies in perception itself. The knowing and taking peculiar to perception is not that of intending, which is simply let loose and continues so, absorbed in its this and remaining enslaved to it. Rather, contradiction must be shown to be in perception itself; there must be in taking itself something opposed to "this." "Taking" takes the object as true. But since taking has the consciousness of deception, it knows in a certain way that taking itself *and not the object* is what is true. Perception is exactly what it is by living from this contradiction, without being serious about it, without knowing it as contradiction, and without sublation. However, we, who should know perception absolvently as a mode of consciousness, must seek the truth of perception in just this contradiction. What matters, then, is on the one hand to show in a general way how perception contradicts itself in the stated manner, how it turns around in a circle, as it were—and on the other hand to bring to light explicitly the contradictory character of perception, on the basis of both the essence of its object, projected in the process of absolvence, and the manner of its knowing. After that it must be shown how in itself perception, by contradicting itself, points beyond itself and thus is in itself mediation. It yields something else to be disclosed, something which can again only be a mode of knowing—and that is understanding.

a) The possibility of deception as the ground of the contradiction in perception as taking and reflection

The point is to experience, in and with an actual perception, how things are arranged in it. *We* undergo an experience. Or: We let perception undergo an experience with itself. This is to say that the transposition to an "actual perceiving,"[1] wherein consciousness should undergo its experience, takes place *only now*, after we have constructed the object of perception.

What do I take when, in an actual perceiving of this white, tart salt, I take its true? *And how* is the taking itself? I take this white salt. At first the object presents itself *"purely as a one."*[2] But I am forbidden to take the object that

---

1. II, 89 [GW IX, 74; Hoff., 93; E.T., 70].
2. II, 89 [GW IX, 74; Hoff., 93; E.T., 70].

way, forbidden by the property, which is the universal. Thus, *I* did not take the object truly; the untruth coincides with taking because the object is indeed the true. However, if I do not take the object purely as one, but as the "also," which in each case is required by the universality of properties, then it immediately becomes manifest that even in this way I do not take the object correctly, because properties are *determined* and mutually exclusive. Thus, I take the object as a "one" which is exclusive. But if I take the object thus, in the universality of the "also" and of the "one," then I take, not the object, but its medium, wherein there are many particular, determined properties for themselves. Thereby I take the particular property *for itself*. If this happens, then I take the property neither as it is in the "one" nor as it is in the relation to another, and thus not at all as a property. Rather, I take the particular this—white—immediately. But this immediate taking of the this is an intending. The knowing of the object, my perceiving, has become an intending.

Thus, in the face of the object of actual perception, we undergo the experience that the apprehending was not correct; taking passes over into an intending. But intending has already crossed over into perceiving. Hence, in this experience perceiving *returns into itself*. Perceiving does not take up the true in a simple apprehending, but it takes the true back into perceiving and thus takes the truth of what is perceived *in* and *upon itself*. Thus—corresponding to sense certainty—the truth that was originally situated in the object is taken back into knowing.

Thus, consciousness as perceiving is pushed back upon itself in the experience which it undergoes with itself—an experience which is, of course, to be understood in the light of the absolvent projection. But in what way is it pushed back upon itself? Not as that which would simply be the true, but rather pure apprehending has proved itself to be thoroughly incorrect. Thus, consciousness arrives at the point of distinguishing its apprehending of the object *from* the untruth of its perceiving. Taking itself needs proper guidance. Insofar and *only insofar* as the untruth of taking is now "corrected,"[3] does the correction, the *truth* of perceiving, fall into perceiving. Thus—and to put it initially as a quite general observation—perceiving as consciousness has emerged as something which does not merely take or limit itself to taking, but as something which is conscious of its own reflection in itself, its bending back upon itself. A taking that reflects is a taking which does not simply take; but a taking which does not take is a contradiction in itself.

This contradictory character must nevertheless be worked out absolvently. This means that we must not understand Hegel with the methods adopted by Hegelianism, which was dead from the beginning. We must not

---

3. II, 91 [GW IX, 75; Hoff., 95; E.T., 72].

violate Hegel with the fading and already consumptive witchcraft of an unbounded dialectic. What is important is to heed "the seriousness of the concept reaching into its depth {the depth of the matter at issue},"[4] of which Hegel speaks in the preface to the *Phenomenology*. The point is concretely to disperse the contradictory character in the essence of perception—in what constitutes the true for it, in its object, in the thing—and to unfold this contradictory character in the whole of its being driven against and beyond itself. The experience is thus made that the object as such is finally exploded by the way in which perceiving itself tries to come to terms with and to preserve what is true for it.

But this break-up is not a simple scattering into pieces, but an annihilation within an already—if unacknowledged—actual attachment of the essence of perception to a higher truth. In the experience which we allow perception to undergo in its arguing with itself, we bring perception near to its absolvent truth. The unfolding of its contradictory character is the sublation of the truth of perception, both in the sense of its elimination and as the raising of it to its actual essence. The task now is to go through each individual stage where the truth of perception, its object, the thing, is run aground, in order to see finally what new realm perception enters in this running aground.

b) The reciprocal distribution of the contradictory one and "also" of the thing to perceiving as taking and reflection

The object of perception is the thing, the one which has many properties. Perceiving itself, as we saw, is not a mere apprehending, but, to the extent that consciousness of the possibility of deception belongs to perception, includes a reflection on its own activity, its way of taking. Both apprehending and reflection belong to perception, so much so that perception separates both from each other; not only that, but in perceiving and in securing the true taking of the true, perception plays one (reflection) against the other (apprehending), and vice versa.

This arguing which takes place in perceiving itself constantly reveals contradictions in perception, which it tries to eliminate again and again by turning itself to the one side and by alleging that the separate, other side is inessential and nothing. We shall pursue this game, holding on to the one-sidedness and keeping them opposed to each other. We shall then see *how* perception runs aground in itself.

Immediately and initially, what is true in perception is the thing, and that means the one, the *single one*. If we come across something else in this single one, like the plurality of properties—the white and also the tart—then this

---

4. II, 6 [GW IX, 11; Hoff., 12; E.T., 3].

"also" must be taken up by consciousness. For only by keeping the "alsos" as the many separate from the one, can the one be maintained purely in its truth. The argumentative understanding can take the one as one only if it omits the many from the thing. Consciousness takes upon itself the many "alsos"—and that is indeed quite all right and plausible, for white is the thing only insofar as it is seen by *our* eyes, tart insofar as it is touched by *our* tongue, cubical insofar as it is touched by *our* feel. We take this variety of properties upon ourselves insofar as the eye, the tongue, etc., are kept apart in us. We are the universal medium which forces apart and provides a place for the "alsos"; and if we take back into *us* these many "alsos" from the thing, then we preserve for the thing its unity, its pure identity with itself.

This is the one way in which perception comes to terms with the twofold character of the thing as the one and as "also," by crossing out the "also" and transposing it into taking. But properties are what they are as determinate, as opposed to others—white to black and so on. Because of these determinate properties, the thing is itself just the one that it is and is *not* another thing. Insofar as it is one, the thing by itself does not have these many determinate aspects and thus the oppositions. The unity of the thing is its mere identity with itself, on the basis of which the thing as one is identical with every other one. In order to be contrasted as the *one*, in order *not* to be *the other*, the thing must have its determinateness in itself. Thus, the thing must itself be the "also" and the many; it must be the universal medium wherein the many properties exist apart from one another indifferently.

But again, in order for perceiving to preserve the "also" for the thing itself—as was required above—it must take the unity upon itself. The argumentative understanding can take the many as many only if it omits unity from the thing. By contrast, the placing of the many into one, which the thing also is in each case—also white, also tart—belongs to taking, to consciousness as it takes the thing as white *insofar as* it is *not* tart, and vice versa. With the help of this "insofar as," the separation of the many is maintained even as consciousness takes all of them together into one, the thing. In principle, oneness claims perceiving in *such* a way that what is called property "is represented as *free matter*."[5] Thus, the thing turns out to be a "collection of matters";[6] and the one becomes the mere surrounding surface, which comes from taking.

Thus, there is on the one side the one which is void of the many, and on the other side the "also" which is dissolved in independent free "matters." Where one emerges and is to stay, the other will be driven away, and vice versa.

If we survey all of this, then we see that perceiving turns its taking

---

5. II, 93 [GW IX, 76; Hoff., 96; E.T., 74].
6. II, 93 [GW IX, 76; Hoff., 97; E.T., 74].

alternately into one and then into the "also" as well as the thing sometimes into the "also" and sometimes into the one. For the thing itself, which still counts as the true according to the sense of perception, this means: The thing has in itself "an opposing truth."[7]

At the beginning the thing was simply the true; then it became manifest that, insofar as "taking" is unhomogeneous, the thing is the true and self-identical. Now it turns out that taking, too, is reciprocally what the thing is. What applies to the thing applies also to taking. *Truth is thus this reciprocal alternation of the entire movement of the one-sided distribution of one moment—* of the "also" or the one—*to taking or to the thing.*

What results from this for the thing, to which perception in all of its vacillation, of which it is not specifically and explicitly aware, returns again and again? The mirroring of this movement in the thing indicates that the thing is in itself contradiction. But perception cannot admit something like this, because perception cannot tolerate the contradiction. Perception cannot tolerate it because, limited to itself, perception is a finite knowing. Accordingly, wherever perception encounters contradiction—and especially in what is the true for it—there it must look carefully so as not to let the contradictory elements loose against one another but to distribute them and to put them aside. Reflection carries out this distribution in such a way that it again adds the "insofar as" and thus separates the contradictory moments.

Our task is to see how and whether perception can maintain this separation and thus defend itself against contradiction.

c) The contradiction of the thing in itself—being for itself and being for an other—and the failure of the reflection of perception

The thing is one as well as the "also," the manifold of others. However, it is one only for another; and because it is for another, the one is itself an other. Being one and being other both belong to the thing, but in different respects. The thing is other only insofar as it is not related to itself but to another. Perception says that the other is responsible for the one's being also the other. For example, the chalk and the eraser: Chalk, the one, is also the other only because there is an eraser which itself can be the one over against which the chalk is now the other. The chalk is the other only because of the eraser. Perception does not understand that the one is not also the other because of the other, but because it is the one. As one it is not the other— *not* the other. That means that it is precisely in itself related to the other, whether this other factually exists or not. Assuming that there were only one single thing, this one would nevertheless be an other, because the term

---

7. II, 93 [GW IX, 77; Hoff., 97; E.T., 74].

sole [*einzig*] means *no* others, but also no *others*. Given the means for understanding at its disposal, perception does not understand something like this.

The unity of the thing (its self-identity) is, as far as the apprehension of perception is concerned, not disputed by the specific thing but by other things, by virtue of the fact that they also exist. Contradiction is thus allotted to differing things. In perceiving, the different things are posited in each case as for itself. Each is an other through the other; each is the other of the other and from consciousness of it; each is different. But in this way each thing has been differentiated. If each is differentiated, then the difference belongs to the thing itself; as such, as one, the thing is an other. The adduced "insofar as" (insofar as there are other things) fails. It cannot keep from the thing *its* being-other and thus must allow the contradiction in the thing itself to prevail.

But argumentative perception makes one final effort against the contradiction by seeking help once again from an "insofar as," namely, the "insofar as" of the difference between essential and inessential. For perception cannot and will not see that what constitutes the essence or the being-for-itself of the thing is exactly what should run the thing and its truth aground. And so perception goes on to argue that the thing in its being-for-itself and being-one is indeed differentiated, but that this differentiation is *not* an opposition in the thing itself. On the contrary, it is for itself simply the determinate that it itself is. Its essence is simple determinateness for itself. Certainly the thing is differentiated in itself insofar as it has a manifold structure. However, that by which the thing is itself and differentiates itself from others is its "simple determinateness."[8] Over against this, then, the multiplicity extant in the thing and necessarily belonging to it is *inessential*.

However, even this final "insofar as" cannot hold its ground. For what does it mean that in its simple determinateness the thing *necessarily* includes being-other, but that this being-other is inessential? What does "necessarily inessential" mean? This is something essential. Thus, the contradiction rests in the ownmost essence of the thing itself, precisely insofar as the latter is simple determinateness: Precisely insofar as the thing is being-for-itself—and in no other respect—it is also being-other. Pure being-for-itself is absolute negation, in which the thing differentiates *itself* from all others and in this differentiation is for an other, that is, related to an other. In this absolute negation the thing is related *to itself*, and this relating to itself is the sublating of itself in that it indicates that it has its essence in the other. The relation to the other belongs essentially to being-for-itself, and it is this relation which is annihilated by the independence of pure being-for-itself. "With this, the last 'insofar as' that separates being-for-itself from being-for-

---

8. II, 94f. [GW IX, 78; Hoff., 98; E.T., 75].

another falls away; more properly, the object is *in one and the same respect the opposite of itself: It is for itself insofar as it is for another, and it is for another insofar as it is for itself.* It is *for itself,* reflected into itself, one; but this *for itself,* reflected into itself, this being one, is posited in a unity with its opposite, with *its being-for-another,* and hence posited only as sublated; in other words, this *being-for-itself* is just as *inessential* as that which alone was supposed to be inessential, namely, the relationship to another."[9]

Thus, the object of perception suffers the same fate as the object of sense certainty, although the history of its running aground is different. The object of sense certainty, the this which is intended, proved itself to be in truth the universal. However, this universal, the what of the thing in its properties, which perception takes as its true, is now in its turn sublated. And it had to be sublated because, from the very beginning and in keeping with its origin in the sensible, this universal was not the *pure* self-identical universal. The universal which resulted from the absolvent interpretation of sensibility was *the universal of the particular.* This particular, as that to which the universal as universal is related, is preserved *in* the universal as its other. But with that it remains the other which exists for itself in relation to the universal. This universal is conditioned by the particular and, in keeping with this conditioning, is burdened by an opposition to the other. Hence, the universal as the object of perception (the thing) had also to split into the *one* of the properties and the "also" of free matter.

However, these pure determinate properties of the thing, the one and the "also," which seem to present the quiet essence of the thing, are manifest in the constant restlessness of the reciprocal opposition or indeed conflict which resides in the essence of the thing itself. Being-for-itself as such is burdened with being-for-other. The being of the thing is basically for-itself and for the other at the same time. But perception and its reflection cannot grasp this unity, the unity of what is contradictory, in which both are essential. Perception is incapable of thinking the contradiction. Insofar as perception thinks, it thinks only so as to avoid contradiction. The principle of avoiding contradiction is precisely the fundamental law of "sound common sense." But insofar as unity finally becomes manifest there, the result is referral to another realm—not that of perception, but of understanding. With this unity of the one and the "also," of the for-itself and the for-other, universality, too, becomes different, a universality which is no longer conditioned by an other as something alien, but is unconditioned, *absolute* universality. Thus, perception, as the mode of consciousness which lies in the middle, is what first mediates to the absolute and the unconditioned.

Looking back, we now see just what perception, when it is left to itself, looks like in the light of absolvent construction. Unlike sense certainty,

---

9. II, 96 [GW IX, 79; Hoff., 99; E.T., 76; Hegel's emphasis].

perception does not maintain itself in an apprehending in which it loses itself; rather, perception *takes for itself* the true and is thus reflected *into itself*. But in this reflection, perception takes its object now in this respect and now in that. The act of reflecting is guided by various ways of the "insofar as" and by different perspectives: the for-itself and the to-an-other. Whichever point of view reflection calls to for help in each case, it always works one-sidedly and separated from other possible perspectives. Reflection operates with and is guided by mere abstractions. The reflective understanding of perception seems thereby to be guided entirely by the concrete wealth of the thing and its properties, whereas basically it is operating in terms of nothing but empty partialities. Perception pretends to be the richest and most concrete thinking, but it is basically the poorest. Perception is only the appearance of understanding; it is that understanding which never tires of praising itself as "sound common sense."

Perception, entangled in itself, is not as such penetrated for what it is by this drive to reflection. By contrast, if perception is placed in the light of absolute knowledge and grasped absolvently as a mode of knowing, then it becomes manifest that there is basically no truth in this perceiving—not no truth overall, but *no* truth in the *radical* sense that perception yields now the one and now the other as its truth. In terms of absolvence—and only so— perception and its drives can and must be designated as "sophistry."[10] The innermost essence of sophistry does not consist solely and primarily in this constant reciprocal reversal of the one-sided one into its other, its equally one-sided opposite; rather, it consists above all in the fact that this drive resists something that comes to light precisely in this very drive itself—the possible unity of what is partial and abstract in something truly concrete. Perception, or the common understanding, resists this bringing together and this attainment of pure unconditional universality as the genuine truth of consciousness. The common understanding resists the essential and actual understanding. But on the other hand, through this resistance, perception already bears witness to understanding as something higher than itself, which it is not equal to, but into which it must now be mediated through absolvence—since, in keeping with Hegel's basic principle, nothing relative remains standing in absolute knowledge.

It should be noted that we understand the transition from perception to understanding only if we register in advance that, as a mode of knowing, perception is already placed in the perspective of absolute knowledge; only then is further advance a necessity. This progress is directed toward the third mode of consciousness: understanding.

---

10. II, 97, 99 [GW IX, 79, 80; Hoff., 100, 101; E.T., 77, 78].

Chapter Three

Force and Understanding

§10. The absolute character of cognition

a) Absolute cognition as ontotheology

Speculative mediation is the way of absolvent knowing. The former, which is, as it were, determinately related to the mediating middle, is already reaching out for a possible mediation and for that toward which the mediated is mediated. Thus, in the course of the mediation—which each time begins with what is not mediated—*that unto* which it is being mediated is for the first time ascertained through the middle term. What is to be ascertained as such through mediation is speculative truth. What is mediated is the true as it is actually attained by speculative knowing and is what is truly ascertained and is that to which the mediation actually belongs.

Hence, absolvent cognition proceeds in three stages. The threefold character of the stages results from conceiving speculative knowing *absolvently and logically*. More precisely, what is logical—or proper to λόγος—is initially the simple determination of something as something: a is b. Herein the relation of b to a is posited as its determinateness. Thus, the logical relation is one-sided. However, one-sidedness is the sworn enemy of the totality, the absolute; for it will not be eliminated by merely positing the other side *in addition*. So what does "removal of the one-sided relation" mean primarily? It means above all the reverse: that the relation of a is shown to be that of a to b. But with this what is posited is not only two different and in each case one-sided relations, but the opposition of both *in themselves*. However, as oppositional, they point beyond to what is not one of the two one-sided relations, each taken for itself, or what is extant alongside them as a detached third, but to that which, as a higher absolute unity, supports them in their very opposition.

97

In the simple proposition, a is b, the *is* is stated. But this "is," being [*Sein*], obtains its actual, true, and absolute meaning only as the speculative "is," which is stated in mediation. However, the "simple," one-sided proposition does not by itself reach the speculative form unless the term *is* is given in advance the meaning, not of a one-sided, but of a sublated-sublating unity. This unity as the unity which sublates all dissension, and along with it all unhappiness, is the absolute as happiness. It unties the entanglement and appeases the conflict. Happiness, entangling, untying, and redeeming—these are determinations which resonate in Hegel's concept of the absolute. What is happy in this sense, what reconciles, is the true being [*Seiendes*]; and it is according to *its* being that all beings are determined in their being.

Ontology is the speculatively conceived and *thus* speculatively grounded interpretation of being, but in such a way that the actual being [*Seiendes*] is the absolute θεός. It is from the being [*Sein*] of the absolute that all beings *and* the λόγος are determined. The speculative interpretation of being is *onto-theo-logy*. This expression is not only meant to say that philosophy is guided by theology or even that philosophy is theology, in the sense of the concept of a speculative or rational theology, which we already discussed at the beginning of this lecture course. In this respect Hegel himself at a later date says in one place: "For philosophy, too, has no other object than God—and thus is essentially rational theology—and service to God in its continual service to truth."[1] We know also that Aristotle already brought philosophy in the genuine sense in very close connection with θεολογική ἐπιστήμη, without being able to explain by a direct interpretation what the relationship is between the question concerning ὂν ᾗ ὄν and the question of θεῖον.

With the expression "ontotheology" we mean that the problematic of ὄν—as a logical problematic—is guided from beginning to end by θεός, which is itself conceived "logically"—logically in the sense of speculative thinking. "But without knowing at least something of the concept of the concept, without at least having a representation, nothing can be grasped of the essence of God or of spirit as such."[2] According to the matter at issue, it is the essence of God as spirit in general that pre-scribes the essence of the concept and thus the character of the logical.

Hegel once wrote the following in a "theological" manuscript of his early period ("The Spirit of Christianity and Its Destiny"): "God cannot be taught and cannot be learned, because he is life and can only be grasped through

---

1. *Vorlesungen über Ästhetik*, X 1, 129 [trans. T. Knox, *Aesthetics* (London: Oxford University Press, 1975), I, 101].
2. *Vorlesungen über die Beweise vom Dasein Gottes*, XII, 413 [trans. E. B. Spiers and J. B. Sanderson, *Lectures on the Philosophy of Religion* (New York: Humanities Press, 1974), p. 211].

living."[3] No matter how immense the transformations are that Hegel underwent—with no consideration for himself—up until the time of the *Phenomenology of Spirit*, no matter how different his overall attitude from which that statement originated is, there is in principle no difference between what is said later in the lecture course given in Berlin ("On the Proofs for the Existence of God") and the earlier statements. For "concept" here is not simply the crude idea of traditional logic—the meaning of a universal (the species) in relation to many individuals—but rather *the absolute self-comprehending of knowledge*, which Hegel later still designates as life. In the same way the later concept of the concept is also basically "logical," but absolutely logical. To understand something of the essence of God means to understand the truly logical character of the logos, and vice versa.

That the Hegelian concept is the sublated concept of traditional logic—which serves as the guideline for ontology—is shown, however, in the same way: The essence of God for Hegel is what presents itself finally in the specifically Christian consciousness of God, in the form in which it has passed through Christian theology and above all through the doctrine of the trinity—which dogma of Christian theology is inconceivable without ancient metaphysics.

Hence, with our expression "onto-theology" we refer in various ways to the primary relation of the basic problem to the ancient inquiry into beings, which has its basis in the λόγος (cf. my basic position on traditional "logic"). This title has been interpreted to mean that I wanted to expel and eliminate the logical from philosophy; it is now becoming customary to say that my philosophy is "mysticism." It is both superfluous and useless to defend oneself against this; we mention these opinions only by way of explanation. "Whatever is not logical is mystical; whatever is not *ratio* is irrational." To say this is only to show that one does not understand anything about the problem and has not made it clear to oneself or really questioned *why* and with what justification ὄν is related to λόγος. Is it so obvious then? The use made of the word *ontology* is characteristic of the fact that today one does not yet feel the inner necessity of this basic question of philosophy. In this usage, which was in part introduced in the nineteenth century and after that by present-day phenomenology—and circulated above all by Nicolai Hartmann—"ontological" means an attitude which allows beings per se to stand as completely independent of any subject. Thus, "ontological" means the same as "realistic." If one understands "ontology" and "ontological" in this way, then they serve even less as a title for a real problem than they did in traditional metaphysics, which at least

---

3. *Hegels theologische Jugendschriften*, ed. Nohl, p. 318 [trans. T. M. Knox, *Early Theological Writings* (Philadelphia: University of Pennsylvania Press, 1971), p. 274].

still had a conception of ontology that inherently and in certain of its intentions overlapped with ancient philosophy. Today everything has fallen victim to superficiality and to merely working with philosophical schools and slogans.

With respect to the title "Being and Time," one could speak of an *ontochrony*. Here χϱόνος stands in the place of λόγος. But were both of these only interchanged? No. On the contrary, what matters is to unfold everything anew from the ground up, by taking over the essential motive of the question of being. It is important to show—formulating it with Hegel—that it is not the concept which is "the power of time,"[4] but it is time which is the power of the concept. (We should, of course, note that by "time" Hegel certainly understands something different from what we do: He basically understands time as nothing other than the traditional concept of time that was developed by Aristotle.)

The expression "onto-theo-logy" should not point to a connection with a discipline called "theology," but should indicate to us the most central thrust of the problem of being. The logical is theological, and this *theo*-logical logos is the λόγος of the ὄν, whereby the term *logical* means at the same time "speculative-dialectical," proceeding in the three steps of mediation.

The outcome of such a mediation, a speculative truth, is certainly a genuine one only if this truth is not isolated again and placed on the side, in order to be delivered, handed over, and offered as a result. On the contrary, as speculative truth it is by itself under the direction and dictates of a mediation which now sublates it, and so on. The expression "and so on" should not be taken in the sense of an unlimited continuation. Rather, we should note what is already posited in speculative cognition: the absolute, in which the manner, the extent, and the range of the first point of departure and of the concluding sentence of speculation (which returns to that starting point) are determined.

We can also regard what is expressed here in Hegel in such a way that we say that being is here determined as infinity. Being is not the infinite itself. Rather, "being in infinity" means that in the speculative proposition being carries the fundamental meaning of being posited. If, by contrast, we say "being is finitude," this does not indicate a simple antithesis, as if we wanted to maintain—against Hegel—that being is being-posited in the simple proposition a is b. Rather, interpreting "being is finitude" in the same formal way, we can say that being is the horizon of ecstatic time. With this reference I want only to say not only that, compared with Hegel's interpretation, our interpretation of being is a different one in terms of content,

---

4. Cf. *Enzyklopädie*, Section 258 [trans. A. Miller, *Philosophy of Nature* (London: Oxford University Press, 1970), p. 35].

but also that the basic thrust of the interpretation itself—in terms of logos and time—is fundamentally different. Thus, it is not a simple or formal either-or. A philosophical debate simply cannot be reduced to such an "either-or." With this reference we wanted only to have indicated from which dimension we come when we meet Hegel in the question of being.

At this juncture of the interpretation—in the transition to "Force and Understanding"—it was appropriate to recall the problem and the character of absolute cognition. Why just at this point will be shown immediately. The discussion of speculative cognition was deliberately carried out in a formal way, and so nothing was said about the inherent character of its object. "*The* science" means for Hegel *absolute* cognition and knowledge; and science *is* only as absolute knowledge in and as system. The system has two parts—more precisely, it is communicated and presented in two versions. The first is the science of the phenomenology of spirit; and its object is speculative dialectical cognition: knowledge. The second is the science of logic, which presents just this absolute knowledge in which what constitutes for it the entirety of those determinations through which whatever is speculatively known is to be known in advance. To put it externally, the science of logic presents the categorial content of what is known of the absolutely knowable. But the modes of absolute knowledge and the manner in which something is known in these modes are not two separate items, but one and the same and belong together. This *one* whole that is absolute knowledge is the object of speculative cognition. This is to say that this object does not stand opposed to speculative cognition as a second object; but rather, this object is cognition itself, absolute self-consciousness, spirit.

b) The unity of the contradiction of the thing in its essence as force

The first object of the phenomenology of spirit is consciousness, the knowledge which initially relates immediately to its object as the other of itself, without knowing that the object is the other when considered against the self of consciousness. Immediate consciousness (sense certainty) is thereby thematized as knowledge of its object and is correspondingly designated by the names "this" and "intending." What evolves out of sense certainty as its opposite is perception, which is also characterized, correspondingly, by the two expressions "thing" and "deception." As a designation for the perceiving knowledge, the expression "deception" is used, in order to indicate—and it should be clear from the preceding—the reflexive, self-deceiving character of perception, and to make clear that the taking of the true is no longer a blind seizing but an accepting unto itself, a certain going-into-itself of knowing. The speculative mediation of sense certainty and of perception yields the first speculative truth of the *Phenomenology*: the absolvent cognition of knowing as consciousness. This knowing is *under-*

standing, and Hegel designates its object with the initially strange expression "force."

The truth of the this is the thing, and the truth or essence of the thing is force. The this of sense certainty is the particular; the thing of perception is the universal, the universal which is determined by something other than itself, by the particular, as to what it is. The particular conditions the universal of the thing. Its universality is a conditioned one, and hence— because it is related to an other beside itself—it is finite, not absolute. Now, the universal, however, is the true of the object of immediate knowing. But this true is really true only when it is not a finite conditioned universal, but an unconditioned absolute universal. Hegel designates as *force* this unconditioned universal, which does not have the particular beside or under itself but in itself and itself unfolds necessarily into particulars. This designation, and even more the essence of the thing so designated, is not readily intelligible. In order to see clearly here, the general context must be recorded. I shall develop this context above all historically; the inherent and thus essentially packed context will unfold from out of the interpretation of the third part of Section A.

Force is the essence of the thing. Accordingly, it is a question of the determination of the essence of extant beings—speaking in terms of the tradition of metaphysics, which here as well as everywhere is determinative for Hegel, without his speaking extensively about it. These are initially particular things, subsisting and inhering in themselves, the so-called substances. The substantiality of the substance expresses *how* the thing is extant as what it is. According to the traditional terminology, it expresses the manner of its existence—in Kant's terms, the character of its existence, its actuality. How then—as a historical question—does Hegel come to bring the problem of the essence of actuality of the thing under the title "force"?

In the *Critique of Pure Reason*, Kant opened up the problem of an ontology of nature—the question of how to determine, in an essentially appropriate manner, extant and accessible beings as to *what* and *how* they are. The determinations of the being of beings are called "categories." Kant calls by the name "mathematical" the categories which determine the *whatness* of things extant, their *essentia*, their possibility. He calls "dynamic" those categories which determine how things are in actuality. Δύναμις is here what is effective, or force. According to Kant, the first group of dynamic categories comprises the following three:

1. Inherence and subsistence (*substantia et accidens*)
2. Causality and dependence (cause and effect)
3. Community (reciprocity between agent and patient).

It is clear that two categories are always mentioned here, but not simply numerically two—rather, two in relation to each other. That is why Kant places this first group of the dynamic categories under the general title *"relation."*

Hegel already took account of the first relation—*substantia* and *accidens*—with the corresponding transformation in the interpretation of the thinghood of the thing as object of perception. And now one could assume that the object of understanding would be the next dynamic category as the truth of the thing, the category of causality. This category *is* mentioned in Hegel's discussion, but at the same time everything stands under the designation of "force," a category which Kant does not know in this form and function. And yet the Hegelian determination of the truth of the thing or of substance as force shows precisely how with it the Kantian problem of the dynamic categories is first genuinely grasped from the ground up and speculatively penetrated.

Therefore, it is not at all an adequate understanding to say that Hegel took from Kant in a certain way the categorial determination of the essence of the thing as force. This statement is correct; but as long as it remains only correct, it does not say anything. One can fill volumes with statements about what Aristotle took from Plato, Descartes from the Scholastics, Kant from Leibniz, and Hegel from Fichte. But this pretentious and presumptuous precision of historical statements is not only superficial. (If it were only that, it could be left quietly to its unsurpassable self-satisfaction and harmlessness.) It is also misleading. Such historical explanation pretends to state how things have really been in philosophy, without itself having been touched in the least by the actuality of philosophizing. Our statement that the Hegelian determination of the essence of the thing as force goes back to Kant is correct, but does not say anything. It would not say any more even if we would try to explain the meaning of the concept of force for the substantiality of the substance by looking back to Leibniz or looking ahead to the effect on Hegel of Schelling's philosophy of nature and his *System of Transcendental Idealism* of 1800. What matters is to see how Hegel took up and penetrated all these issues and transformed them *into his* problematic—*"his"* understood not in terms of personal intellectual production, but *his* as the material completion and unfolding of what came earlier.

I have already emphasized the broad basis of the investigations upon which the *Phenomenology of Spirit* rests and have indicated that we do have some insight into that basis through manuscripts from the Jena period. When circumscribing the concept of infinity, I indicated that the Jena period was, among other things, taken up with a confrontation with Kant's doctrine of categories. But Kant had set up the table of categories on the basis of the table of the forms of judgment, the modes of logos. Therefore, by critically working his way toward a more comprehensive beginning, Hegel too develops the speculative interpenetration of the categories in the "logic." At that time he still distinguished logic from metaphysics, although for him "logic" had already taken on an entirely different form from that of traditional scholastic logic. It took the form of a logic which was really carried through in transcendental terms, wherein Fichte had already preceded him. Hegel too conceives the threefold of substantiality, causality, and reciprocity with the title of what he calls, terminologically, *Verhältnis* [*relation*]. *Verhältnis* is a very definite speculative concept. It is for Hegel not simply an indifferent title that merely indicates what is common to it, being unconcerned with whatever is subsumed under it—as it is for Kant. Hegel develops the so-called categories *in terms of* the essence of relation; he uncovers the essence of relation through this development. This whole speculative development is carried out under the guidance of the concept of "force."

"Force itself {expresses} the idea of relation."[5] The speculative thrust of the concept of force is *relation*—relation itself therefore comprehended speculatively. If we attempt to visualize such a concept of relation, then we see that relation is nothing other than the *unconditioned*, absolute universal, which does not have the particulars indifferently under it, but has and *holds* the particulars within itself and is their unity and ground. Relation is no longer the indifferent connection which, so to speak, is accidentally drawn over the items connected; rather, it is the holding which as such "relates" the items, holds them in such a way that they can be what they are. The members of the relationship are defined in terms of this "relating." But force as relation should also not be identified with causal relation; rather, force expresses this only along with it: "The concept of force rises above . . . the causal connection; force unifies in itself both the essential aspects of the relation: being-identical and being-separate, the former as the identity of being-separated or of infinity."[6]

But what is sought is the unconditioned universal, insofar as the conditioned universal, as the truth of the thing of perception, is to be sublated in the unconditioned universal as the object of understanding. If relation is the object of understanding under the title "force," then understanding as a mode of knowing of this object is speculatively determined along with it as infinite, and the intelligible, finite conception of understanding in Kant is overcome. Therefore, Hegel says that for understanding the principle is the "unity that is in itself universal"[7]—not the unity that ensues from the connection of two independent extremes, but the unity which itself unfolds into that which unifies the two and, as unifying, is their relation—to such an extent that the unified are themselves the relation.

Whereas for Kant the presentation and arrangement of the table of

---

5. *Jenenser Logik, Metaphysik und Naturphilosophie*, ed. Lasson, p. 50 [GW VII, 52; *Logic and Metaphysics*, 55].

6. Ibid., pp. 49f. [GW VII, 51; *Logic and Metaphysics*, 54].

7. II, 114 [GW IX, 92; Hoff., 115; E.T., 91].

categories was guided by the already-made table of judgments, put together from many undeveloped elements in the tradition, for Hegel (1) the table of judgments becomes problematical (because the proposition as such becomes questionable), and (2) the speculatively oriented determination of the essence of the judgment and its possibilities turns out to be the *speculative origin* of the categories themselves.[8] Thus, the Kantian treatment of the connection between judgment and categories is taken up by Hegel in a genuinely philosophical manner and developed anew from out of an independent problematic. However, the connection between the judgment (λόγος) and the categories is that connection which has always been vital since antiquity and catches the eye if we consider that *the* basic form of the λέγειν of the λόγος is κατηγορεῖν.

For Kant in the *Critique of Pure Reason*, especially in the second edition, understanding is not only that which determines what is given and is determinable in intuition—is not only determinative [*bestimmende*] in the sense of being at the service of intuition—but is also determinative in the manner of the dominant element of cognition. But cognition is cognition of what is extant, of nature, of things, of the manifold of individual items which are manifest to us in their general existence. But for Hegel it is precisely the task of a speculative interpretation of consciousness to develop the essence of thinghood *in terms of* the this and in turn to develop the thinghood of perception *into* the object of understanding, an understanding which thinks the thing as substance, causality, and reciprocity—as relation. The title for *relation* is the expression *"force."*

This is how we understand the title of the third part, "Force and Understanding," from out of the historical context of the problem of the *Phenomenology*.

c) Finite and absolute cognition—"Appearance and the Supersensible World"

The title of the third part still contains the words *appearance* and *supersensible world*. We readily infer from these titles a further relation to Kant and to his distinction between appearance and thing in itself (the intelligible object, the intelligible as counter-concept to what is "sensible"). But, of course, the Kantian concepts cannot simply be transposed here under Hegelian titles; rather, these Hegelian expressions must be developed *in terms of* the problem of the concept of force. On the other hand, the Kantian terms *appearance* and *thing in itself* are also not self-evident concepts, but rather need to be explicated in terms of the guiding problem of the *Critique of Pure Reason*, which is the guiding question of metaphysics.

---

8. See below, pp. 116ff.

Let me here refer to what I say in my book on Kant.* I assume at this point that what I said in that work is understood and now mention only one thing: The distinction between appearance and thing in itself is rooted in the distinction between finite and infinite (absolute) cognition. Now, when in the heading of the third part of Section A Hegel mentions the difference between appearance and supersensible world, this indicates that, along with the speculative interpretation of the object of understanding as force, at the same time the step is taken from finite, relative knowing to the realm of absolute knowledge and that the first manifestation of *reason*, of the absolute, is accomplished. Or, as Hegel puts it at the conclusion of the entire Section A (which deals with consciousness): "This curtain {the appearance as naively understood} is therefore . . . drawn away {namely, from the absolute}."9 With this step, however, the absolute is not simply to be stared at, as if it were present on a stage, because the speculative comprehension now first begins.

Therefore, the phenomenology of spirit as consciousness, as the manifestation of the truth of consciousness in understanding as such, has a central historical and factual significance for Hegel, (1) in the sense of a confrontation with the one-sided philosophies of understanding and of reflection, which are stuck in the finitude of logos and understanding, so that in the face of this finitude the task arises of bringing the understanding to reason, and so comprehending the understanding absolutely, and (2) in the sense of preparing the explicit grounding of the absolute position of idealism.

Whereas the first part of the title—"Force and Understanding"—simply indicates the third form of consciousness in view of what is known in it and in view of the manner of knowing, the second part of the title—"Appearance and the Supersensible World"—expresses how, by having appearance as its object, understanding precisely goes beyond the sensible world, the world of the senses. This should be taken to mean not only that understanding as a mode of consciousness sublates *sense certainty* as the immediate mode of consciousness, but essentially something more than that. Sense certainty as the knowing of the this is still—albeit sublated—in the thing as object of perception, as also in the object of understanding. Wherever there is still consciousness, wherever the known is *an* other for knowing (and not *its* other), there is sensibility. The character of sensibility encompasses all three modes of consciousness; and just because of this, these modes are all of one essence: relative knowledge. When in understanding the transition beyond sensibility toward what is supersensible begins, then understanding is at the same time *the* mode of consciousness

---

*[Heidegger refers here to *Kant und das Problem der Metaphysik*, first published in 1929.]
9. II, 129 [GW IX, 102; Hoff., 128; E.T., 103].

which raises itself above itself by sublating sense certainty and perception. Put more precisely, the raising of understanding above itself becomes *manifest* by and in the history of the sublation of consciousness but without yet being specifically accomplished through knowing itself.

Given these indications as to the central role of the concepts of "appearance" and of the "supersensible world" and their connection with the problem of understanding, it would be appropriate to characterize these concepts briefly before offering a thematic interpretation of the third part of Section A. At this point this can be done only in an external report. For this purpose, we begin with the naive explication of the difference between the sensible and the supersensible world which was still current in Kant's and Hegel's time and of which Kant gave a certain metaphysical formulation with his *Critique of Pure Reason*, without further making this explication explicitly problematical. Hegel's critique of Kant also takes its bearing from this the usual interpretation.

Things as we represent them, the appearances, are in this interpretation something like a string of extant things. Similar to the way in which we represent the appearances, we represent what is supersensible as what is extant behind the appearances. The fact that this background is not accessible to our sensible representation means only that accessibility is thought of as a representing that fundamentally has the same character as the representing of sensible things—the only difference being that it goes further and gets behind the things of the senses. Thus, appearances are present at hand, and in their interior there is again something present at hand. Taking his bearing from this the usual representation, Hegel speaks frequently, and in a certain sense terminologically, of an *inner*, whereby the inner certainty has a deliberate orientation to the inner in the sense of the interiority of the subject. For the moment we will not explain further how this the usual view is not that of Kant.

But when Hegel now attributes to consciousness—and thus to some extent to Kant—this way of apprehending the relation between appearance and the thing in itself, then in his speculative critique he arrives simultaneously at connections which, while not identical with the real intentions of Kant, still do justice to them. Hegel rightfully emphasizes that there are no appearances for themselves, nor is there anything that for itself may be called appearance. Appearance, taken *as* appearance, is the appearing of *something other than itself*. Insofar as what appears is what primarily and immediately shows itself, *as* this self-showing it shows what appears in its own way. Appearance as what shows itself—what appears as the emerging view—is, namely, an other, above all and actually this other. What appears as the self-showing which shows the other is the immediate; and, as what shows the other, it is at the same time mediating. And so the concept of appearance again jumps into the specifically speculative character of the objectivity of knowing as such. But even with that we have not yet grasped a *single* basic character of the Hegelian concept of appearance, which shows first of all how Hegel relates this concept, as the concept of a being, to his speculative concept of being in general.

That which appears is related as mediator to what is to be ascertained. But the latter taken speculatively is always the higher and the genuine truth. Therefore, when Hegel takes appearance *as* appearance, he must necessarily comprehend the supersensible world which the appearance shows as the *true* of appearance, in which the appearance itself is sublated. From this the further point follows—and it is decisive for the Hegelian interpretation of the concept of appearance—that appearance as what appears is not only *that which shows itself.* To show itself is *to rise up.* Appearing means arriving or coming, and not-appearing means staying away. Thus, taken as a whole, appearing means *rising up and disappearing.* With this we grasp the specific *character of movement* in appearing. Thus, appearance is taken in its specifically *dialectical* character and in this way attains its *suitability as a* basic speculative concept whose significance is expressed by its position in the title of the work: appearance, phenomenon, phenomenology. Consequently, appearing means rising up *in order to* disappear again, disappearing in order *thereby* to make room for another, for something higher. It means the affirmation and negation in transition, to which we referred when we defined the concept of appearance in connection with the clarification of the title *Phenomenology.*[10]

Now, Kant is of the opinion that, insofar as and because what *we* experience is appearance, the object of *our* cognition is *mere* appearance. By contrast, Hegel says that, if appearance is what is primarily accessible to us, then our true object must be the supersensible. Once the phenomenal character of the objectivity of consciousness is posited, precisely then the knowability of the things themselves, of the supersensible world, is fundamentally proven. This is the way to understand the juxtaposition of "appearance" and "supersensible world" in the title. It says that they are not differentiated, but in the speculative sense are the same. "The supersensible is therefore *appearance,* as *appearance.*"[11]

However, it would be quite wrong to put Hegel's thesis on the knowability of the thing in itself on a par with the knowability, or rather unknowability, of the supersensible that is maintained by common sense—as though Hegel were affirming that the representing simply and immediately penetrates the curtain of appearance to what is hanging behind it. Rather, the phenomenal character of appearance is solely and in advance to be grasped *speculatively-dialectically as the mediating middle.* Here we come

---

10. Cf. above, pp. 24f.
11. II, 111 [GW IX, 90; Hoff., 113; E.T., 89].

across a new characteristic of the "middle." The ancient doctrine of λόγος as συλλογισμός (syllogism) already mentions a middle, μέσον. With this connection in mind, Hegel conceives the essence of appearance as a middle and at the same time conceives mediation as μέσον of a syllogism, whereby *syllogism* too is not supposed to be understood in the formal, logical sense of a simple deduction of propositions, but in the speculative sense of *joining together* in a higher unity, as synthesis of thesis and antithesis. The syllogism is what actually draws together, joins, as it were, two ends or extremes in such a way that the middle leads from one extreme to the other. And indeed, understanding, on the one hand, and the thing in itself, on the other, are supposed to be joined—truly grasped in their relatedness to each other and in their belonging together as the same.

Thus, appearance as that which joins together is the dovetailing middle and central segment of *understanding* as a mode of *knowing* which is constantly "our {absolved} object" in the *Phenomenology*. "*Our object* is thus from now on the syllogism, which has for its extremes the interior of things and the understanding and for its middle term appearance; but the movement of this syllogism yields the further determination of what understanding catches sight of in the interior of things through the middle term, also yielding the experience which understanding has of being joined in this relation."[12] And corresponding to that: "Raised above perception, consciousness presents itself as joined with the supersensible by means of the middle term of appearance, through which consciousness gazes into this background."[13]

Two things should again be pointed out: (1) Catching sight of the interior of the thing in itself does not mean going directly behind appearance, as it were, through a back door, leading straight to the interior of the thing in itself. Rather, it always means going solely and precisely *through appearance as a middle*. Appearance must be grasped *as* appearance, as a middle. (2) This going through the appearance is therefore possible only where the middle as such is intelligible as mediation. But mediation is absolute knowledge itself. *Only absolute cognition knows things in themselves.*

Kant and Hegel share this conviction, the only difference being that Hegel claims that absolute knowledge is possible *for us*, whereas Kant denies to human beings the possibility of an ontic theoretical knowledge of the absolute. Certainly the absolute knowledge which Hegel claims is not to be put on a par with theoretical knowledge as it is usually understood; to this extent Hegel is like Kant, who from a practical point of view and intent also concedes that human beings can know the absolute. (It is superfluous to explain in detail how, when Hegel speaks of appearance as the middle term

---

12. II, 110 [GW IX, 89; Hoff., 111f.; E.T., 88].
13. II, 129 [GW IX, 102; Hoff., 128; E.T., 103].

of a syllogism, he does not intend to claim that our knowledge of things themselves is a "syllogism" [*Schluss*] with whose help we *infer* [*schliessen*] the interior and the background from what lies at the exterior. This way of inference, which is often invoked today as a precondition for accessibility to the things in themselves, is the most superficial finite way of cognition— *finite* in the worst sense of the word—and is by no means the appropriate way for knowing the absolute. To give one example: I infer from the rising of smoke out of the chimney that there is fire in the house. But it is still dubious whether this is a syllogism at all, as is often claimed.)

For Hegel the thing in itself is truly accessible, but only when we are serious about absolute knowledge. But when the thing in itself is the object of *absolute* knowledge, then this object can no longer be that which stands over *against* us, that which by itself no longer stands *over against* absolute knowledge as *alien* or *other*. In such a case this knowledge would not be absolute. It would have no power at all over its known, but would be relative in the sense that was explained earlier. If the thing in itself is absolutely known and knowable, then it loses its *oppositional* character, becomes truly *in itself*, having the character of an *itself* or of a for-itself [*ein Sichhaftes, Fürsichhaftes*]. It defines itself as belonging to a self, which knows itself as itself. What we who know absolutely know as the thing in itself is what *we ourselves* are, but always as those who know absolvently. What is known absolutely can only be that which knowledge knowingly lets emerge and which, only as emerging thus, stands in knowing; it is not an object but an emergence, as I have said elsewhere.[14] The correlate of absolvent knowing is this emergence. More exactly, emergence is no longer a correlate, because it is no longer relative—absolute knowledge is *self*-comprehension, or "concept." Something that we let emerge in such knowing is not a relative ob-ject [*Gegen-stand*] but an absolute emergence [*Ent-stand*] which is maintained only in its emergence and as such in the history of absolute knowledge. What is absolutely knowable can never be an object but exists only as emergence, and as such stands in the emergence by means of knowledge itself. We ourselves, as those who know absolvently, bring the thing in itself to a stop. What we know in the thing in itself is *our spirit*.

Thus, if the supersensible is to be seen, we must ourselves go there, as we who know absolvently. We ourselves must go there, not only so that the access to the supersensible is really accomplished and so that seeing is accomplished in truth and absolutely, but also so that there *is something* there—something of ourselves as those who know absolutely—where we gaze knowingly. For only in this way *is* there the absolutely knowable—if the thing in itself is indeed absolutely knowable. In this sense Hegel

---

14. Cf. *Kant und das Problem der Metaphysik*, pp. 29ff. [trans. J. Churchill (Bloomington: Indiana University Press, 1962), pp. 36ff.].

emphasizes at the conclusion of the entire Section A, which deals with consciousness: "It is manifest that behind the so-called curtain which is supposed to conceal the interior of things there is nothing to be seen unless *we* go behind it ourselves, as much so that we may see as that there be something behind there which can be seen."[15] If the term "we" is grasped simply as a pronoun which indicates the readers who happen to come across the work in the full soundness of their common sense, then everything becomes totally absurd. Put the other way, it is crucial that this "we," its meaning, and its role be meditated upon from the first sentence of the work and repeatedly thereafter.[16]

In the speculative experience of the essence of understanding, it turns out that its true object is the thing in itself, which is, however, something belonging to the self of self-consciousness. But because understanding presents itself now as *consciousness*—and can only present itself as such—and because it *is* not self-consciousness, understanding is incapable of recognizing itself in its true object. Understanding does recognize the thing *in itself* and *is* thus related to itness [*Sichheit*], but understanding is not capable of comprehending this itness as selfhood [*Selbstheit*]. Therefore, Hegel says: "To begin with, therefore, *we* must step into its place and be the concept which develops and fills out what is contained in the result. It is through this completely developed object, which presents itself to consciousness as a being, that consciousness first becomes explicitly a consciousness that comprehends."[17]

As we know, already at the beginning of the *Phenomenology* Hegel says that "we" have to take our place in immediate knowledge, in consciousness, since otherwise the relative for itself would not move from the spot; it is indeed something peculiar to the relative to stick to its own place. But here, too, Hegel does not simply say again that we have to take the place of understanding (qua relative knowledge). Rather, he adds "to begin with," by which he indicates that as soon as knowledge gets so far as to know itself absolutely, then "we" become superfluous. But that only means that the difference between a knowledge which does not yet know itself absolutely (but is basically still absolute knowledge) and one which knows absolvently vanishes insofar as the position of absolvence is itself alive for itself when knowledge which knows itself absolutely is reached.

Thereby the perspective of this section, which is so crucial for the entire work, should have become visible in its basic outline. This section offers the systematic presentation and justification of the transition of metaphysics from the Kantian foundations and problematic to that of German Idealism;

---

15. II, 130 [GW IX, 102; Hoff., 129; E.T., 103].
16. See above, pp. 47ff.
17. II, 101 [GW IX, 82f.; Hoff., 103; E.T., 80].

it presents the transition from the finitude of consciousness to the infinity of
spirit; and viewed in terms of the special problem of understanding, this
section presents the transition from the *negative* determination of the thing
in itself to its *positive* determination.

The task now is to follow the main steps and to go along with the
movement in which understanding in its knowing relatedness to its object—coming from perception—sublates perception along with the sense
certainty included in perception, in order to elevate itself and thus consciousness as a whole into the truth of consciousness, which is basically *self-
consciousness*.

§11. The transition from consciousness to self-consciousness

a) Force and the play of forces: Being-for-itself in being-for-another

What is required now is to go along with the movement of understanding. What do we mean by this "going along"? We do not mean observing
the procedures of something like the crude activity of understanding vis-à-
vis an object as something roughly intuited. Rather, we mean following
absolvently and intelligently the mutuality and multiplicity of the inner,
essential relations of this mode of consciousness, which Hegel calls understanding, *to the essence* of what is known therein, and the other way around.
Do we mean, consequently, "the dialectic of understanding"? Yes, but what
does this dialectic mean? Should we now apply dialectic—the sequence of
the three steps of thesis, antithesis, and synthesis—to understanding? But
how? What is understanding, and what is its relation to what is known in it
like?

Certainly, "dialectic" is a magnificent thing. But one never finds *the*
dialectic, as if it were a mill which exists somewhere and into which one
empties whatever one chooses, or whose mechanism one could modify
according to taste and need. Dialectic stands and falls with *the matter itself*,
just as Hegel took it up as the matter of philosophy. To speak more clearly,
one cannot be enthusiastic about dialectic and involve oneself in the revival
of Hegelian philosophy while at the same time pushing aside—with a wink
of the eye and a pitiful smile—things like his Christianity, his Christology,
and his doctrine of the Trinity. If one does this, then the whole of Hegelianism turns into a mendacious prattle; and Hegel himself becomes a ridiculous figure. In the present case, understanding is not our theme because we
know something somehow about understanding and, in the dialectic, want
to shuffle these known properties around and oppose them to one another.
Rather, what understanding is is already determined in advance in the
absolvent beginning and becomes visible *through* dialectic.

For Hegel *the whole* of knowledge—as every page of the *Phenomenology* shows—is anticipated in the absolvent construction which itself has received its genuine impulses from the inner history of the guiding problem of metaphysics. The task is to unfold from within this construction the modes of knowledge, each in terms of its *own* inherent content. Thus, we will see that perception is not so readily mediated to understanding—only to have something else leap out—but that the real work on a real, absolvent clarification of the essence of understanding confronts us. Even if we had no knowledge—from the manuscripts of the Jena period—of how often only a few concentrated sentences of the *Phenomenology of Spirit* rely on very extensive and penetrating investigations as their foundation, even if we did not know this, it would become clear from the wealth of relations which are articulated in the work.

Understanding, which is supposed to be our theme now, has already announced itself in the absolvent essence of perception as that which perceiving constantly resists insofar as it does not really concern itself with bringing together the essential determinations of its object. The object of perception is the thing. The thing as such is the thing which has many properties. The thinghood of the thing is that whatness of the particular this, the universal. This universal (thinghood) includes the following essential moments: the "also" of many properties and the one of the unity of the independent object, which we now call thing. The "also" and the one are reciprocally brought forward over against each other in perception and favored one-sidedly, although both belong with equal weight to the essence of perception. The one essential moment is the universal, which, however, is conditioned by the other essential moment. The universality is not an unconditioned one; the togetherness of both moments of the object—the "also" and the one—is not a real unity such that this unity could ground and support their separation. Rather, these moments simply go asunder. Only in the truly mediated unity of these moments, in their *inner* unity, would the universality be the unconditionally mediated simplicity, the absolute universal, and thus the truth of the object of consciousness.

It is important to examine whether and to what extent the object of understanding contains this *unconditioned universality*. The referral of the moments to the *inner* unity, in which the moments return into themselves, indicates that here there is a "reflection." But this reflection exists only objectively for understanding as a mode of consciousness. Understanding hits upon the interior, but the latter must remain *empty* for understanding. Understanding does not know *itself* as that which in its object constitutes objectivity or this unconditioned universality. Since understanding is also a mode of consciousness and since, according to its own sense of knowing, it has its truth in the object, we must begin again with the question of the essence of understanding as the question concerning the essence and truth of its object.

In our anticipatory and largely external or historical elucidation of the title of the third section, we explained that the object of understanding is *force*. Now we must raise the essential question: To what extent does force have a connection with the objectivity of perception, and thus with an unbalanced breaking up of the "also" and the one, such that force at the same time constitutes the possible unity of what breaks up—in such a way that this unity is an unconditioned unity? Is there a movement in which the moments do not go asunder at all, but unfold while remaining *in* a unity, in order to return at once from the unfolding back to a unity? Such a movement would be a reciprocal transition. "But this movement is what is called *force*."[1]

The proof of the thesis is presented in the following manner, which I now outline briefly by way of anticipation. We are dealing again with *constructing* the object of understanding (force) by proceeding from the common representation of it. What is required for the true actuality of the absolute essence of force must become visible in the absolvent construction.

Hegel proceeds from the universal, immediate representation of force. But the issue is not force as a representation in the sense of what is represented. Rather, the point is to show force as the truly actual in the *actuality* of things in themselves. But if we think of force in accordance with its conceptually predetermined essence as actual, then we are forced to assume two or more actual forces in each case. But then we fall back into the actuality of the object of perception, in the multiplicity of particular, extant things as they are in themselves. However, it becomes manifest that the multiplicity of two forces qua forces is possible only as a play of forces. The *play* between both forces is their genuine actuality. But play is a *relation*; and as explained in the logic of the Jena period, relation is the *unconditioned universality*. Thus, it is force which sublates—or, seen absolvently, does not permit—the breakup of the moments in the object of perception. Their separation is shown only to perception, which has not yet arrived at understanding. When seen from the viewpoint of absolvence, which has not lost understanding but has retained it in absolute knowledge, the separation of single forces is only the unfolded unity of something higher. We must now show this more concretely.

Taken simply, what is force? What do we mean when we immediately represent to ourselves force in general? A force confronts us in its *externalization*; externalizing itself, it breaks up, so to speak, in the manifold of what has been effected. It is here that we first come across force and become attentive to it. However, we genuinely represent force to ourselves when we take it *for itself*, as something withdrawn—or more exactly, driven back in itself from its possible externalization. But in this being-driven-back-into-

---

1. II, 102 [GW IX, 84; Hoff., 105; E.T., 81].

itself there is at the same time a *being-driven-toward-externalization*—being tense, being drawn back into itself, being poised and ready. Force is both together at the same time: *being-driven-back-into-itself as the drive-toward-externalization*. And again, in its externalization, force remains in-itself as well; for *it* can externalize itself only as long as it remains in itself.

With that the inner connection with the preceding discussion is already announced. The externalization of force corresponds to the way in which the multiplicity of the "also" is spread out in the object-realm of perception. In the same way being-driven-back-into-itself over against a multiplicity of possible effects corresponds to the being-for-itself of the thing's oneness. But force is *both of these at once*. Force is reflected *in itself*, driven back to itself, so much so that force as such pushes toward the outside, toward externalization—whereby it then exists *for the other*, on which it has an effect and which it effects. Force is being-for-itself *and* being-for-another.

But we have thus developed only the simple concept of force, and it might seem as though force is something for itself, something purely simple so that the difference which we made between being-for-itself and being-for-another would be only an imagined one, a difference which would be brought to the object only by our representation. Against this it is important to see—and this is Hegel's second step—that *in its actuality* force itself *is* this difference between being-driven-back-into-itself and being-driven-to-ward-the-outside. This means that the externalization of force is not op-posed to force and is not extant alongside force, occasionally stepping in as its realization—so that force would be only what is *possible* and not yet existing. On the contrary, force is just that in which the being-for-itself of what is driven back into itself and the being-for-another (the being of the other itself as such) have their subsistence at the same time. *Force is the relation*, identical with itself in its externalization. It is *force* which has externalized itself. What comes forward as an other upon which force has an effect and what looks as if it for its part enticed the force to manifesta-tion, that is force itself, as the disquieting, the irritating (the solicitous). So this is the result: Where there is force or an actual effectual relationship, there are necessarily *two forces*, each one independent. And thus, by de-veloping the concept of force—the speculative concept of force—we would have the same state of affairs as we had in perception, where the object is split into a multiplicity of independent things—"substantialized extremes" (partialities)—only with the difference that these things are now endowed with force. Thus, the characterization of the thing as force does not achieve what it is supposed to achieve. Force does not provide the sought-for absolute, self-relying unity of the things in themselves.

But is it then simply the case that, where the concept of force is actualized, necessarily two forces are actual, the solicited and the soliciting one? Certainly. But if force is actually real in the actuality of *two* forces, then both of these independent forces are not simply extant in the medium of the "also." Rather, their actuality consists precisely in movement against each other. They force each other to disappear reciprocally into independence. This disappearance should not be taken naively as a thing-like event but must be understood speculatively, so that they *remain* together in taking effect but disappear as independent. One only has to be serious about the realization of force into forces in order to see that the forces are not extremes existing for themselves as extremes which, as Hegel says figuratively, "would transmit to one another in the middle term and in their contact a merely external property; on the contrary, what they are, they are only in terms of this middle and in this contact."[2] What is actual is the *play* of forces, and not individual forces as substances. The truth of force consists precisely in *losing* its actuality as "substantialized extreme." What we sensibly and objectively represent as force, as dynamite on hand, as it were, is immediate and is the *untrue*. *The true is the play, the middle*, not the extremes—the middle which relates the extremes in their comportment to each other and is *relation*. The forces do not dispatch something, from each of them, into the middle lying indifferently between them. Rather, the forces are related precisely by the middle, such that only in this way they can be what they are. Force is in its actuality exactly as understanding had already represented it in its concept, the relation of being-for-itself *in* being-for-another, but that means the original, conditioning unity of the "one" *and* the "also" and *thus* the "true essence of things."[3] We see the essence of the thing[4] through the middle of the play of forces; only through this mediation does consciousness arrive at things as they are themselves, at the *supersensible*. And this consciousness is the *understanding*.

b) The appearance of the play of forces and the unity of the law

How are we to grasp positively the mediated essence of the thing through the middle of the play of forces? First of all, what is the mediated middle itself which we come to know as *the play of forces*? Or: How is understanding related to the interior through mediation? What happens by way of this mediation? How does understanding unfold its essence, which indeed holds as its principle that for understanding the universal unity in itself is the true?

As has been frequently stated already, with this speculative interpretation of understanding Hegel has in mind *the* conception of understanding which determines the problematic of Kant's *Critique of Pure Reason*. Understanding is the faculty of concepts, of judging, of representing of something in

---

2. II, 107 [GW IX, 87; Hoff., 109; E.T., 85].
3. II, 108 [GW IX, 88; Hoff., 110; E.T., 86].
4. Cf. II, 109 [GW IX, 89; Hoff., 111; E.T., 87].

general—as the faculty of rules—understanding as thinking which always unfolds as "I think." But this "I think" is "I think *unity*," or, as Kant says, "I think substance, causality, reciprocity, and so on." I think the categories; or better formulated: I think categorially.

Categories are representations of unities which bind in advance the capacity of understanding to connect and to judge. In itself "I think" means to take a view toward the unity under whose guidance and regulation the act of connecting is carried out. Thus, the inner, essential interrelation of judgment and categories is indicated; and the essential ground for the inner unity of judgment and category is shown, as Kant put it in the *Critique of Pure Reason*. Though guided by this concept of understanding, Hegel develops it now speculatively. I think unity, a unity which does not depend on some kind of concrete collecting, but is an a priori, final unity. The principle for understanding is the universal unity in itself, a unity which constitutes the objectivity of its object.

The questions raised above turn knowing, which as understanding determines its object, into a speculative problem. The speculative characterization of the object of understanding as force has been carried so far up to this point that it became apparent that the actual, which understanding thinks in its knowing, is not made up of individual forces "which offer each other only an oppositional extreme."[5] Rather, the actual is the middle of these forces, *the play of forces*. What does this mean for force, which was initially taken up as an individual agent? The particular force vanishes in the play. The *being* of force is the *vanishing*, namely, the vanishing of what force at first pretended and seemed to be. In this vanishing the being of force is itself a *non-being*, a mere show which vanishes, so much so that something else emerges; this means that the mere show is *appearing* [*Scheinen ist Erscheinen*].

It is important to remember again that Hegel does not take the essence of appearing only as self-showing, as becoming manifest, as manifestation. Rather, appearing also means a *mere*-showing and vanishing. There is in appearance a moment of negativity, which is most intimately connected with the character of appearance as movement. But this means that appearance is not merely a showing, but that also in the vanishing something makes its appearance. What emerges is nothing other than what is retained in the arising and vanishing of the sensible, what is brought along with appearance in itself, the interior or the *supersensible*. At first we saw only that the play of forces (the appearing) is *not* in itself. Thus, there is in appearing a negative indication of the *in-itself*, of the enduring interior, whereby we simultaneously know positively that this interior becomes graspable only through mediation—that appearance *as appearance* returns itself into itself.

---

5. II, 107 [GW IX, 87; Hoff., 109; E.T., 86].

The in-itself is still empty and remains empty as long as understanding is left to itself. By itself understanding is incapable of understanding any *more*. But the task is to grasp the speculative essence of understanding; this means that *we* must take its place and that we have already done so. The empty interior (the in-itself) becomes fulfilled by the return into itself of appearance as appearance, by way of the speculative sublation of appearance. Going beyond the initial characterization (which says that in appearance itself there is a non-sensible [*Nicht des Sinnlichen*]), the supersensible is determined positively.

This fulfillment of the initially empty supersensible is accomplished in two stages for understanding, which *we* again leave to undergo its experience with itself. Thus, Hegel distinguishes a first and a second supersensible,[6] or the first truth of understanding over against the second truth,[7] or the one side of the supersensible over against another side.[8]

According to all that we now already understand, we can expect that the distinction between a first and second supersensible is not a crude juxtaposition, but rather a speculative subordination in the sense of a dialectical belonging-together. The second supersensible is, namely, the reversal of the first one, but *this* does not mean an opposite which is merely placed alongside the first one. Rather, it means that inversion [*Verkehren*] which in its turning takes the other into itself and thus determines itself in a higher way.*

We shall now ask about *the first supersensible*, about what initially results when we let the *appearance as appearance* return into itself. We shall ask what the play of forces makes manifest in absolvence, when understanding accepts this play, *not immediately*, but as understanding. But the principle of understanding as determined by Kant—and this determination is crucial for Hegel—is *unity*. In its own way understanding takes the appearance— the arising and again vanishing manifold—when it simplifies and reduces to unity the manifold of appearance, the play of forces. This simplification of the manifold as the basic function of understanding in terms of appearance takes place when understanding, according to the *Critique of Judgment*, "thinks toward laws." The play of forces finds its uniformity in law. But the reduction of appearance to laws as the ground of the play and its mode is *explanation*. The primordial function of understanding, the mode of its knowing, in which the known object manifests itself as law, is explanation.

The following speculative construction of appearance as appearance (of

---

6. Cf. II, 121 [GW IX, 96; Hoff., 121; E.T., 96].
7. Cf. II, 114 [GW IX, 91; Hoff., 115; E.T., 91].
8. Cf. II, 124 [GW IX, 98; Hoff., 123; E.T., 98].
*[The German word *verkehren*, used here several times, has two meanings: (1) to turn, to invert, to reverse (thus reversal), to pervert, and (2) to mix, to communicate, to associate.]

the play of forces) is supposed to complete this absolvent knowledge of the essence of understanding, and thus of the essence of consciousness as such. It follows accordingly that *law* and *explanation* play a central role. Hence, we also see now already the possibility of illuminating an interconnection, which we will expect as long as we have not prematurely lost sight of the guiding problem.

Already in the form of sense certainty, the universal as the true object of consciousness confronted us as the mediated simplicity which can be "this" as well as "that" in the sensible particular and yet which is neither "this" nor "that." As long as universality is confronted, as was shown in perception, with the manifold of particulars (alsos) in their arbitrariness, the universal is conditioned by the particulars in their independence. But the true *mediating* universality is not conditioned in this way—that universality which is itself the ground of the individualization of particulars, so that the particulars exist only in the universal. It is only this universality which is the true, absolvent universality.

The next question concerns how understanding arrives at the law at all and how law is initially determined. This is the same question in another form as the following: What does the play of forces testify to when it is taken by understanding in accordance with its principle? And how is the appearance *as appearance* sublated into its truth through the thinking of understanding? Hegel says: "Understanding, which is our object, finds itself in just this position, that the interior [of things] has initially come into being for it only as the universal, still unfilled *in-itself*. The play of forces has {up to this point at least} only the negative significance of not being *in itself* and only the positive significance of being that which mediates, albeit outside the understanding. The connection of the understanding with the interior [of things] through mediation is, however, its own movement through which the interior [of things] will be filled out for the understanding."[9] By looking ahead to the decisive result of the *whole* of the *Phenomenology*, the following interpretation will especially emphasize the isolation of individual steps from one another. And this means that it will stress the divisions within the movement of dialectics, wherein we together with Hegel let understanding absolvently unfold itself to in-finity.

The play of forces testifies to the manner in which the particular forces move as cause and thus effect and so are made effective. When a force, which we initially represent as driven-back-to-itself and poised, is effective, it externalizes *itself*. But the externalization in itself simultaneously effects the *other*. Thus, the other which is effected is itself manifest. This second one thus becomes self-externalizing as the first force was; and vice versa, with the externalization of the second one the first force is simultaneously

---

9. II, 112 [GW IX, 90; Hoff., 113; E.T., 89].

driven back into itself, becoming what the second one initially was. The play of forces is their arrival on the scene, in which the players exchange back and forth the determinations which they initially showed. This immediate exchanging in which one becomes reciprocally what the other was, indicates *what* the forces *are*, seen from the play. But *what* they are, namely, the difference constantly given back and forth against each other, is simultaneously the *way in which* they are. Content and form coincide; and in keeping with this coinciding in *one*, something unified stands out in which all special forces constantly vanish. This one, which constantly belongs to each force reciprocally, this universal simple into which the play of forces returns in accordance with its essence, is the law: the way or the how of being effective as the what of what is effective. Appearance or the play of forces does *in* itself retain the disappearance or the instability, but in such a way that, in this instability of exchanged differences, what is stable is present as law. Thus, the law is what is constantly the same in contrast to what is constantly not the same. What appears in the sensible, in the appearance, namely, the same *over and beyond* [*über*] what is not the same, is the *supersensible* [*das Übersinnliche*]. The interior of things, that which determines their externalization, their reciprocal back and forth movement, is a *"serene realm of laws."*[10]

Thus, the first supersensible is obtained. But this serene, enduring universal can be taken only as the first, not as the ultimate, truth of understanding. For *over against this* universal, the law so conceived, stands again absolute change, the play of forces; and as another it thus conditions what lasts. The law is then the unconditioned universal only when it itself, in itself and by itself, contains the absolute change. Or, to say the same thing from the other side, the side of the appearance: Appearance as changing retains something on its side which the law does not have; appearance retains for itself the principle of change. Thus, seen speculatively, the law has a lack and with this lack cannot yet be designated as unconditioned. And, on the other hand, appearance remains the counter-image of the supersensible, is not the appearance *of* the supersensible, thus is not yet the supersensible itself. Hegel plays here deliberately with the ambiguity of the genitive. Appearance of the supersensible—as an objective genitive—means that appearance is another, over against that which appears in it. But this appearance of the supersensible must now become the appearance *of* the supersensible in the sense of the subjective genitive: the supersensible appears. Appearance is itself only something which belongs to the supersensible and exists only with and in the supersensible.

As we determined law so far, why is it not capable of taking into itself the appearance as such? Because the law, *conditioned by appearances*, is at the

---

10. II, 114 [GW IX, 91; Hoff., 115; E.T., 90].

moment related only to a certain multiplicity of appearances. This means that the law itself is in each case only one particular law among others. The application of the law until now shows an indefinite number of extant laws. But a multiplicity of laws is, in the light of understanding's own thinking in terms of law, *against* the principle of understanding and is thus a deficiency, because the principle of understanding is unity. Hence, understanding must allow this plurality of laws to come together into one. But this one in turn exists only by putting aside the determinateness of the many unities. The one is not the many; an example of this—to name a law which plays an important role both in Kant and in Schelling's philosophy of nature, and which Hegel naturally has in mind here—is the law of universal attraction, which defines the fall of bodies with respect to the earth as well as the motion of the earth itself in connection with heavenly bodies.

The concept of law as the universal unifying principle is attained with this universal law. And yet this "*concept* of the law . . . goes *beyond the law* as such"[11] and turns against it. The law of gravity, as what heaviness is in itself, has its necessity only through gravity itself, through force. But now force is no longer taken in the sensible immediacy as one extant among others, but as that which in law as law unfolds itself initially into the differentiated, which law as such regulates. Thus, precisely here, when it seems as though the true universal, the universal law, has now been found, we come across a duality: force (gravity) and the law which has the force in itself. Here again force is what is indifferent *to* the law. Thus, also in this manner we have not yet obtained the simple unconditioned universality. And obviously this universality cannot be obtained along the way that we have just followed, if we consider that understanding arrives at the universal law only by setting others aside. However, this is typical of the one-sidedness of abstraction, in which a most universal sameness, the most universal law, did emerge just now, but only in such a way that the non-identical many on the other side came to a halt. The one unifies the many, but in such a way that the many, as the other which conditions the one, are given in advance, as it were, to the one. The necessity of unification is understandable in terms of the principle of understanding, but not the necessity of what is to be unified as such. Thus, there remains an *indifference* which Hegel tries to make visible from still another angle, namely, with reference to the essence of *movement*, by starting from the thought of law as the law of motion.

If we again see things in their immediacy, movement in general is co-determined by space and time, a thought which Hegel developed speculatively in his manuscripts from the Jena period, in his philosophy of nature—a lecture course which to a large extent is very obviously nothing but a speculative paraphrase of Aristotelian physics. Aristotle already ex-

---

11. II, 115 [GW IX, 92; Hoff., 116; E.T., 92].

presses this peculiar co-determination of motion by space and time when he says that, in order to grasp the λόγος of κίνησις, it is necessary to employ the λόγος of the place, of the empty, and of time (προσχρήσασθαι . . . τῷ λόγῳ . . . τόπου καὶ κενοῦ καὶ χρόνου).[12] In the speculative consideration of the essence of movement, in the philosophy of nature of the Jena period, motion is dealt with in the closest proximity to the system of ether and then to the system of the sun. (Hegel's concept of ether encompasses the basic meaning which Hölderlin has in mind when he speaks of ether, rather than that of present-day physics, which is, so to speak, denaturized.) This discussion culminates in showing how the essence of movement in and by itself requires space and time, such that movement implies that space goes over into time, and vice versa. The thrust of the whole context is that in this intimate relationship [Zugehörigkeit] of space and time to the essence of movement, the essence of the infinite is announced. Merely to illustrate what is stated at this point in the *Phenomenology*, I would like to quote a few sentences from the philosophy of nature of the Jena period, which show, at least approximately, the direction of these observations: "Time and space are the opposite of the infinite and of what is identical with itself in nature as the idea of the infinite, or they are the infinite itself in the determinateness of absolute self-identity. The reality of space and time or their reflection into itself is, as separated, itself the expression of the totality of moments. But what is thus separated in them remains immediately in the determinateness of the simple. What is different is posited in such a way that it would be indifferent and thus not have any essential determinateness at all, whereby it would deny its relation to its opposite and be for itself. On the contrary, this relation remains their essence. They do not face each other as substances; but their determinateness is as such immediately the universal, and not as something opposed to the universal—thus not as a self-sublating but immediately posited as something sublated, as ideal."[13]

The brief mention of movement with the determinations of space and time, in the discussion of the object of understanding in the *Phenomenology*, corresponds to this fundamental thought. In the law of motion it is posited that movement divides itself in time and space and is determined by speed (velocity) and distance. This division pertains to movement in itself. But the parts themselves (space and time), seen in their immediacy, are independent and indifferent as far as movement is concerned, when in opposition as well as when together. The necessity of the division lies in movement,

---

12. Aristotle, *Physics*, Γ 1, 200b 19ff.
13. *Jenenser Logik, Metaphysik und Naturphilosophie*, ed. Lasson, 202/3. [GW VII, 193–94].

but—seen again in their immediacy—the necessity of the divided *parts* is not already posited for each other so that they originate together from out of the one. Movement is not *difference in itself*. It is not a unity which divides in such a way as to let the parts spring forth only in order to keep them back within itself at the same time.

As long as the object of understanding is not posited as difference in itself, the actually true (the unconditioned universal) is not attained. The object of understanding was initially posited as force, which of course dissolved itself into the play of forces. Now, by arriving at that to which the play of forces testifies, we come across law. By trying to grasp this as law in the universal, we again encounter force, now as the basis of law. Force as well as law shows itself as *object* of understanding; and the question is: How does understanding now understand that it is grasping force as the basis of law? What manner of knowing does the activity of understanding manifest? In anticipation we said that this manner of knowing is "explanation." What does this mean? We formulate a law, e.g., the law of electricity from lightning; and this law is differentiated from force, from electricity itself. But force itself is thereby constituted exactly as the law itself. The difference which we make regarding the content is fundamentally revoked again. The movement of explanation is pure tautology[14] and as such is absolute change. It is in itself the opposite of itself. A difference is posited, force reduced to law, law reduced to force—and yet one still says at the same time that there is no difference.

Up to this point we found the absolute change only in appearance, and not in the interior of the object of understanding, in the law. Now, in any case, a further step is revealed: absolute change is also in understanding itself. But force as the ground of the law is the concept of the law. But this concept is a concept of understanding. Thus, the change which is in understanding arrives at its own matter, at the interior or, according to what we have said so far, arrives at the law. So far the law was that which stands with constancy and stability over against appearance in its restless play. But now this identical [law] becomes unequal, the unequal of itself—becomes force. But appearance as unidentical becomes as law unequal to itself, i.e., identical with itself.

When compared with the result of the first truth of understanding, everything is now inverted. The unequal, appearance, is equal; the identical law is non-identical (change). However, this inversion should not be understood such that what is inverted (the law as unequal to itself and the appearance as equal to itself) would still exist as a differentiation which has

---

14. On the tautology of explanation, cf. *Jenenser Logik, Metaphysik und Naturphilosophie*, ed. Lasson, 47ff., 58ff. [GW VII, 49ff. and 59ff.; *Logic and Metaphysics*, 52ff. and 62ff.].

been solidified. The inversion is not a turning away. Rather, the inversion as inversion encroaches upon the first supersensible and receives it into itself. The inverted world is this world itself and its opposite, in a unity.

But this unity, which differentiates itself and in the difference is itself the un-differentiated, is the difference in itself, the inner difference—*infinity*. "The simple character of law," the truth of the object of understanding, "is infinity."[15] This infinity is the *unconditioned universal*. But for ordinary representation the universal is already the concept. The named infinity is the *absolute concept*; it is that universal which is no longer relative to the extant particular which is subsumed by it; it is that universal which *is* the differentiated in its difference and *is* simultaneously unity. Hegel says of the absolute concept that it is "the simple essence of life, the soul of the world,"[16] but *we* can say that it is the *essence of being*.

Infinity coincides with what Hegel calls absolute restlessness; and now it can be admitted that this infinity "has already been the soul of all that has gone before."[17] But this infinity could not freely emerge, not only because in the first modes of consciousness the object was the other to knowing, but also because this other was initially taken and meant as that which it immediately presents itself to be—and can and must present itself to be— as long as we are to avoid thinking the contradiction. But if the difference in itself, the opposition in itself, is to be thought, then the contradiction must be thought, too.[18]

c) The infinity of the I. Spirit as λόγος, I, God, and ὄν

In order to assess the interpretation of the essence of understanding, it should be observed that by itself understanding is incapable of grasping infinity as such. Understanding happens upon infinity and comes against it, but it does not discover infinity as such. The concept of infinity is only for us; it is accessible absolvently. Understanding testifies only that consciousness is struggling with infinity, as it were, without conceiving it as such and that it can grasp infinity only in a new form of consciousness, such that consciousness specifically gets to know what in itself [*in sich*] is the inner difference in itself [*an sich*]. This happens in such a way that consciousness becomes aware of the *I* which differentiates itself from itself and thus knows that it is not differentiated from itself. Consciousness knows consciously of the inner difference, since consciousness is consciousness of the I and of the self—is self-consciousness. Or, to express it in the style of Fichte—but

---

15. II, 125 [GW IX, 99; Hoff., 124; E.T., 99].
16. II, 126 [GW IX, 99; Hoff., 125; E.T., 100].
17. II, 127 [GW IX, 100; Hoff., 126; E.T., 101].
18. Cf. II, 124 [GW IX, 98; Hoff., 124; E.T., 99].

Fichte understood on the basis of the Hegelian inquiry—we can say that by saying I, I is posited as I: I = I. But I "equals" I is just the difference which has to be made, solely in order basically not to be a difference. Since this inner difference has the character of an I [ichlich] and since the I posits itself, it differentiates itself at the same time from the not-I. More precisely: As I, the I posits what has the character of the not-I [Nicht-Ichheit]; by understanding itself as I, the I understands what has the character of the not-I in general; and along with this the I understands the possibility of objectivity in general. With this there opens up for the I as I a realm for encountering this or that being which has the character of a not-I.

This relationship, which I have presented in the style of Fichte, shows nothing other than—to use an expression of Husserl's—the "ego-logical" justification that and how consciousness of the thing, thinghood, and objectivity is possible only as self-consciousness. So much so that this self-consciousness does not present merely an additional condition for consciousness, but is in the unity of mediation the truth of consciousness, the truth of the three shapes of consciousness which have now been sketched.

In the same connection in which understanding shows itself absolvently, infinity is the actual object for understanding. When understanding understands force as such and comes to understand absolvently—at the very place where force manifests itself in its equality and inequality with law as the truth of appearance—at that very place understanding as the truth of perception is driven beyond itself. Insofar as understanding as the truth of consciousness still seeks its true in the object, but at the same time, taken absolvently, is driven beyond this truth, this can mean only that consciousness as such must become another; it can no longer remain only consciousness. The *interior of things* into which understanding penetrates is the interior of the genuine interior, the *interiority of the self*. Only because the interior of things is basically the same as the interior of the self, is understanding constantly satisfied with its explanation. In the belief that it is doing something else in its explanation, understanding "in deed" hovers around only with itself and enjoys itself.[19]

The objectivity of the object of consciousness is dissolved in the unconditioned universality, in the inner difference, which exists only as "I." When the objectivity of the object, and along with it the object itself, thus lose their seeming independence, there is nothing more left for consciousness in which it could abstractly lose itself as in something other and alien. The *relative* is now not only almost given up, left behind, and abandoned to itself—so that consciousness could withdraw into itself—but in the entire previous history of the phenomenology of spirit, that is to say, in the

---

19. Cf. II, 128 [GW IX, 101; Hoff., 127; E.T., 101].

dialectic of consciousness, the *possibility of relativity* is eliminated. The illusion of the relative is dissolved in the truth of the first simple absolute, in the truth of the *infinite*.

At the same time, something decisive becomes visible: Being determines itself *logically*, but such that the logical proves to be *egological*. We see this egological determination of being gradually unfolding since its beginning in Descartes, until via Kant and Fichte it receives its comprehensive and explicitly absolvent justification in Hegel's *Phenomenology*. Thus, right at this juncture the decisive approaches and lines of inquiry into the problem of being in Western philosophy are gradually gathered in one. The inquiry into the ὄν was onto-logical ever since its beginning with the ancients, but at the same time it was already with Plato and Aristotle onto-theo-logical, even if it was correspondingly not conceptually developed. Since Descartes the line of inquiry becomes above all ego-logical, whereby the ego is not only crucial for the logos but is also co-determinant for the development of the concept of θεός as it was prepared anew in Christian theology. The question of being as a whole is onto-theo-ego-logical. It is important in this regard that the term "logical" is repeated everywhere. The apt expression of these relations in their original formation and their concise justification lies in the fact that for Hegel the absolute (i.e., the true being, the truth) is *spirit*. Spirit is knowledge, λόγος; spirit is I, ego; spirit is God, θεός; and spirit is actuality, beings purely and simply, the ὄν.

Only when we see the Hegelian problematic in terms of the whole of Western philosophy—and not only externally but also in the sense of the inner coincidence of the mutually determining perspectives of the question of being—only then do we have the basis for really understanding Hegel. We must work out this inner motivation of the Hegelian position as the completion of Western philosophy; and above all we must be receptive to this motivation in the decisive stages of the history of phenomenology itself.

Though hidden from itself, consciousness is self-consciousness. The absolvent presentation of knowledge thus does not arrive at something alien and other. On the contrary, this presentation in an initial, decisive movement has taken knowledge back from an alienation with the object—namely, *knowingly* taken it back, insofar as we obtain the essence of absolute knowledge only through knowing.

SECOND PART

Self-consciousness

•

§12. Self-consciousness as the truth of consciousness

a) "The Truth of Self-certainty"

The first main section of the *Phenomenology of Spirit* carried the title "A. Consciousness," without—let it be noted—being defined any further. By contrast, the titles of section B and C are defined further: "B. Self-consciousness: The Truth of Self-certainty," and "C. Reason: The Certainty and Truth of Reason." This is not by accident. In Section A we do not yet have any truth at all, and therefore none can be named. And we do not yet have any truth in Section A because truth is constructed in advance in view of the whole as the truth of absolute knowledge. In Section A *knowledge* is not yet at all the true. Rather, the true is only the *object* as the alien other of knowledge, so that, in terms of knowing, the object is not known at all as what is other than knowing. This is because knowing knows in accordance with its own sense and so forgets *itself* and is lost exclusively in the object. The truth *of knowing* (knowing as the true) is reached only when knowing becomes an object for *itself*, when knowing is a knowing for itself, when certainty is no longer the certainty of the sensible, but *"certainty of its self."* Certainty, it should be said as a reminder, does not mean here an insight into the security of a knowing or even certainty as certainty of the I in Descartes's sense of a *fundamentum absolutum inconcussum*. Rather, certainty means knowing in the unified form of the how of knowing and the what of the known. Only where knowing or certainty knows *itself* is there the *possibility* of truth at all, insofar as truth is grasped absolvently in advance. Hence, truth and certainty are not placed beside each other. Rather, it is the "truth *of* self-certainty" that must be dealt with.

Considering the unprecedented power and confidence of the construction of the entire work, it is no superficial observation to say that Section A does not yet carry a more precise thematic title of the kind first given with Section B. The genuine rigor peculiar to the philosopher is manifest in the inner concentration and discretion for what is appropriately demanded by the whole of the work of each of its parts. Compared with this rigor, all the so-called rigor of the sciences remains an arbitrary, limited procedure governed by permanently inadequate perspectives and ideals. Hence, it always leads to an inner perversion of philosophizing when the latter is reduced to such ideals, and all the more so when these ideals reveal the dubious form of the nineteenth-century concept of science.

However, this "petty detail" concerning the difference between the titles of Sections A and B shows its significance, and at the same time proves to be something which Hegel quite clearly knew, when we reflect on the words which he wrote in the introduction to Section B: "With self-consciousness, then, we have, therefore, entered the realm where truth is at home."[1] Hegel often employs the expression "at home" [einheimisch], above all in a crucial passage of the preface to the Phenomenology[2] where he speaks of the "concept" as "truth ripened to the form in which it is at home," the form in which knowledge has absolutely returned to itself. The concept presents the absolute self-comprehension of reason in the sublated history of the essential forms of knowledge—concept understood, not in terms of traditional logic as the simple representation of something in general, but as absolute knowledge.

With self-consciousness truth is generally at home, on its own ground and soil.By contrast, in the sphere of consciousness truth is in a foreign land, is alienated from itself, and is without a ground. As the interpretation of perception showed, absolute truth, in which contradiction is really to be thought, is what is strange for consciousness, against which consciousness defends itself, and which consciousness tries to avoid.

However, here we must immediately keep something else in mind. Seen absolvently, self-consciousness is the middle between consciousness and reason, which, when developed as spirit, is the true absolute. Self-consciousness is the middle with whose help spirit is disclosed in the history of the experiences which knowing undergoes with itself. As this mediating middle, which, sublating itself, is delivered over to spirit as the absolute truth, self-consciousness points not only in the direction of the origin [Herkunft] from out of consciousness but also simultaneously in the direction of the future [Zukunft] which is its due and comes to it as spirit. (We deliberately take zukommen in a twofold way: (a) We take it in the sense of "belonging" or "being due": As spirit belongs to self-consciousness, spirit is due to self-consciousness as its true. (b) We take it in the sense of "arriving at something, which is not yet at our disposal but will be.") Accordingly, as soon as the absolute essence of self-consciousness is unfolded, spirit must show itself in self-consciousness.

Now, in the introduction to Section B, Hegel presents a sketch of the phenomenology of self-consciousness as such, and in the final stage of this introduction, which is indeed a transition, "the concept of spirit is already extant for us."[3] Hegel concludes this preliminary look into the speculative essence of self-consciousness with the significant statement: "It is in self-consciousness, as the concept of spirit, that consciousness first reaches its turning point, where it steps forward, out of the colorful lustre of the

---

1. II, 132 [GW IX, 103; Hoff., 134; E.T., 104].
2. II, 56 [GW IX, 48; Hoff., 57; E.T., 43].
3. II, 139 [GW IX, 108; Hoff., 140; E.T., 110].

sensuous here-and-now of the empty night of the supersensible beyond, into the spiritual day of the present."[4] Every word here needs the interpretation that is concretely given in the work itself, and initially in Section B.

The absolvent history of self-consciousness allows spirit to appear. But self-consciousness in turn has emerged by way of the absolute history of consciousness. In this history *we* who know absolvently played a peculiar role. We had continually to take the place of consciousness and thus bring it forward, since, left to itself, consciousness turns directly away from self-consciousness, from the intrinsic difference, and from the infinite. Now, the more genuinely knowing is unfolded as absolute knowledge, the more *we* give up this role of proxy. It is not that we as mere onlookers would be excluded. On the contrary, we are always more fully and more originally involved as the ones who execute the history of consciousness. The more consciousness and knowing return *into* absolute knowledge *from out of* consciousness's alienation in itself, the more genuine consciousness becomes that which we ourselves are from the beginning. This means that absolute knowledge, which has absolvently come back to itself, takes *our place*; *it* actually fills our position now; and there is no longer anything which we for our part could or should be proxy for. We ourselves, the "we," are brought to our true selfhood. We have played out the role that we had at the beginning of the *Phenomenology of Spirit*—a role which frequently had to change in the course of the history of the phenomenology.

Now, the first change takes place in the transition from consciousness to self-consciousness. But the real "turning point" is located at the point where self-consciousness conceives itself *as spirit*. After this turning point the work proceeds, as it were, in its own clarity, a clarity continually deriving from the work itself; and from this point on, the work leaves behind all the central philosophical difficulties insofar as knowing, having been *clarified* in its absolute essence, is now in itself and only with itself.

b) The significance of the transition
from consciousness to self-consciousness

The being of the object has now become the possession of self-consciousness. The truth is thereby attained of what was already announced in the course of the interpretation of intending: namely, that the intending is not simply lost in the object, but also begins to take back into its own possession what it comprehends, albeit only quite extraneously.

Thus, with the interpretation of the truth of the object of consciousness, deliberation itself enters the realm in which truth is at home, without, of course, already traversing this realm. And traversing is possible only if the

---

4. II, 139–40 [GW IX, 108–109; Hoff., 140; E.T., 110–11].

first step in this realm is measured with full clarity concerning its peculiarity. In other words, for everything else—for the form as well as the
fullness of content—it is crucial to comprehend the inherent essence of the
transition from consciousness to self-consciousness. This is to say that this
transition is not to be represented according to the practice of common
understanding. When one approaches Hegel's problem with representations stemming from that understanding, any intelligibility is hopelessly
undermined; just as the first sentence of the work and all the other statements about consciousness must remain closed off as long as one assumes
that Hegel is concerned with transforming our natural attitude about things
into a philosophical posture or with offering an epistemology.

Just as the decisive step in our interpretation of Section A consisted in
clearing away these prejudices and defining what it means for immediate
knowing to be *our* object, so now we must undertake for Section B the still
more difficult and no less important interpretive step which will place the
phenomenology of self-consciousness in the proper light. Everything else
after that is only a supplementary explanation which has to see to it that the
course that has been taken and the horizon that this course has opened be
maintained.

In order to render intelligible in advance what is peculiar to the Hegelian
(i.e., absolvent) transition from consciousness to self-consciousness, we first
want to contrast this transition with common representation. By common
representation we do not simply and primarily mean pre-philosophical
opinion, but precisely the philosophical view, which takes spirit and existence as something extant and explains them by way of what is extant. This
view was prevalent in philosophy for a long time and, through the domina-
tion of positivism, gained power precisely in the post-Hegelian period of the
nineteenth century. Naturalism in the sense of a biological or even mecha-
nistic explanation of spirit is only a consequence of positivism. Even where
naturalism is set aside or does not even appear at all, there is no guarantee
that positivism is overcome. On the contrary, positivism, in the form of the
psychology attributed to Nietzsche, has spread more than ever. The influence of a *psychologically interpreted* Nietzsche (an influence which is just
beginning) is *the* barrier which excludes us today from knowledge of the
essence of philosophy and pulls us down into a psychologization of everything spiritual.

In terms of a current, so-called "unprejudiced" point of view, one might
be inclined to say initially that the Hegelian transition to self-consciousness
is considerably complicated and thus artificial. It is a going back and forth
from object to consciousness, by reciprocally playing one mode of consciousness against the other, in order finally to arrive at the thesis according
to which understanding basically has its truth in self-consciousness—a
thesis which, in spite of a vast expenditure of dialectical differentiations and

sublations, is not even truly discerning. Should not the Hegelian procedure be juxtaposed with the experience—clear, unequivocal, and above all immediately corresponding to actuality—that we are constantly related to our acts of consciousness and lived experiences as our own and as thus belonging to us? And does not this relation unmistakably announce that our consciousness is simultaneously also self-consciousness? This experience is so elementary that it could not escape philosophy from early on. It had already occupied Aristotle expressly; and the *reditus in se ipsum* is almost the commonplace of all human inquiry. Descartes gives expression to this in his proposition that all *cogitare* means an act of consciousness. Every consciousness of an object is simultaneously a consciousness of consciousness of the object, and is thus self-consciousness. Hence, seen from this perspective, the Hegelian transition might not only be seen as complicated, artificial, and thereby undiscerning; but, moreover, Hegel mistakes *the proper character of self-consciousness of consciousness*, in that he does not give to the *immediacy* of the knowing of this relation its due. And he does so although, precisely in the history of philosophy from Descartes to Kant, it had become always more clearly and more significantly explicit that each *perceptio* is at the same time *apperceptio*. Certainly it can be admitted, or in any case discussed, that we occasionally deceive ourselves in our self-conscious, reflective observation and consideration of our own acts of consciousness and that lived experiences with their transient character are not so palpably graspable as the things around us. However, this does not contradict the basic fact that consciousness of things outside us always goes together with consciousness of events in us. Being conscious of external things, we are aware of this consciousness itself; we are even aware of this consciousness of things. Therefore, it might still be said that on his way Hegel from the beginning neglected an essential peculiarity of the *matter* (of self-consciousness) and that he cannot make up for this negligence with a multilayered dialectic.

We do well to review these arguments, because they are the ones that immediately intrude whenever we talk about consciousness and self-consciousness and indeed the relation of both. We must now make clear to ourselves the peculiarity and fundamental intention of the Hegelian transition from consciousness to self-consciousness, over against these "evident" considerations.

In the first place, Hegel does not at all wish to prove that our consciousness is *at the same time also* self-consciousness and that both always occur together. Just as little does he want to dispute that consciousness immediately knows about itself and discovers that in the extant human being a stream of consciousness and the flow of time drain away. Hegel does not want to prove the one or dispute the other, because his problematic does not move at all in this dimension of the "natural attitude." Hegel would say that the entire discussion that is put forward here and which we can visualize in an exemplary fashion in Descartes's "*cogito sum*" operates in the sphere of *consciousness*. This means that the self, too, is something that at the same time is connected with the consciousness of objects, is extant, and can be known objectively by us. In such a knowing of consciousness as self-consciousness, we move entirely and continuously in the realm of what is relative and abstract. This is not a transition of consciousness to self-consciousness, but a dragging of self-consciousness out into the field of what is only immediately known. But—Hegel would have to say—an inquiry into and speculative presentation of the relation between consciousness and self-consciousness would not be grasped at its roots if one were to understand this relation as though over against the consciousness of objects; and thus, over against objects and things the alterity of self-consciousness, *its unthingly character*, is to be proved, as though it were only a matter of preventing the self from reification [*Verdinglichung*]. The task is a totally different one and with far-reaching consequences. It has to do neither with demonstrating the co-extantness of consciousness and self-consciousness nor with the proof of their alterity, but rather with *revealing the fact that self-consciousness is the truth of consciousness*.

"Consciousness *is* self-consciousness." This sentence must be taken in its speculative import. The "is" does not mean that along with acts of consciousness which are directed at things there is always also extant an act of reflection accompanying them. Rather, the sentence "Consciousness *is* self-consciousness" means that *the essence* of consciousness ("essence" understood speculatively and absolutely) lies in self-consciousness. Consciousness presences [*west*] as self-consciousness. We have something corresponding exactly to this in the universal proposition: "Dissimilarity [*Verschiedenheit*] is sameness." Common sense considers this proposition to be nonsensical: Dissimilarity means just being dissimilar and different and does not mean sameness at all. Philosophy says, "Yes, exactly!" The dissimilarity of two dissimilar things, as dissimilarity, is possible only insofar as the dissimilar things are related to the unity of what is the same; and in view of this sameness dissimilarity can be what it is essentially. In the proposition "Dissimilarity *is* sameness" the expression "is" has the speculative meaning of "has the essence in. . . ," whereby essence is determined in advance speculatively, in accordance with the guiding concept of being in general, as onto-theo-ego-logical. Dissimilarity has its essence in sameness. And, correspondingly, the other way around: sameness does not mean the empty monotonous interchangeability of something with itself, but rather the unity of what belongs together. Sameness is that belonging together, which is in itself at the same time dissimilarity.

The transition from consciousness to self-consciousness is the return into the essence of consciousness, which is essentially self-consciousness and as such constitutes the inner possibility of consciousness, in everything and anything which belongs to consciousness itself. Therefore, this return into the essence of consciousness is to be carried out only within a simultaneous or rather a prior concrete unfolding of the essential structures of consciousness itself, so that *in terms of these* structures and their proper relations the essential relatedness to self-consciousness becomes evident. Thus, we are in fact *not* dealing with the trivial statement that consciousness would be unobtainable without an accompanying self-consciousness.

If consciousness with regard to its own relative truth is thus supposed to be brought back to truth as self-consciousness, then, according to Hegel's approach, the basis is thus obtainable in advance in terms of which what is brought up as a basic fact can be made intelligible and justified, namely, *why cogito = cogito me cogitare* and *must* be that. If Hegel from the very beginning keeps within this dimension of the self, then his starting point is nothing less than the transformation and working out of a fundamental intention of Kant's problematic, which is expressed as the original synthetic unity of transcendental apperception (the "I think" that must accompany all my representations) as the condition for the possibility of all objectivity. Precisely because Hegel pushes for the speculative *absolute* overcoming of the Kantian position, he had to take over Kant's basic starting point. Hegel had to take into account consciousness and the I in its transcendence. Certainly this transcendence undergoes a peculiar contraction and formalization through its orientation toward the relational character of knowledge (thinking, understanding, λόγος), which is already to be found in Kant. But, of course, on the other hand, by this means its absolutization and simultaneously its dissolution become possible in Hegel.

In whatever way we are obliged to take up a critical stance on this, it is crucial above all else that, with the speculative explication of consciousness in all of its forms and with the interpretation of its transition to self-consciousness, consciousness is from the beginning posited and unfolded as *transcendental* (in its transcendence and only in it). In spite of all our fundamental critical reservations regarding the manner of the absolvent overcoming of the finitude of transcendence, we must admire in a positive sense the unprecedented power, confidence, and fullness with which philosophizing here moves in transcendence itself.

Thus, the transition of consciousness to self-consciousness is not simply a re-execution of everyday self-reflection, but the absolvent return from the transcendentally interpreted essence of consciousness into the essence of self-consciousness. But even with this interpretation, we have not yet grasped the peculiarity of the Hegelian problem. The view of the transition which we presented just now can (particularly for us today) awaken the illusion that, although we are not dealing with an ontic bending back of consciousness in perception, we are still concerned with the ways which lead into the essential sphere of the lived experiences of pure consciousness as the sphere of the pure I. It is, after all, not possible that this is what we are dealing with, because Hegel does not want to treat the sphere of self-consciousness as the beginning and end of everything. *Self-consciousness is only a passageway.* It is itself still something relative within infinity, whose full truth is to be grasped in the concept. Thereby it is also true that for Hegel self-consciousness is from the beginning never represented as a realm for finding the essential coherence of lived experiences in the sense of a region of possible research. Rather, in self-consciousness Hegel is concerned with the *actuality of spirit.* Briefly, Hegel is not concerned with the being *conscious* of the self as what is reflectively knowable but with *being* conscious of *the self* as a higher actuality over against the being of the objects extant for consciousness. The task is to render the *being of the self,* or self-being, intelligible in absolvence.

§13. *The being of self-consciousness*

a) The attainment of the self-being of the self in its independence

One must remember that for Hegel the being of the self—as well as the actuality of spirit and of the absolute in general—is primarily determined by "consciousness" and by "knowing," a determination which is closely tied in with the interpretation of being in terms of λóγος. To put it in historical terms, the new orientation toward consciousness in modern philosophy since Descartes is not a radically new beginning over against antiquity, but only its extension and transference to the subject. Because this transference is not understood in terms of its motivations and goals, the question concerning the *being* of the self is gradually and finally buried under the issues of consciousness and knowledge. The egological orientation of the ontological still remains bound to the tradition in the form of the I as "*ego cogito,*" "I think," "I know," and "*I state.*" (The fact that for Descartes the *cogitationes* are not the same as acts of thinking, but that *cogitationes* mean *all* acts and behavior of the I, including its practical as well as emotional behavior, is not operative at all in what is decisive for the foundation of his philosophy. For precisely the calling of *all* acts *cogitationes* proves that the being of the self, in all its dimensions, is primarily conceived in terms of knowledge.)

But although Hegel, too, conceives the I in terms of *cogito* and *self-being* in terms of self-*consciousness,* one must keep in mind the drive toward the absolvent comprehension of self-*being* in order to understand the entire section on self-consciousness, and particularly the difficult introduction to it.[1] Yet this introduction only *opens* the door to the rest of the whole work,

---

1. II, 131–40 [GW IX, 103–109; Hoff., 133–41; E.T., 104–111].

whose absolvent questioning is now no longer concerned with the objectivity of objects, but with the essence of the stance and standing of the *self*,
i.e., with its *independence*. The formal regularity of the dialectical progress
and transitions here too conceals the fundamental posture of Hegelian
philosophizing and provokes the unfortunate illusion that we are dealing
only with an expository presentation of forms of consciousness and with the
appearing of types of knowing. Basically, however, we are dealing with *the
transmission of knowing into the absolute self-reliance of the knower, the effecting
of the self-unfolding of the actuality of spirit.*

If we fail to grasp this transposition of the entire questioning as it takes
place in this transition, then we understand nothing of this work. But if we
grasp this transposition, then it suddenly becomes clear that, for example,
Kierkegaard's entire critique of Hegel collapses as irrelevant. Only when we
keep in mind the independence of the self, *self-being*, as the guiding problem
does the transition of "A. Consciousness" to "B. Self-consciousness" lose its
strangeness. In all other cases this strangeness remains. Above all, we
should not talk ourselves into believing that this transition is self-evident—
perhaps by an appeal to the popular view that now, after "theoretical"
consciousness is dealt with in A, the "practical" one has its turn.

In fact, the transition is strange as soon as we pay attention to the new
title. After discussing sensibility, perception, and understanding, there
follow sections that are entitled "Independence and Dependence of Self-
consciousness: Lordship and Bondage" and "Freedom of Self-consciousness: Stoicism, Skepticism, and the Unhappy Consciousness." But if we
keep in mind that nowhere in the *Phenomenology of Spirit*—not even in
Section A as already discussed—are we dealing with "epistemology" but
that already here it is solely a question of the true *actuality* of spirit, then we
have no cause to wonder if, in the transition to self-*being*, we run into
various shapes of *freedom*. In keeping with the Kantian inquiry, freedom is
indeed a kind of causality. But causality is the determination of a being with
regard to its Dasein, its existence.

If, on the basis of what we have said provisionally now, we keep in mind
what we have claimed to be the fundamental direction of Section B, then
there is no risk of passing over the crucial part of the introduction to Section
B: On pages 133–39 [GW IX, 104–108; Hoff., 135–40; E.T., 106–110]
Hegel undertakes nothing less than *to develop a new concept of being.* So, on
the contrary, we can infer from the appearance of such passages that, if *such*
considerations are necessary by way of introduction, the *entire* section must
be devoted to an essential problem of being. (Here we must take note, with
respect to terminology, of the corresponding issue which we already mentioned about the use of the term *concept* [*Begriff*]. This term stands sometimes for "representation" and sometimes for "concept" in the traditional
sense. But sometimes it is also used in the Hegelian coinage of "absolute

concept." Correspondingly, being (1) means the indifferent substantive of the neutral "is" *as copula,* (2) is the designation for each and every being as actual, and (3) means, in a limited sense, *the objectivity of the object of consciousness.*)

In connection with the explication of the new concept of being, this introduction provides us with a preliminary view of the essence of self-consciousness as it is in and for itself. One sees at this point how little the appeal to reflection contributes to the clarification of this essence. Reflection is so little taken into consideration that the essence of self-consciousness is constructed by way of *being-for-another.* The moment of reflection (not in terms of knowing and consciousness, but as a mode of being) is admittedly not excluded. On the contrary, it is asserted in a more original form. The *to-itself* [*Zu-sich*] which belongs to the being-in-itself of the self—the return into itself as truth—is grasped as *desire,* as the passion of the self for itself. This takes place in such a way, it is true, that the satisfaction of this desire takes place by way of the consciousness of objects and hence does not arrive at its goal, always producing new desires. This means that the self is not simply extant, to be met in a reflective gaze, but rather that the self must in its being *become* necessary for itself. However, these moments of self-consciousness—being-for-itself and being-for-another—are not two determinations that simply stand side by side. Rather, they belong to each other in a way that, in keeping with what was said earlier, can be expressed as follows: Consciousness of the object is not left behind and given up as consciousness returns to itself and becomes self-consciousness, but is sublated and drawn into consciousness's knowledge of itself. This means that, in keeping with its essence, self-consciousness has a "double object,"[2] in the sense that (1) the I posits itself as particular vis-à-vis another particular, and (2) the I takes into itself this doubling and thus manifests in itself a relation to the absolute. This doubling is the decisive phenomenon for the speculative construction of self-consciousness—seen not only in its closest aspect (insofar as we approach from the side of consciousness and its object), but also in terms of the guiding problem of *independence.*

In the preceding discussion we have presented, negatively and in individual stages, the peculiar character of the transition from consciousness to self-consciousness as follows:

1. The transition is not simply accomplished through inner perception.

2. It is no proof that consciousness and self-consciousness are together extant.

3. It does not establish the unthingly character of self-consciousness in distinction from the thingly character of the objects of consciousness.

---

2. II, 133 [GW IX, 104; Hoff., 135; E.T., 105].

4. It does not secure the sphere of pure lived experiences as the realm for observing essences.

5. It does not refer transcendental consciousness to its transcendental presupposition as self-consciousness in the sense of the Kantian transcendental apperception.

Expressed in positive terms, the transition means the *attainment of the self-being of the self in its independence*. And with this the most inherent problematic of the entire movement of the phenomenology is intensified and becomes really explicit for the first time—a problematic which is nothing other than the *disclosive attainment of the absolute actuality of spirit*. A paragraph in the introduction to Section B, in which Hegel develops the new concept of being, meets the crucial significance of the transitional stage with reference to the possibility of the speculative exposition of the independence of the self. We must now make this problem more acute in the following way, in order to understand the manner of its treatment.

The outcome of Section A was that truth cannot be at home in consciousness, because there, according to the most proper requirement of knowledge, truth must reside in the object of consciousness, an object which remains an alien other to knowing. Truth is unconditioned universality, the *inner* difference which *exists* as I. In being an I, the self-identity of being-other-than-itself has its native realm. This thesis grows out of the speculative interpenetration of consciousness. But it also immediately reveals a thorny new problematic. For is not the I, in its being an I, precisely the outstanding and first of all real *particular*? Can a reified this ever be as particularized as the I, which though being an I, though being in the self as an I, nevertheless accomplishes *knowing*, the true and knowing realization of particularity? Precisely because being is defined in terms of being known and in that way stands so much higher, and in each case is more genuinely knowledge, for that reason *being an I* must be the true being of the *particularized particular*. This is exactly the opposite of what resulted at the end of Section A, according to which the interior is the universal.

We can reduce the new problematic which has now emerged to the following questions and then place the approximate answers alongside them: (1) In what manner alone can the I be absolute truth, assuming that the I has to be the truth at all? Answer: Only in such a way that the particular I as self-consciousness *is* in itself absolute being [*Wesen*]. But the second question arises at once, in relation to this answer: (2) Can self-consciousness as such *be* absolute truth at all? Does self-consciousness dispose in itself *the* knowledge which can know the absolute absolutely, in order to *be* absolute in such knowing? Answer: The inner difference, the absolutely true in knowing, does indeed exist for self-consciousness; but self-consciousness is not completed thereby. Precisely because self-consciousness knows the absolute in *itself* [in self-consciousness], the absolute still remains for self-consciousness the other, or its extreme.

The absolute remains the extreme for self-consciousness. Knowing itself *thus*, self-consciousness knows itself as a knowledge which essentially struggles for the absolute, but in this struggle fights its way to a constant subjugation. "Consciousness of . . . its existence and activity is only an agonizing over this existence and activity"[3]: the knowledge of failure in what drives its own essence. Thus, self-consciousness is unhappy, just at that place where it unfolds unto its own essential character; it is *the unhappy consciousness*. Self-consciousness cannot really conceive and grasp itself as that which it already in a certain way understands its own truth to be, as something absolutely unchangeable, which finds itself (its truth) neither in the object nor exclusively in the subject of this object. It finds itself rather in a higher self, which knows itself as the unity of the first self-consciousness and consciousness of the object, or as spirit, or—in its preliminary form— as reason. If this occurs, then "*a self-consciousness exists for a self-consciousness. Only thus is it in fact self-consciousness; for only in this way does the unity of itself in its otherness become explicit for it.* . . . With this the concept of *spirit* is already extant for us."[4] For "reason is the certainty of consciousness {i.e., of self-consciousness} that it is all reality."[5]

Granting all the reservations and reductions, we have here a relation which corresponds to what was already announced in perception. Perception stands and mediates between sensibility and understanding in such a way that perception takes up sensibility and already attests to understanding, although in the negative way of resisting it. Correspondingly, in a higher connection, self-consciousness (B) is located between Consciousness (A) and Reason (C). Self-consciousness takes up consciousness in itself as its truth, but in such a way that self-consciousness simultaneously attests to reason—this again only in the [negative] way that, as it continually attempts to overpower reason, self-consciousness drives itself to continual defeat and remains unhappy in this failure.

The unhappy consciousness is neither simply unhappy nor first made unhappy afterwards. Rather, this consciousness is *not yet* happy, but in such a way that it *knows* about happiness precisely in knowing about its *unhappiness*. The knowing of unhappiness is not a relative, abstract confirmation that a disagreeable condition is extant. It is knowing's restlessness, the disruption of not being able to achieve happiness. Thus, in a certain manner true being (the absolute) already arrives at certainty in self-consciousness.

---

3. II, 160 [GW IX, 122; Hoff., 160; E.T., 127].
4. II, 139 [GW IX, 108; Hoff., 140; E.T., 110].
5. II, 175 [GW IX, 133; Hoff., 176; E.T., 140].

b) The new concept of being as inhering-in-itself, life.
Being and time in Hegel—*Being and Time*

Unhappy knowledge constitutes the being of self-consciousness. Just as in the construction of perception we had to anticipate the understanding already in the form of deception and what lies therein, so too the construction of self-consciousness now needs the anticipatory determination of *absolute being*. Only in the light of absolute being can the stages of self-consciousness be grasped absolvently and above all can the final stage, unhappy consciousness, be determined in its speculative being. To put it more clearly and more appropriately: It is only from out of this genuine being that self-being in its various stages unfolds to its own truth, to *spirit*, which is the absolute, so much so that spirit is concept.

The passage in the introduction in which the new concept of being is developed in a preliminary way runs from pages 133–39 [GW IX, 104–108; Hoff., 135–40; E.T., 106–111]. We divide this passage into two parts: (1) on page 133 [GW IX, 104; Hoff., 135; E.T., 106], beginning with "The object which . . . " and continuing to page 137 [GW IX, 107; Hoff., 138; E.T., 108] "Since we started from the first immediate unity," and (2) page 137 [GW IX, 109; Hoff., 138; E.T., 109] beginning with "This other life, however" and continuing to page 139 [GW IX, 108; Hoff., 140; E.T., 110] "With this the concept of *spirit* is already. . . . "

As we said, we are dealing here with the explication of *a new concept of being*. This can only mean that we are dealing with an understanding of being in another sense than that to be found earlier in the *Phenomenology*, and indeed in a sense which complies with the meaning of the absolute concept of being for Hegel. Intrinsically, this concept of being is and must be old, as old as Western philosophy in its two main stages, which we designate externally with the pair of names Parmenides-Heraclitus and Plato-Aristotle. Hegel's crucial step consists in unfolding in their own essential import the fundamental motifs which were predetermined in the ancient point of departure, namely, the logical, egological, and theological motifs. The new concept of being is the old and ancient concept in its most extreme and total completion. Thus, with the passage just mentioned we arrive at a point where we can really substantiate for the first time *that and to what extent the science of the phenomenology of spirit is nothing other than the fundamental ontology of absolute ontology*, or onto-logy in general. The *Phenomenology of Spirit* is the last stage of a possible justification of ontology.

To put the same thing in historical terms, we can say that since antiquity—in Aristotle no less than in Plato, and in Parmenides in a preliminary form, of course—the being of beings is determined as εἶδος, ἰδέα, *idea*, and thus related to seeing, knowing, and λόγος. Therefore, philosophizing as inquiry into the being of beings is *idealism,* a title which should not be taken as the label of an epistemological orientation and viewpoint, but as a designation for the basic approach to the problem of being, and thus to what lies on this side of all ordinary, so-called epistemological factions. In this respect we can say that the *Phenomenology of Spirit* is the deliberate, explicit, and absolute justification of idealism of which Hegel speaks subsequently.[6]

Finally, we can clarify the same thing in yet another way, with reference to a problem which we have frequently touched upon earlier.[7] Since Aristotle the determinations of being are called categories, and the problem of being has the form of the problem of categories. Kant arrives at the multiplicity of categories and thus at the same time at the unitary character of the determinations of being by taking as a guide the table of judgments, which comes from traditional logic. With reference to this procedure by Kant, Hegel states, from his position of absolute knowing: "But to take up the plurality of categories again in some way or other as a discovery—for example, from the judgments and thus to be satisfied with them—is in fact to be regarded as an offence against science. Where else should the understanding be able to demonstrate a necessity, if it is unable to do so in its own self, which is pure necessity?"[8]

This harsh judgment of Kant by Hegel is justified and intelligible only if we understand him to mean an "offence against *the* science" in the sense of *absolute* science, which to Hegel is the essence of philosophy. For his part Kant speaks of a "scandal of philosophy" in another, although basically the same, respect. Both judgments concern, not persons, but rather the course of the most intrinsic problematic of philosophy, which is always "scandalous" when measured against that which in human machinations at any given time boasts of being philosophy.

What has been said should once again clarify initially the entire range of the passage and of the context whose interpretation occupies us. We shall try now to elucidate the first part of the specified passage.

The explication of the new, that is, the proper, absolute concept of being is nothing other than the clarification of the "result" which emerged from the dialectic of consciousness. For consciousness being had the character of the object and basically meant the simple "presence" of this object to the immediacy of sensible-intelligible knowing. Now, however, the result is that the object of consciousness is not the universal which is merely present and hovering above the particular. This universal is not at all what is truly *immutable and permanently self-subsisting.** At first this universal revealed

---

6. II, 175ff. [GW IX, 132ff.; Hoff., 175ff.; E.T., 139ff.]
7. Cf. above, pp. 77f., 102ff., 116ff.
8. II, 178f. [GW IX, 135; Hoff., 179; E.T., 142f.].
*[Because of a printing error, this sentence was wrongly typeset in the original German. We are grateful to Prof. F.-W. von Herrmann for providing us with the correct formulation,

itself as "unconditioned universal," as the "inner difference," as "*absolute concept,*" as the universal which is no longer relative to its particulars. Already near the end of Section A Hegel says: "the absolute concept is the simple essence of life."⁹

Why suddenly here the talk about "life"? Aristotle has already responded to this question in his treatise on the essence of life: τὸ δέ ζῆν τοῖς ζῶσι τὸ εἶναί ἐστιν.¹⁰ Life is a manner of *being*. Thus, we understand why, in developing the genuine concept of being, there can emerge the term *life*. Hegel himself already uses the term *life* in a special sense in his *Theologische Jugendschriften*.¹¹ There Hegel states unequivocally: "pure life is being."¹² Still, why is it "life" that stands for genuine being in the *Phenomenology*? To grasp this, we must again go back to Aristotle: ζωὴν δὲ λέγομεν τὴν δι' αὐτοῦ τροφήν τε καὶ αὔξησιν καὶ φθίσιν.¹³ Here the determination δι' αὐτοῦ is crucial; self-preservation and growth and decline through itself. And we must bear in mind that these determinations, which easily appear to us as worn-out and insipid, at that time required an unprecedented exertion in order to be seen purely in themselves in terms of the phenomena. Later Hegel once said, and with justice: "Aristotle's books *On the Soul*, with his treatises on special aspects and conditions of the soul, are still . . . the most excellent or the only work on this subject which is of speculative interest."¹⁴

Life means the *being* which produces *itself from out of itself* and maintains *itself* in its movement. From this we understand to what extent genuine being is called "life." It is a determination in view of which the essence of this being can be "characterized";¹⁵ for this is what matters most. The "inner difference," the "unconditioned universality," refer to that being in which all the differences are not extinguished but are sublated and maintained in their origin. Unity is "self-repose as absolutely self-subsisting infinity."¹⁶ Being is grasped as self-subsisting *independence*. Therefore, Hegel maintains: "*Being* no longer has the significance of *abstract being* {like the sphere of objectivity of consciousness}, nor has their pure essentiality

---

which reads: "Der Gegenstand des Bewusstseins ist nicht das nur vorschwebende und über seinem Einzelnen schwebende Allgemeine; dieses ist noch ganz und gar nicht das wahrhaft *unwandelbare beständige Insichständige*."

9. II, 126 [GW IX, 99; Hoff., 125; E.T., 100].

10. *De Anima,* B 4, 415 b 13.

11. *Hegels theologische Jugendschriften* ed. Nohl, "Der Geist des Christentums und sein Schicksal," pp. 302 ff. [trans. T. Knox as *Early Theological Writings* (Philadelphia: University of Pennsylvania Press, 1977), pp. 253ff.].

12. Ibid., p. 303 [E.T., p. 254].

13. *De Anima,* B 1, 412 a 14.

14. VII 2, 6 [trans. *Philosophy of Mind*, Paragraph 378, p. 3].

15. II, 136 [GW IX, 105; Hoff., 136; E.T., 106].

16. Ibid.

the significance of *abstract universality*; on the contrary their being is precisely that simple, fluid substance of pure movement within itself."[17]*

And now without preparation, as if self-evident—right in the middle of the elucidation of the concept of being, where he offers the first comprehensive definition of this concept—Hegel adds in apposition "the simple essence of time, which, in this equality with itself, has the pure shape of space."[18] At first sight this is strange, and yet basically it is not. This concise proposition, which is not further explained, is, it is true, not readily intelligible by itself alone. But this proposition is one of those many compressed statements made in the *Phenomenology* which are the results of entire treatises and investigations written in the Jena period, and through which, as frequently noted, insights are given. That is the case here. This sentence from the *Phenomenology*, which stands entirely isolated, reproduces what in the manuscript from the Jena period is treated on pages 202–214.[19] And what is the theme there? Motion within the thematic of the solar system, which is the basic theme of the philosophy of nature.

It must be pointed out emphatically that, from the beginning and throughout his entire philosophy, *time and space* are for Hegel *primarily* problems of the *philosophy of nature*; this conforms entirely with the tradition. And whenever Hegel speaks about time in connection with the problematic of history and even of spirit, this happens each time in a formal displacement of the concept of time beyond the philosophy of nature into the realms of history and spirit. Conversely, the problematic of time is not primarily developed in terms of history and even spirit, for the simple reason that this would run as counter to Hegel's basic intention as anything could.

After I myself had in the first place pointed to a remarkable connection in Hegel between time and the I, several repeated attempts have recently been made to prove that the problematic of "being and time" already exists in Hegel. This exercise is perfectly acceptable so long as the aim is energetically to find fault with my presumed originality. This business of degrading and belittling or, what is worse, of giving grudging recognition is for a long time now the chief pleasure of historians of philosophy. For this is also the easiest thing to do. By contrast, to see the positive aspect here, one must have already put in the effort of actual work, directed from the inner will. The energetic efforts to prove that *Being and Time* is an old story should be a wholesome and moderating factor for its author. This moral concern for the modesty of the author is entirely acceptable. It is, however, quite

---

17. II, 134f. [GW IX, 105; Hoff., 136; E.T., 106f.].

*[The word "their" (*ihre*) refers to "the differences" (*die Unterschiede*) which Hegel mentions just prior to the passage cited by Heidegger.]

18. Ibid.

19. *Jenenser Logik*, ed. Lasson, pp. 202–214 [GW VII, 193–205].

different and decisive whether with such devious tricks we do Hegel a favor or even honor him. This must, of course, be called into question. If reading the problematic of *Being and Time* into some other text is ever nonsensical, then this is the case with Hegel. For the thesis that *the essence of being is time* is the exact opposite of what Hegel tried to demonstrate in his entire philosophy. The Hegelian thesis is the reverse: Being is the essence of time—being, that is, as infinity. And this is exactly what is as clear as daylight in the passage in the *Phenomenology* that we just mentioned.[20] The text there is concerned with life qua being in the sense of the "inner difference." And it is stated: "The *essence* [*Wesen*] {the genuine being} is infinity as the *sublatedness* of all differences . . . , " and then Hegel says further: "the simple essence of time . . . , " which is to say that *the essence of being is the essence of time*. Or to speak in terms of time, we can say that time is *one* appearance of the *simple* essence of being qua infinity. And time has such an essence as being only insofar as time "has the pure shape of space."

Conceived logically and thus really onto-*logically*, the essence of being is being-identical-with-itself in being-other. The egologically conceived essence of being is the "inner difference" as I = I, *the relation to something which at the same time is not a relation*. The theo-logically conceived being is spirit as absolute concept. In the light of this onto-ego-theo-*logical* concept of being qua infinity, time proves to be *an appearance* of being, in fact one which belongs to nature, "which is opposed to spirit as absolutely real."[21] (Cf. what is said about *absolute matter*, the basic essence of nature, and about *ether*: "The identity of ether with itself is infinite; and the manifestation [*Ausdruck*] of infinity only means that the ether does not have this infinity as an inner which is absolutely reflected in itself, without {thus} the movement of reflection nor—what is the same—as an exterior movement of reflection which is foreign to ether, i.e., does not have infinity in itself at all in this manner."[22] The moments of ether—as this alien and external element—and its motion are *space and time*. Accordingly, time is what is *alienated* from the absolute and thus from the essence of being itself.)

Just as the abstract being of the objectivity of consciousness is without spirit, so is time an appearance of being in that sphere which is void of spirit. But insofar as what is *void* of spirit is also determined in its nature as spirit, time can and must be grasped by the formalized concept of absolute being. But this means the extent to which spirit itself, if it has to exist, must fall *into time* is simultaneously rendered intelligible. The actual being can enjoin the form of inauthentic being, not because time is the essence of being, but the

---

20. II, 134 [GW IX, 105; Hoff., 136; E.T., 106].
21. *Jenenser Logik*, ed. Lasson, p. 187 [GW VII, 179].
22. Ibid., p. 202 [GW VII, 193].

other way around: because being is the essence of time and hence is capable of appearing in time and as time—and indeed only because the time itself is referred to space in order to become an appearance of absolute being.

Therefore, we have to say that Hegel, in keeping with his entire view of time, not only has treated time in the proximity of space (like the entire tradition before him since Aristotle) but also has intensified this proximity still more in that he connected the essence of time essentially with the essence of space, so that time exists only as space and vice versa. This is clearly explicated in the manuscripts from the Jena period. The same view is expressed in the brief mention of time which occurs in this passage of the *Phenomenology*. We really understand this passage only if we read it integrally and if we grasp what is stated here, namely, that the true essence of being, infinity, is the essence of time, which has the shape of space.

We must forego here an interpretation of the essence of time in Hegel's manuscripts on the philosophy of nature from the Jena period. Only one thing should be pointed out here: For Hegel the former time, *the past*, constitutes the essence of time. This corresponds to the fundamental view of being according to which what is a genuine *being* is what *has returned to itself*. If this is understood absolvently, then it means that being is what has already occurred, in the face of which nothing can be earlier, and everything always comes later or too late. (The a priori as the original past, as what is antecedent and simply prior to time and thus beyond time, as what is in advance, prior, reposed in itself, as the past which has become quiet.)

Time and space can here be connected with the true essence of being, since, in keeping with the course of the *Phenomenology*, the essence of being experiences its initial, preparatory, and most external determination in the transition from the alienated objectivity of consciousness. The reference of the essence of being as it encounters its initial externalization should help to prepare and initiate the transition into the interior and genuine essence of being, which is selfhood as *spirit*.

To summarize in the form of theses, we can say: For *Hegel*, being (infinity) is also the essence of time. For *us*, time is the original essence of being. These are not theses which can be simply played against each other antithetically. Rather, the term *essence* [*Wesen*] says something fundamentally different each time, precisely because being is understood differently. For essence is only a consequence of the understanding of being and its concept.

(Philosophy is unfortunately not so easy that one simply picks up something called *Being and Time* and then subsequently moves around at random in the history of philosophy, in order to flush out similarities as proof that the matter has already been said a long time ago. It is characteristic of this posture that precisely at that juncture—where in fact the problematic of "being and time" flares up for the first and *only* time, namely, in Kant— people *refuse* to see the problem and speak rather of my arbitrarily reading my own views into Kant. There is something peculiar about the lack of understanding in our contemporaries by virtue of which one can become famous all of a sudden, and indeed in a dubious sense. Fame is not only the ridiculous way we are honored nowadays by being bandied about every-where. Fame also has hidden tricks of its own, which R. M. Rilke once stated in the following way: "For in the end fame is only the sum total of all misunderstandings that gather around a new name."[23])

If I may speak further about *Being and Time*, then I would say that it is not an advertisement for a new panacea which one could or should try out, but is the name for a task, for a way of *working* whereby we can perhaps once again become worthy of venturing a confrontation with *real* philosophy in its core. This does not mean negating philosophy, but rather affirming its greatness by *actually understanding* it.

Hegel's explication of the genuine concept of being—in the passage just indicated, where time is mentioned—is nothing less than leaving time behind on the road to spirit, which is eternal.

The essence of being is life, the restlessness which reposes in itself, the *independence* of being-for-itself,[24] which in its fluidity contains the division of individual forms in itself by continually taking these forms back into this independence from out of disunity. Such "circulation" is the essence of life, and its moments may now be more closely differentiated.

The first moment is the persistence of independent forms. This means a denial of differentiation. For by itself differentiating is nothing other than becoming related to something, being held in relation to something, being *not* by itself and having *no* persistence.

Conversely, *the second moment* is the subjugation of that persistence by the infinity of the difference.

Hegel shows that each of these two moments of life is turned into its opposite, so that four moments of life thus result: (1) immediate continuity, (2) the individually persisting form, (3) the universal process of these forms as such, and (4) the simple summary of the three moments just mentioned. However, life does not consist in the immediate summation of these four moments, but rather is "the self-developing whole which dissolves its development and in this movement simply preserves itself."[25] This unity of the whole, which results from the movement itself, is the higher and

---

23. Rilke, *Auguste Rodin*, 1903, WW IV, 299 [trans. G. C. Houston, *Selected Works*, vol. I (London: Hogarth Press, 1967), p. 95].
24. Regarding the problem of independence, cf. above, pp. 136ff.
25. II, 137 [GW IX, 107; Hoff., 138; E.T., 108].

genuine unity of life and is thus other than the immediate unity. But this higher unity does not get split off for itself, as it were, as a result which persists for itself. Rather, life in its higher unity *refers* to what is the higher of the high, wherein everything is sublation, sublation to a knowing which must now be life itself and independence. This other life is self-consciousness; and it is unfolded by being guided by the moments of life that were presented and that are grasped as moments only if they are taken back into the circular movement.

Conclusion

I close by breaking off and foregoing an artificial summary. Everything should remain open. You are not supposed to snatch up a fixed opinion about this work, or even a point of view for judging it. On the contrary, you are supposed to learn to understand the task of the confrontation that becomes necessary here—what it is and what it requires.

Here we are confronted with a position of philosophy which *proves* itself through this work, by presenting itself in its actuality.

But this position does not prove itself in the original sense of grounding its possibility. And yet is not its impossibility most acutely refuted by its actuality, which establishes its possibility at the same time? Yet *is* the absolute really actual in the *Phenomenology of Spirit*?

If so, then the absolute must *be* actual *before* the beginning of the work. The legitimacy of the beginning cannot be established by the end, because the end is itself only the beginning. Thus, is the leap into the whole of the absolute all that is left? In that case, does the problem not become simply the factual issue of executing or re-executing the leap?

Certainly. But rightly understood, this issue is in itself the question: What should man do as an existing being? *Where* does he stand, that he should or should not make the leap and so become something other than man?

Where does man stand? Does he stand at all in such a way as to be able to determine his own standpoint and to fathom whether or not to *leave it behind*? Or perhaps man does not stand at all and is rather a transition? And is man as such a transition wholly incomparable, so that he would be driven *before being*, in order to comport himself, as the one who exists, toward beings as beings?

Can and should man as transition try to leap away from himself in order to leave himself behind as finite? Or is his essence not abandonment itself, in which alone what can be possessed becomes a possession?

The first and proper indication that you have understood something of what was essentially unspoken, but constantly at issue here, can only take the form of awakening in you a will to do justice to the work in its innermost demand—each for his part and according to his ability and measure.

149

Editor's Epilogue

The lecture course on Hegel's *Phenomenology of Spirit* was given in the winter semester of 1930/31, meeting two hours a week at the University of Freiburg. The text is fully written out, with only a few parenthetical remarks in outline form. The text of the lectures has forty-eight pages with numerous additions, some of which are designated as insertions and some of which summarize briefly the reviews of each lecture session. The division of the text of the lecture course grows out of its relation to the work being interpreted. After thirteen pages of introduction, the second title again reads: "Phenomenology of Spirit." After the following five pages of preliminary observation, the subsequent portion of the text is entitled "I. Sense Certainty or the This and Intending." Further titles are familiar from the *Phenomenology*, going up to "B. Self-consciousness. IV. The Truth of Sense Certainty."

The basis for this edition, which Martin Heidegger himself entrusted to me in March, 1976, were, in addition to his own manuscript, a transcript belonging to Curd Ochwadt and another found in the literary remains of Helene Weiss. Both of them are totally identical texts, except for the absence of the Greek quotations in the transcript by Helene Weiss.

Moreover, I could rely on a transcription by Ute Guzzoni, made from the original text of the author with the support of the *Deutsche Forschungsgemeinschaft* in 1961/62. This transcription was carefully compared with the original by Ute and Alfredo Guzzoni in cooperation with Martin Heidegger. In this transcription all insertions and additions were taken into consideration. From the first, a few alterations were made. Most of the "ands" at the beginning of sentences and frequent expletives, such as "just" [*eben*], "exactly" [*gerade*], and the like, were deleted. In some instances a stylistic revision of the text was accomplished by placing the verb according to the rules of grammar, whereas the placing of the verb in Heidegger's text was more for the sake of immediate clarity. [An example of this is to be found on page 191 of the German text, regarding the place assigned to the verb *entgegengehalten werden.**] In one copy of this transcription there are addenda which originate in a revision made at the same time by Ute and Alfredo Guzzoni. This revised version already has all of the above-mentioned transpositions of the verb. There are additional cases in which the

---

*[The example given by the German editor cannot be reproduced in English.]

place of some words has been altered in order to achieve greater intelligibility. Repetitious words were changed according to their meaning. The paragraphs were often arranged differently from the handwritten text. Wrongly deciphered passages were corrected, and what was omitted out of negligence was reinstated. Quotations were for the most part already corrected, and in some rare instances short insertions were added to the text to make it more intelligible. The latter are found to be identical in the transcript.

This transcript is very well prepared and leads to the assumption that the lectures were written down in shorthand as they were originally presented, since many expletives and series of adjectives, etc., are identical in the manuscript and in the text of this transcript. Deviations are so evident in style that one notices how the oral presentation itself deviated from the text—sometimes abbreviating or explaining, sometimes referring what was said then to what was said earlier, for the sake of clarity, sometimes adding a still more precise formulation to the text. Exceptions to this are a few mistakes clearly made in listening to the lecture or in understanding it. In this transcript the only passages not included are those in which Heidegger responds to the polemic directed against him.

In preparing the manuscript for publication, those stylistic changes from the transcription which helped to clarify the text or to avoid misunderstanding were adopted. Alterations which served merely to regulate Heidegger's writing style were not always adopted—at any rate, not in those cases where constant clarity in reading longer sentences suffered. According to Heidegger's instructions in the guidelines, those insertions and explanations were adopted from the transcript which served to clarify a passage formulated with difficulty or to introduce an especially novel formulation. Likewise, repetitions were adopted from the transcript which briefly and precisely express the thrust of the interpretation.

Insertions placed in square brackets within quotations are explanatory additions made by Heidegger.*

In the table of contents which I prepared, I have tried to focus on the essential themes dealt with in the interpretation, although the variety of these themes could have been surveyed only by titling each page or through an index.

Setting aside the preface and the introduction, the lecture course explicates Sections "A. Consciousness" and "B. Self-consciousness" of the *Phenomenology of Spirit*. It explicates these sections precisely because they can be considered as the further development and overcoming of Kant's position in the *Critique of Pure Reason*. Here the section "Force and Understanding, Appearance and the Supersensible World" has, according to Heideg-

---

*[These insertions are marked in the English translation by { }.]

ger, a crucial significance for Hegel, both historically and objectively—first as a confrontation with the philosophy of reflection, which remains bound to the finitude of what is extant and the finitude of understanding, and second as a preparation for and justification of the absolute position of idealism. In this section of the *Phenomenology*, Heidegger sees "the systematic presentation and justification of the transition of metaphysics from the Kantian foundations and problematic to that of German Idealism; it presents the transition from the finitude of consciousness to the infinity of spirit," as he states in a note added to a summary of one of the lecture sessions.* Moreover, in regard to this "justification of idealism" in the transition from the section on consciousness to the section on self-consciousness, Heidegger stresses Hegel's efforts which aim at not only grasping self-consciousness in terms of knowing but also bringing into sharper focus the *ontological sense* [*Seinssinn*] of self-consciousness. Central for Heidegger in the section on self-consciousness is Hegel's inquiry, no longer into the objectivity of objects, but into the essence of the "stance of the self," of independence, and of self-being. "We are basically dealing with transmitting knowing into the absolute self-reliance of the knower and with bringing about the self-unfolding *actuality* of spirit."** In view of this, the last section of the lecture course explicates the *Phenomenology of Spirit* as the "fundamental ontology of absolute ontology" in the sense of absolute "idealism"—"idealism" understood as the orientation to ἰδεῖν and λόγος at the beginning of the problem of being.

But here the interpretation of Hegel's position is a confrontation on the basis of a relatedness [*Bezogensein*]. The core of this confrontation consists in the notion of transcendence as it is developed in Heidegger's lecture course *The Metaphysical Foundations of Logic* of 1928† and in "On the Essence of Ground": transcendence understood as transcendence of Dasein beyond beings, insofar as Dasein is being-in-the-world. In certain respects Heidegger sees his own intention vis-à-vis Kant (namely, the presentation of the possibility of an a priori understanding of being from the unified ground of selfhood) operating also in Hegel's dialectical development of consciousness to self-consciousness. On the other hand, Heidegger contrasts the dialectical overcoming of the finitude of the opposition of consciousness (the dialectical absolvence from the relative) to the transcendence which occurs beyond beings toward selfhood. He contrasts the infinity of absolute knowing to the finitude of transcending Dasein. "Is the understanding of being absolvent and is the process of becoming absolute

---

*See above, pp. 111f.
**See above, p. 137.
†[Published by the Indiana University Press.]

the *absolute*? Or is absolvence *transcendence* in disguise, i.e., finitude? Our confrontation with Hegel arrives at this crossing which is located between finitude and infinity."* Heidegger's interpretation of Hegel in the lecture course of 1930/31 is marked by an antithesis, held together in an affinity between, on the one hand, the transcending of man, conceived in his finitude and detached from beings, and, on the other hand, a dialectical detachment of absolute knowledge from its relation to the objectivity of beings.

My thanks are due to Mr. Ralf-Peter Lohse, Cand. Phil., and to Mr. Hartmut Todt, Cand. Phil., from the *Philosophisches Seminar* of the University of Kiel, for their careful reading of the proofs.

Ingtraud Görland

---

*See above, pp. 65.

Glossary of German Terms

This glossary intends to list those German expressions in Heidegger's text which are philosophically the most significant and/or the most difficult to render into English. Cross-references are meant as a directive to the reader to gather certain words together and in that gathering of *words* to be provoked unto the *work* of thinking. (The mere cross-referencing does not itself do that philosophical work.) What appears in brackets in this glossary is offered as an elucidation and will generally not be found in the translation text. Parenthetical remarks appear in parentheses.

die Abseitigkeit: aloofness

das Absolute: the absolute [literally: not relative]

absolvent: absolvent; detaching; in the movement of the absolute, in the process of being absolved, in the process of becoming absolute

allgemein: universal, general

aufheben: sublate [*tollere*/cancel, *elevare*/elevate, and *conservare*/preserve]

der Auftrag: mission

aufzeigen: show up

der Ausdruck: manifestation; expression

die Äußerung: externalization

der Begriff: concept

besorgen: procure [Latin *curare*]

bestimmt, die Bestimmtheit, bestimmen: determinate, determination, determine

bewahrheiten: verify; come into its truth

bewähren: confirm

bewährt: tested

die Bewegung: mobility, movement

das Bewußtein: consciousness

das Diese: the this

diesig: having the character of a this [of a *dieses*]

die Dingheit: thingness, thinghood

das Einfache: simplicity [the "one-fold"]

einheimisch: at home

154

die Einseitigkeit: one-sidedness
das Einssein: being-one
einzeln: particular [rarely: individual]
einzig: sole
der Entstand: emergence
erfahren: experience, undergo an experience, learn
die Erfahrungswissenschaften: experimental sciences [literally: experiential sciences]
die Erinnerung: internalization
die Erkenntnis: cognition (see *wissen*)
die Erscheinung, das Erscheinen: appearance; appearing

das Fürsichhafte: for-itself (see *das Sichhafte*)

der Gegenstand: object; what stands opposed to
geschichtlich: historical
gleichgültig: indifferent or (taking the word in its root sense) with equal weight or force

die Herkunft: origin

die Ichheit: I-hood, egoity
ichlich: having the character of an I

das Meine (see also *meinen*): mine, my own
meinen, das Meinen (see also *das Meine*): intend [more usually: mean]
merken: mark
die Mitte: middle term, middle (see Translators' Foreword, p. xv)

real: concrete
rein: sheer; pure

der Sachgehalt: inherent content
die Sachgestalt: inherent form
sachlich: inherently
scheinen: show, appear
das Seiende: beings; a being
das Sein: being
das Selbst: the self
das Selbstbewußtsein: self-consciousness
die Selbstheit: self-hood
das Selbstsein: self-being

das Sichhafte: having the character of an itself
die Sichheit: itness
das Sinnliche: sensible [something which is sensible]
der Schluß, schließen: "syllogism"; infer
die Sorge: care

das Übersinnliche: the supersensible (see *das Sinnliche*)
das Unmittelbare: the immediate, immediacy
der Unterschied: difference, differentiation; (less frequently) distinction

die Verdinglichung: reification
das Verhältnis: relation
verkehren: reverse, turn around
vermitteln (see also *die Mitte* and *das Unmittelbare*): mediate
die Vermittelheit: mediatedness
die Vernunft: reason
die Verschiedenheit: dissimilarity
die Verteilung: allotment, distribution
vorhanden: extant

wahrnehmen, die Wahrnehmung: perceiving/perception; (sometimes in the
   more root-sense) taking-for-true
das Wassein: whatness
wesen: presence (see *das Wesen*)
das Wesen: essential character; essential unfolding ["essential" in the sense
   of "root"]
die Wirklichkeit: actuality
wissen, das Wissen (see also *die Erkenntnis*): know, knowing; knowledge
die Wissenschaft (see also *das Wissen*): science
die Wissenschaftlichkeit: scientificality

zugrundegehen: run aground, go under; be annihilated [this word, as used by
   Heidegger, carries with it much the same diversity as *aufheben* does in
   Hegel]
die Zukunft: future
zu-sich: to-itself